Library of
Davidson College

APPLIED LANGUAGE STUDY

New Objectives, New Methods

Papers from the 1983 Conference
at Oklahoma State University

Edited by

John Joseph

UNIVERSITY
PRESS OF
AMERICA

LANHAM • NEW YORK • LONDON

Copyright © 1984 by

University Press of America,™ Inc.

4720 Boston Way
Lanham, MD 20706

3 Henrietta Street
London WC2E 8LU England

All rights reserved
Printed in the United States of America

ISBN (Perfect): 0-8191-3858-4
ISBN   (Cloth): 0-8191-3857-6

All University Press of America books are produced on acid-free paper which exceeds the minimum standards set by the National Historical Publications and Records Commission.

To the memory of

JONATHAN C. BOOKOUT

(1930-1983)

Associate Professor of Spanish

Oklahoma State University

ACKNOWLEGEMENTS

On behalf of the thirty-one scholars whose work is collected in this volume, I wish to extend appreciation to a number of people without whose time, faith, and generosity the Applied Language Study Conference, and this book, could not have been.

Smith L. Holt, Dean of the College of Arts and Sciences of Oklahoma State University, is gaining nationwide notoriety for his enlightened, outspoken belief in foreign language study as a core element (he is a chemist; hence the metaphor) of a sound high school and college education. We have enjoyed his full support, together with that of Associate Deans Neil J. Hackett and Richard C. Powell, from the first planning stages in 1981.

A conference highlight was the appearance of Pierre Shostal, Dean of the Language School of the U.S. Foreign Service, who wrangled time away from Washington (on his birthday, no less) despite obvious inconveniences-- but to our great profit.

Many thanks to our colleagues at OSU who contributed their energy toward planning and ground arrangements, especially the late Jonathan C. Bookout, Charles E. Chase, Sabrina M. Chase, Santiago Garcia-Saez, Janice Krenz, Mary Susan McCarthy, Robert L. Maurizzi, John L. Schweitzer, David N. Wigtil, and Harry S. Wohlert; also to Fran Mihura, who prepared this manuscript. The corps of students who worked diligently during the conference days earned the gratitude of all present.

Finally, we wish to recognize those who participated in panel presentations which are not included in the book (except insofar as the interchange of ideas they generated inspired the final form taken by these papers): Mervin Barnes, Mustapha K. Benouis, Rosemarie A. Benya, Joseph F. Byrnes, G. Truett Cates, James Fife, Michael J. Folk, Mark G. Goldin, Joan Grimbert, Helga Madland, A. Allen Rowe, Dorothy L. Schrader, David Stout, and Harry S. Wohlert.

J.J.

CONTENTS

Foreword, by **John A. Schillinger** — ix

Introduction, by **John Joseph:** "What Is Applied Language Study?" — xi

PART ONE: FROM THE CLASSROOM TO THE WORLD

Renate A. Schulz: "Foreign Language Proficiency for the Real World: Wedding the Ideal to Reality" — 3

Willard E. Hiebert: "Foreign Language and Business Administration: An Integrated Approach" — 13

Philip S. McKnight: "Foreign Language Study: Bankruptcy and Merger" — 19

Elaine K. Horwitz and **Gloria Contreras:** "A Survey of the Foreign Language Needs and Use of Texas Business" — 31

Christiane E. Keck: "Business German: A Developing Discipline" — 41

Barbara E. Kienbaum: "A Practical Approach to Business German" — 45

Arlene J. Russell: "A Model: Purdue Calumet's Foreign Language International Studies Program" — 49

Sidney Pellissier: "Functional FL for the Non-FL Specialist: Curriculum Design and Instructional Strategies for an Entry-Level FL Program Geared to the Workaday Needs of a Targeted Group of Non-FL Professionals" — 53

Kevin J. McKenna: "The 'Contextual Approach': An Innovative Methodology for Attracting Science Majors to Our Language Programs" — 63

Signe Denbow: "Foreign Language Instruction for Singers" — 69

Kyoko Hijirida: "A New Curriculum Design in 'Japanese for Travel Industry Management Majors'" — 77

Gertrud G. Champe: "The Place of the Translation Laboratory in the University Curriculum" — 85

Cida S. Chase: "Applying Oral and Translation Skills in the High School" — 91

PART TWO: FROM THE WORLD TO THE CLASSROOM

Richard L. Frautschi: "Some Aquarian Objectives in Applied Language Study"   101

William L. Easterling: "Can College Students Actually Learn to Speak and Understand French?"   115

Thomas Deveny: "Tradition and Change: New Trends in Teaching Spanish in a Liberal Arts Environment"   123

Fritz H. König and **Nile D. Vernon:** "Culture x Language = Short Course Abroad"   131

Henk Kroes: "Upgrading Second Language Skills: Manpower Development in a Developing Country"   137

John J. Deveny, Jr., James D. Wells, Thomas Deveny, James F. Ford, and **Alfred Gage:** "Toward a Definition of Intermediate Applied Language Study"   149

Pierre Trescases: "From Theory to Practice and Back: How Recent Functional Methods Give Form to New Objectives in Second Language Teaching"   159

Fritz Hensey: "Translation/Interpretation in Special-Purpose Second-Language Instruction: An Experiment"   167

Nancy A. Zeller and **Bernice Melvin:** "Strategies for the Use of Authentic Materials"   173

Anthony D. Northey: "Developing Motivation and Spontaneity in Conversation: Ideas on the Design of Classroom Dialogue and Games"   185

Jonathan J. Webster: "The Metalex Project"   195

Kurt Kraetschmer: "Practical Applications of Current Linguistic and Psychological Theories on Second Language Acquisition"   223

John J. Deveny, Jr.: "Intensive Language Programs: Past, Present, and Future"   231

Index   237

FOREWORD

John A. Schillinger
Head of the Department of Foreign Languages & Literatures

Oklahoma State University

Oklahoma State University's Conference on <u>Applied Language Study: New Objectives, New Methods</u> in February 1983 provided an excellent forum for the exchange of ideas among participants from across the nation. For all who came to investigate new directions and approaches it was an unqualified success.

But of greater importance is the fact that Oklahoma State's Applied Language Study Conference is indicative of a new national trend. Now, more than ever before, Americans are beginning to understand the fact that foreign language study is the key to the future. The mere fact that this conference took place in Oklahoma, a state now energetically developing its foreign language programs after years of neglect, speaks volumes.

As Oklahoma moves to take its place among those states known for their support of foreign language studies, it reflects a burgeoning national awareness displayed by the appearance of strengthened foreign language requirements, expanding enrollments, increased attention in the news media, and growing public support.

Clearly, this February conference was a harbinger of an approaching spring. As Americans come to understand the vital significance of communicating with the rest of the world, the necessity of achieving a global awareness to insure the social, political, and economic future of our nation, foreign language studies in the United States will achieve the stature they have had throughout the rest of the world.

And it is in the application of these languages to virtually every field of human endeavor that the goals of this conference will be realized.

INTRODUCTION

WHAT IS APPLIED LANGUAGE STUDY?

John Joseph

Oklahoma State University

Normally the tenor of a conference is defined by its subject. Sometimes the opposite occurs--the conference defines the subject. This is largely what was happening in the Theatre and Case Study Rooms of the Oklahoma State University Student Union on February 18 and 19, 1983. Applied language study is the authentic materials approach, the contextual approach, foreign language study for singers, the translation laboratory, black education in South Africa, Business German, intermediate and intensive training . . . all of the subjects this book addresses itself to. When a category is so broadly inclusive, one questions its usefulness. Categories, after all, are meant to be selective, discreet, like little file drawers where information can be organized and more easily handled.

But is applied language study a category? Let us "apply" ourselves a moment to considering the words. Among the people with whom I have corresponded about the Conference is Jacques Derrida of the Ecole Normale Supérieure at Paris; he is also affiliated with Johns Hopkins and Yale Universities in this country. Derrida's business is deconstruction, and I discussed with him how the purpose of the conference was to "deconstruct" second-language training in general and applied language study in particular. Let us proceed to the second of these tasks.

Applied language study consists of three words, but of only two terms: applied, and language study. Study is a neutral element, signifying only that the student is supposed to be actively doing something, the matter of which is language. One strategy for clarifying a term is to look for its opposite, or for other terms that could fill the slot. What is the opposite of applied language study? unapplied language study? What does that mean?

We have to go to the history of the whole name. "Applied language study" was coined, I believe, on the model of the earlier term applied linguistics--itself modeled on "applied" studies in such areas as physics, chemistry, mathematics. These studies were created in essence to bring the subjects "down to earth," out of the lofty theoretical spheres into which their most brilliant practitioners had taken them. Other practitioners, not necessarily less brilliant (and possibly much smarter) felt the need to end the concentration on abstract number play and to train students in the relevance of their findings to the human experience--in <u>applying</u> theorem XYZ to some concrete task with a clearly recognizable advantage to be gained.

The analogy to linguistics is easy enough to see. Applied linguistics came predictably into vogue just as the forefront of the field was busy reorganizing along the lines of a new theoretical orientation.

But what is "theoretical" language study, in connection with second-language acquisition? Not the study of literature, I think, since this is itself an application, and is generally agreed to be useful toward any advanced language/training goal. The only possible context I can think of is the following:

Teacher A asks, "Are your students learning French?"
Teacher B replies, "Theoretically."

We've all known <u>that</u> feeling, and if this is what theoretical language study means, we would surely agree we want nothing to do with it. But again, if applied language study means only <u>good</u> language study, with the students applying themselves and having some corollary interest in the study besides simply wanting to know Spanish for the sake of knowing Spanish, then it fails as a category.

I think we must admit this failure. We cannot say very much about what is not applied language study, and far too much about what is.

Not a category. What then? Well, for one thing, a curriculum, a plan of study. German for Business. Italian for Singers. Latin and Greek for-- uh, never mind.

But something more is involved. It ties in with the fact that the German for Business course will never be the same as the regular German course (German for Pleasure?) or the German for Teachers course. Because--and this is the main point I wish to make--applied language study is also a state of mind. We want to be in the position of being able to convince students that majoring, or at least co-majoring, in Spanish, will enable them eventually to eat, to eat fairly well. Our interest in doing so is not merely to increase our enrollments (though this should happen, giving us, in self-generative fashion, more future customers for the very teachers we are training now). But just as important, the students we do have, be they many or few, will be <u>motivated</u>. The difference between teaching to motivated and unmotivated students, to me at least, is equivalent to the difference between painting a canvas and painting a garage, between creating a mosaic and laying bathroom tile.

So our useless category has become a very useful concept. Many of the persons in whose hands the development of this concept lies have

Joseph

contributed to the present volume. I urge them, and those of you reading their work, to keep applied language study at the fore of the research agenda. We will all be the richer for it.

PART ONE

FROM THE CLASSROOM TO THE WORLD

FOREIGN LANGUAGE PROFICIENCY FOR THE REAL WORLD: WEDDING THE IDEAL TO REALITY

Renate A. Schulz
University of Arizona

The professional literature abounds with statements on the value of foreign language knowledge for practically any career, as well as with descriptions of courses, methods, procedures, and techniques which aim at developing functional language skills for general or specific purposes. My comments are in no way meant to belittle or to discourage these efforts. Rather, I hope that they will stimulate a critical review and discussion of our only sporadically successful efforts in equipping our students with second language proficiency for the real world.

"Applied language study," the study of a language for practical purposes, is based on the underlying premise that the learner will want or need to use the language for acquiring information, and/or for interaction and communication with people outside the classroom, often for job-related purposes. Employers with international interests--be they in business, industry, government, the military, communications, academic research, or in service and social service related fields--look for individuals with considerable fluency in the desired language. "Familiarity with" or "acquaintance with," "exposure to," or a certain number of academic credit hours in a language are usually not sufficient to represent the interest of an employer in international dealings.

In fact, criteria for evaluating language proficiency in international business here and abroad are demanding. In 1981, for instance, the Chamber of Commerce of the Federal Republic of Germany reported that only 46 of 104 individuals who took its language test received certification.[1] 75% of the 31,000 government positions requiring second language knowledge specify "minimum professional proficiency" (Foreign Service Institute [FSI] Proficiency Rating S-3/R-3) or "limited working proficiency" (FSI Proficiency Rating S-2/R-2); 7.5% require "full professional proficiency" (FSI Proficiency Rating S-4/R-4, or "native or bilingual proficiency" (FSI Proficiency Rating S-5/R-5).[2] This type of proficiency (FSI rating of 3 and above) is practically impossible to reach in a conventional foreign language program[3]--or, at the most, it is reached only by exceptional individuals.

Brod (1982) points out that even under optimal conditions--using small classes, intensive instruction, and involving highly motivated students such as one finds at the Foreign Service Institute--students of commonly taught Western European languages need approximately 480 hours of instruction to achieve an FSI rating of S-2 (limited working proficiency). And these 480 hours need to be increased considerably to reach a similar proficiency in a non-Western language. 480 instructional hours translated into the traditional college curriculum mean eight four-credit semesters of language study with a predominant and intensive focus on language skills development.

One major task facing the profession is to help change the totally unrealistic expectations of the lay public regarding what it takes to gain proficiency in a second language. This expectation is fueled by commercial enterprises which promise instant success with a set of records, other gimmicks, or a two to three-week "crash" course. We are perpetuating a fraud on students if we promise them "proficiency" in a traditional two to four-semester sequence.

If, indeed, language proficiency is the goal in "Applied Language" or "Language for Special Purposes" (LSP) courses, we need to examine the necessary conditions for gaining language proficiency and we need to investigate if and how these conditions can be created in a formal school setting to enable a larger number of learners to reach that goal than is now the case. Little is yet definitely known on how second languages are learned, but three conditions appear to be prerequisite to success:

1) large amounts of comprehensible input in the language;[4]

2) motivation (need for skill); and

3) extended periods of exposure and practice time.

The difficulties of providing these conditions in the traditional curriculum are obvious: input is limited, often with the teacher as sole contact with the language. Further, input often is limited not just by time but by the teacher's insufficient language fluency. Many teachers lack the self-confidence and proficiency to use the language as medium of communication, and employ it solely for grammatical problem solving. The time factor is equally problematic, particularly for students who are majoring in disciplines other than a foreign language. Most professional schools leave their students very little room for electives. And finally, the motivation for learning is often negatively affected by the students' knowledge that their native language has become the lingua franca of most international business and government transactions.

The U.S. education system (secondary and postsecondary) has been notoriously unsuccessful in preparing a sufficient number of professionals able to use a second language effectively. Ruchti (1980: 10), for instance, states that only one in five foreign language majors who pass the Foreign Service Examination achieves an S-3/R-3 rating and that "nearly all recruits come with inadequate language skills from the education system."

To enable their personnel to gain adequate language proficiency, government agencies as well as business concerns resort to in-house training or contract for language instruction with private concerns or individuals. Inman (1980) reports that only about 8.5% of the companies which contract foreign language instruction for their employees do so through traditional academic establishments; 59.7% utilize commercial teaching concerns.

These findings should not, however, be interpreted as indicative of low quality instruction. The major reasons for our lack of success lie, in my opinion, not so much with incompetent teachers or teaching, as with the constraints put on second language instruction by traditional curricular planning. Our curriculum allows and prescribes the same learning conditions for the acquisition of a second language as it does for the learning of historical or geographic facts: three to five fifty-minute classroom periods per week.

The problem is further compounded by a relatively low demand for individuals fluent in a second language. Several surveys indicate that, in general, employers find proficiency in a foreign language desirable but not necessary. First and foremost they look for subject specialists in the area of immediate usefulness to marketing their products or ideas (Inman 1980).

A report on "The United States Government Requirements for Foreign Languages" (Ruchti 1980) indicates that fewer than .5% of the 5.5 million government jobs require a language other than English. One survey (Britt et al. 1980) indicates that only three of seventy U.S. subsidiaries of German firms consider the knowledge of German an essential employment criterion for their managerial staff; fourteen of the seventy consider it "very important." It might be interesting to know that 58% of the respondents to the same survey indicated that "general communication ability" in German was needed, rather than predominantly technical or business language.

Let me state immediately that I am not proposing the development of an extensive battery of LSP (Language for Special Purposes) courses for beginning language students. As I concluded in my final report of the NEH-supported <u>Survey of Successful Undergraduate Foreign Language Program in U.S. Institutions of Higher Education</u> (Schulz 1978), I view the need for individuals with career specific language training as relatively small. According to Inman's study, LSP is rarely included even in corporation sponsored language training. The major need is for professionals in all fields with a general basic language fluency in at least one foreign language and familiarity with the related culture(s). Specialized career oriented foreign language courses for students without such a general basic foundation in a language are emergency, stopgap measures. While valid (and often necessary) as a community service (e.g., Spanish for firemen, police, and health officials), the value of such career specific phraseology courses is limited for the general curriculum.

Despite the relatively low demand for individuals with a second language proficiency, government agencies have nevertheless problems filling the affected positions--especially in the less commonly taught languages. Ruchti (1980) maintains that the problem is a qualitative rather than a quantitative one.

Given these realities, how can postsecondary institutions improve language instruction so that students can actually learn to use the language to meet the demands of the real world? The remainder of this paper will make some recommendations toward this end.

What general minimal foundation skills do individuals in various careers need to be able to use the language as an adjunct skill in their profession? Most of us would agree that there are at least three:

1) adequate proficiency in a language;

2) sufficient knowledge of daily customs and life styles to fit unobtrusively into a cultural setting while performing one's professional functions abroad; and

3) sufficient knowledge of present-day political, social, and economic institutions to have realistic expectations of what can be accomplished, and a perspective for interpreting the meaning of current events vis-à-vis one's own interests.[5]

Let me make some concrete suggestions of how these competencies might be included within the traditional preparatory program of career students in business, journalism, political science, medicine, or whatever.

The conventional four to six semester sequence of language skills courses is, for most students, unfeasible and, in my opinion, even undesirable, since it generally serves a minimally motivated "requirement" population. Most career programs entail a highly structured sequence of courses and leave little time to follow a parallel sequence of demanding courses in a foreign language. Furthermore, such a parallel sequence would assume that students decide on acquiring an ancillary language fluency very early in their course of study. Otherwise it would be impossible to fit in the minimal number of courses necessary. I see only two options to circumvent the insufficient time factor and still have some hope of reaching an adequate level of proficiency: 1) immersion study abroad, and/or 2) intensive language instruction within a foreign language department. An immersion experience abroad, after some initial language instruction in the home country, is clearly the ideal and most efficient way to acquire both foreign language proficiency and cultural awareness. However, this option is open only to a very limited number of students because of financial constraints. We need to look more closely at intensive instruction to simulate a "real life" language learning experience.

Various forms of intensive programs are presently in existence.[6] Their only common definition is that they offer a large number of contact hours with a language within a relatively short time span. The advantages of an intensive course are obvious:

1) They enable students to learn a language without the usual lengthy time commitment. This factor is especially important for individuals who want to acquire a language proficiency as an adjunct skill to their

chosen profession.

2) They provide increased contact time with the language and offer a setting which resembles more than their traditional counterparts a natural language learning situation.

3) They allow a more realistic time frame for achieving language proficiency. The traditional two semester sequence usually consists of 90 to 150 hours of instruction, depending on the number of course credits. Experience has shown that this instructional time is insufficient to achieve even minimal mastery of a language. Some intensive courses offer up to 75% more instructional time than conventional courses for the same number of credits, and there is evidence that they can indeed achieve superior student achievement.[7]

Two eight to ten-week intensive summer courses could provide from 640 to 720 hours of language instruction, approaching the minimum number of hours recommended by the Foreign Service Institute or Defense Language Institute for an S-3/R-3 rating on the FSI examination for Western European Languages. During the regular academic year students would then need only to enroll in a low-credit skills maintenance course in order to keep up and polish language skills acquired during the summer. These skills maintenance courses could be one-hour topical conversation courses focusing on current affairs, daily life, social problems, etc., and be offered as companion courses available during the academic year, not just limited to students bridging two intensive summers.

The program I am suggesting is not just an accelerated one (i.e., offering the traditional number of contact hours per credit over a shorter time period than the regular semester). For optimal effectiveness, the program should simulate an immersion experience, to the extent this is possible, outside the target language culture. This means the availability of foreign language houses--or at least dormitory floors reserved for students of a language--staffed by native speaking assistants. In common living and social areas students would then be surrounded by and could practice the language outside the classroom. An extensive extracurricular program, offering films, taped radio and videotaped television programs, song fests, folk and social dancing, sports and other leisure activities, is a necessity. That the use of computer assisted instruction and other electronic media can be a very valuable asset to language instruction goes without saying. There is, furthermore, no question that the course of study I am proposing will need an exceptionally committed faculty. Program planning, advertising, student recruitment and selection, intensive teaching, materials development, course coordination and planning with other team members, and responsibilities for extracurricular activities will require more time, energy and creativity than traditional language courses. Untenured faculty whose institutions reward strictly on the basis of publications or which do not adequately recognize curricular development and teaching, had probably better stay away from such commitments.

Some more precision is in order regarding the proficiency level I envision as a goal of the proposed course sequence. The American Council on the Teaching of Foreign Languages (ACTFL), together with the Educational Testing Service (ETS) and various government agencies concerned with foreign language instruction, are in the process of adapting the FSI proficiency rating procedure for the formal school setting. The project is supported by a grant from the U.S. Department of Education. Provisional guidelines have already been developed, and two five-day workshops have been conducted to train test administrators on the postsecondary level in French, Spanish, German, and Italian. Another workshop took place during the summer of 1983 to begin training high school test administrators.[8]

The nine levels of the "ACTFL/ETS Provisional Speaking Descriptions" are described in full in Weinstein (1975). ACTFL has combined the upper three levels of the FSI proficiency scale into the classification of "superior," since "full professional proficiency" or "bilingual" proficiency cannot usually be reached by students without extensive experience abroad.

It should be noted that the proficiency descriptions are not bound directly to specific levels of language instruction (i.e., "intermediate" on the scale does not mean that these proficiencies can necessarily be demonstrated by a student in second year language instruction).

One is, of course, tempted to hope for a "superior" proficiency rating for students wishing to use a foreign language for career purposes. However, without an experience abroad, students might actually only be able to reach an "advanced" or "advanced plus" rating, especially in highly inflected languages or in languages not sharing with English a large group of cognates. Anticipated ratings will need to be established and verified experimentally; it is important, however, to keep realistic expectations.

The second minimal language-related skill for a career student-- knowledge of daily customs and life styles--could be made part of these summer intensive courses. I see no reason why the second course in the sequence could not deal with the popular culture of an area by analyzing contemporary values and customs through an examination of various aspects of television, film, popular literature, advertising, popular music, sports, and art in addition to and in conjuction with language study.

Let me emphasize that if the proposed courses are indeed to lead to a proficiency goal, they cannot serve the student who studies a foreign language purely or predominantly to fulfill a requirement. To be successful in a course sequence such as I am suggesting, stringent selection procedures need to be used which consider foreign language learning and general academic aptitude as well as motivation as enrollment criteria. Further, through personal screening interviews students must be made aware that gaining fluency in a second language outside the target language country takes much time, energy, commitment, and plain hard work.

Also, a traditional grammar-based syllabus would be inadequate to teach the desired skills. While sequential grammar instruction will probably always be a part of formal foreign language instruction, the syllabus needs to include notional/functional components as well. Students need to know not only how to conjugate verbs, decline adjectives, and transform the present tense into the past; they must also be able to apologize, compliment, disagree, express doubt, ask for clarification, and so on.

If at all possible, an experience abroad, preferably an internship in which students could practice both their professional and language skills, would be invaluable.

One other practical consideration deals with the communication, interaction, and cooperation of language teaching departments with other departments whose students can benefit from their offerings. To be successful in attracting students, foreign language departments must have the support of other disciplines. Interdepartmental advising and counseling should bring the program to students' attention. Through interdepartmental committees, foreign language departments can solicit input into the program and can keep colleagues in other fields informed of the program's success. Even local businesses with international interests could be involved in the planning. These same businesses might be approached to establish an endowment for scholarships or internships abroad, for funding additional staff, a language house, or the purchase or development of computer software useful to reaching the program's goals.

In summary, if students are properly advised and choose their electives judiciously they could complete the minimum suggested course sequence in two summers and one academic year and could start language study as late as the summer before their senior year.

One final but most important requirement of my proposed scheme is in the area of competence certification. The purpose of the proposed program is to enable individuals to acquire concrete communication skills-- i.e., ability to use the foreign language to exchange information--and sufficient cultural awareness and sensitivity to enable a person to communicate accurately and inoffensively within another culture. Most foreign language departments certify foreign language study only in terms of academic credit hours which are meaningless as an indicator of a student's communicative ability. If we expect to gain credibility in the nonacademic world we will have to provide concrete evidence of what students can gain in our classrooms that will indeed help them in future careers. Institutions must commit themselves to formal proficiency certification and make it a part of a student's credentials.

Certification procedures can be internal, handled by the department according to clearly described criteria and procedures, or they can make use of externally available exams. Internal evaluation could utilize the

ACTFL/ETS guidelines described earlier. External proficiency testing could make use of instruments such as the Zertifikat Deutsch als Fremdsprache, available through branches of the Goethe Institute. If a business language focus is desired, the Chambre de Commerce et d'Industrie de Paris (CCIP) offers the Examen de premier niveau in Business and Commercial French, and the Carl Duisberg Gesellschaft offers the Certificate in Business German. A Spanish examination in business language exists as well.

Starr (1979) maintains that "the only statistic that really counts is acquisition of competence." If we can provide such statistics to other professional schools and to the business world, they might be more willing to make foreign language proficiency an adjunct to their training than they do now, and they might be willing to prepare those sorely needed Americans who will be able to represent us competently and compete for us successfully in diplomatic, military, business, educational, and cultural dealing with other nations.

NOTES

[1] See p. 107 of "Bericht 1981," issued by the Handelskammer Hamburg, Abteilung Information, reported in Trendota (1982).

[2] The descriptions of these ratings are explained in Weinstein (1975).

[3] By conventional language programs I mean the four to five contact hours per week, audiolingual elementary and intermediate courses, and those language courses focusing predominantly on the development of language skills (rather than literary appreciation) available at the advanced levels of language instruction.

[4] Krashen (1981) considers the quantity of comprehensible input the major variable leading to success in second language learning. Several studies indicate a strong positive relationship between the amount of language input and student proficiency. See, for instance, Nord (1980).

[5] Ideally, if time permits, competencies should also include 4) knowledge of the historical background and evolution of a nation to understand present-day social and political constraints, cultural values, and attitudes in the context in which they developed; and 5) some familiarity with the artistic and technological accomplishments of a culture and its contributions to human civilization in order to appear as an interested intelligent, well informed, and appreciative representative of America.

Knowledge of present day political, social, and economic institutions and knowledge of historical background is probably best left in the domain of political science and history departments unless special expertise is available among foreign language faculty. Most institutions already have established courses in history, geography, political science, economy, and anthropology departments which deal with specific cultures or geographic areas and which could easily be made to fit our purposes. These courses might be negotiated to replace other required courses in the general curriculum, again saving time and enabling students to complete career supportive language and area studies training in addition to requirements in their major field.

The fifth competence, familiarity with the artistic and technological accomplishments of a culture, could be taught within the foreign language department, but preferably through an interdisciplinary team approach involving specialists in literature, music, and the fine arts. I envision a one to two-course sequence dealing with the masterpieces of a culture which, if lectures are conducted in English and readings are available in the original as well as in translation, could be negotiated as a requirement option for a humanities course.

[6] For a description of some of these programs, see Schulz (1979a), Benseler and Schulz (1979), and Schulz (1979b).

[7] See, for instance, Kühne and Jordan (1980) and Schulz (1979a).

[8] Readers interested in more information on the project or in obtaining a copy of the ACTFL Guidelines should write to ACTFL, 385 Warburton Ave., Hastings-on-Hudson, NY 10706.

REFERENCES

Benseler, David P., and Renate A. Schulz. Intensive Foreign Language Courses. (Language in Education: Theory & Practice, No. 18). Arlington, VA: Center for Applied Linguistics, 1979.

Britt, Christa, Helmut Roessler, Lilith Schutte, and Elisabeth Zeiner. "German Firms in the United States: A Survey of Managerial and Professional Opportunities and the Matter of Language Competence." ADFL Bulletin, 11, No. 4 (1980), 38-40.

Brod, Richard I. "Building a Language Profession." ADFL Bulletin, 14, No. 1 (1982), 10-13.

Inman, Marianne. "Foreign Languages and the U.S. Multinational Corporation." Modern Language Journal, 64 (1980), 64-74.

Krashen, Stephen D. Second Language Acquisition and Second Language Learning. Oxford: Pergamon Press, 1981.

Kühne, Robert J. and Gerad P. Jordan. "Integrating International Business and Language Training." ADFL Bulletin, 11, No. 3 (1980), 27-30.

Nord, James R. "Developing Listening Fluency before Speaking: An Alternative Paradigm." System, 8 (1980), 1-22.

Ruchti, James R. "The United States Government Requirements for Foreign Languages." ADFL Bulletin, 11, No. 3 (1980), 6-11.

Schulz, Renate A. Survey of Successful Undergraduate Foreign Language Programs in U.S. Institutions of Higher Education. Washington, DC: National Endowment for the Humanities, 1978. Grant No. EH-27125-77-67.

──────────. Options for Undergraduate Foreign Language Programs: Four-Year and Two-Year Colleges. New York: MLA, 1979a.

──────────. "Intensive Language Instruction: How and Where It Works." ADFL Bulletin, 11, No. 2 (1979b), 37-40.

Starr, S. Fredrick. Paper presented at the ADFL Seminar East, Columbus, Ohio, June 1979.

Trendota, Kristina. "International Trade in Commerce with Liberal Arts: One Instructor's Dual Pursuit." ADFL Bulletin, 14, No. 2 (1982), 35-87.

Weinstein, Allen I. "Foreign Language Majors: The Washington Perspective." ADFL Bulletin, 6, No. 4 (1975), 20.

FOREIGN LANGUAGE AND BUSINESS ADMINISTRATION AN INTEGRATED APPROACH

Willard E. Hiebert
Concordia College

Recently there has been a great deal of activity in foreign language departments around the country toward finding new directions or subject matters with which to replace or supplement the traditional literary curriculum, for despite isolated rumblings in the popular press, The Report of the President's Commission on Foreign Language and International Studies, and Congressman Paul Simon's book The Tongue-Tied American (all of which underline America's need for greater foreign language proficiency), students are still not flocking to our classes in large numbers. In a recent article in The Wall Street Journal, Roger Thurow, the Journal's Bonn correspondent, praised the linguistic adroitness of Chancellor Helmut Kohl, but damned the difficulties involved in learning the German language. He concluded his brief article by stating, "It's all enough to make one avoid the bother by doing without good friends in Germany." The Journal's editors must share his views since no German nouns were capitalized, all umlauts were missing, and some German words were misspelled. Unfortunately the majority of Americans, including students, are also of the opinion that if making foreign friends requires us to learn their language, it's just too much bother.

But despite this prevailing attitude, language teachers continue to be optimistic and to try new things. Frequently, one of the new things they try is to introduce a course labeled German in the Business World. Any popularly taught language may be (and often is) substituted for "German" in the title. Such courses tend to concentrate on business correspondence because correspondence deals with language, and language is what language teachers know best. There is frequently little or no cooperation between the language and business departments, and language teachers often do not consider the fact that the student might have to know more about Germany or France or Latin America (not to mention Japan) than about its language, in order to be successful in the world of international business. But even if the language teacher realizes that more than language is necessary, cooperation with the business department is not easily obtained. Most business departments have more than enough students, and most U.S. firms have not yet felt the need for employees with linguistic skills. Thus the launching of an international business program which includes a foreign language component is difficult at best, but it can be done. We in the language field must learn to think like businessmen in order to accomplish the task.

The first step in launching a program is to contact your university's Business Administration Department. At Concordia College we are indeed fortunate that our Business Administration Department is willing to cooperate. You must show the business educators how your disciplines can complement each other. Research journals and the popular press for articles supporting your position. Many good articles have already appeared. A cooperative business department is essential, because most students think of business before they think of language. And if current journal and press articles are at all accurate, the business department will be glad in the future that it cooperated now. You should then discuss which business and language courses should be considered essential in the preparation of future international businessmen.

The second step in launching the program is to do some market research by visiting the consumers of your product. These consumers are firms in your area that are engaged in international trade. Find out what they want. Are the courses which you have selected adequate? If at all possible, representatives of the language and business departments should go together to interview the firms. This shows the firms that you are cooperating and that you are serious about turning out an acceptable product. Much letter writing, phone calling and leg work is involved in this phase. At this point you may become discouraged if you only visit large, well known American firms. With the possible exception of Spanish, most firms are not interested in hiring language specialists. You will be told that language skills are not considered in their hiring practices, that all overseas operations are handled by foreign nationals, and that the company has little or no need for stateside linguists. This is the current situation, but if future projections are correct, it cannot long remain this way. In the areas of German and French, you will have better luck if you visit foreign firms doing business in the United States. They want U.S. citizens who are competent in business and who also speak the language of the firm's main office. They will tell you that they desire applicants with business <u>and</u> language skills. The "and" is very important. A representative of a German company told me that language majors expect him to fall on his knees before them because they speak German. However, he can't use them if they have no business skills.

It is obvious, then, that a strong foundation in business is a must if the student is to get a job in the business world. This means that the student should have at least a minor if not a major in business administration. The course of study should preferably include a course dealing with international trade. All company representatives whom we interviewed stressed the importance of a good preparation in business. Without such a background, the language student is viewed as unskilled and will probably not be hired. The business component of our program at Concordia includes Principles of Economics, Principles of Accounting, Intermediate Accounting Theory, and Managerial Finance. In addition the student must choose one of the following: Statistics for Economics and Business, Intermediate Microeconomic Theory or Intermediate Macroeconomic Theory. Additional courses in international trade are to be taken in the foreign country together with or separate from the internship. The internship will be described later in this paper.

We now come to the linguistic portion of the program. Our program at Concordia has three linguistic branches, one in French, one in German, and one in Spanish. Each linguistic program is designed to fit the specific language and the system of business education in the target culture.

The French program includes French Skills and Culture, French Language and Culture, Advanced Grammar Review, Advanced Conversation and Composition, and Special Topics. The content of the special topics course is geared toward the French business and economic system and is to be taken the semester prior to the semester of study at the University of Rennes in France. Areas for study in France include international finance and marketing, international trade policies, and the psychology of the French consumer. After the semester of study, the student may participate in a six to eight-week internship with a French company.

The German program includes Basic German according to placement, Conversation, Composition, Culture, and German in the Business World. This last course contains some terminology but is mainly directed toward the political, economic and social geography of German speaking countries. Business terminology is included because the foreign internships can precede foreign study. Business correspondence is treated briefly, but the bulk of the course is spent on economics, i.e., the study of business as it is conducted in German speaking countries. Such matters as resources, labor laws and labor unions, the banking systems, and social welfare legislation are also considered. Some time is spent on the various political systems of the separate countries. Cultural questions are also discussed.

Our program is based on our perception that the student needs to know the everyday customs and manners in order to avoid offending the foreign nationals. For example: What are good table manners? What are your obligations when visiting someone socially? Why are all the doors shut? Why, for instance, will men's razors sell in Germany while women's razors will not? Politics is included because it affects the business climate. Good business sense dictates that the students learn a great deal about what is manufactured in the host country, what types of transportation are available, what services are offered, and what resources are present locally. Since there is too much culture to be handled adequately in one course, culture (historical as well as present-day) is stressed in other courses. We feel that the more the students know about a specific country, the better they will be able to do business with its inhabitants. Even a knowledge of the country's literature can be helpful in that it reflects the culture in an artistic form. Therefore our whole curriculum is heavily weighted toward the teaching of culture, as are the curricula of the French and Spanish departments.

The Spanish program includes Spanish in the Modern World, Civilization, Conversation, and Composition. Spanish students also take a special topics course prior to leaving for Mexico. In Mexico they enroll in business courses at the university level and intern in a business simultaneously. Among the courses they take while in Mexico are political and economic history of Latin America, socioeconomic relations between Mexico and the

U.S., and the present-day Mexican economy. They stay with selected families.

We feel our program is integrated well through the foreign experience. For it is while the student lives abroad that both aspects of his or her training become essential. Business skills, language skills and cultural skills are all necessary for survival. The foreign experience is tailored to the specific country. Business education in France and Mexico is more similar to that offered in the United States than is the case in Germany. Because of its unique dual system of business education, specialized business schools do not enjoy a high status in Germany; a fact which makes business study more difficult for the foreign students. Thus the intern program in Germany becomes more important. In the German dual system, those who wish to become business administrators enroll in a program which combines a position in a firm with formal business studies. Thus students in Germany learn and do for a period of three years. Our students are given an opportunity to work in the firms, but not to attend classes. The system is not ideal, but we are striving to improve it. In situations where the student begins in the foreign firm (Germany and Mexico), initial fluency is very important. Firms offering us internships in Germany were very concerned about the fluency of our students. They also insisted that all correspondence be carried out in German. Thus we can observe that, contrary to popular belief in the United States, all the world does not speak English, and even those who do are becoming less willing to use it. In his recently published book, Megatrends, John Naisbitt states, "In everyday life, however, as we become an increasingly interdependent global economy, I would look for a renaissance in cultural and linguistic assertiveness. In short, the Swedes will become more Swedish; the Chinese, more Chinese; and the French, God help us, more French" (1982: 76). I have observed this trend in Germany over the past twenty-two years. In 1961 the Germans used every opportunity to practice their English with me, and it was difficult to speak German with them. In 1983 they never uttered a word of English even though they knew I was American. One frequently hears them say Ich spreche nur Schul-Englisch ('I speak only school-English'). And they are indignant that American-made high tech products come with directions only in English, while those from Japan have been translated into German. They buy our products only when they cannot get them elsewhere. All this leads us to believe that the Germans will have little patience with minimal fluency.

So in order to insure quality of performance and to meet the standards which foreign countries have for our interns, prospective interns must apply for admission to our program well in advance of the foreign experience. In this way their business and language skills can be evaluated independently of specific courses, and the students become aware of what is required of them. Students who successfully complete the program are awarded a special certificate in addition to their bachelor of arts degree.

In conclusion, I would like to say that the demand for programs such as ours seems to be growing. One need only read Congressman Paul Simon's book The Tongue-Tied American to develop a rationale for them. However, many U.S. firms have not yet felt the need for employees proficient in foreign languages. Enrollments in our programs will remain moderate until recruiters from businesses start asking for language skills and rejecting students who do not possess them.

REFERENCES

Naisbitt, John. Megatrends. New York: Warner Books. 1982.

Simon, Paul. The Tongue-Tied American. New York: Continuum, 1980.

Thurow, Roger. "Helmut Kohl's Mother Tongue Is Greek to Most," Wall Street Journal, 27 October 1982, p. 23.

FOREIGN LANGUAGE STUDY: BANKRUPTCY AND MERGER

Phillip S. McKnight
The University of Kentucky

I. Bankruptcy

About a year ago I met a man with degrees in Russian and history who had left academics to go to work for Gold Kist Corp. Exploiting his language skills and his ability to make a convincing presentation, he eventually went to Moscow where he took a $2,000,000 order for Georgia chickens. He earned a much handsomer reward than he had been accustomed to in academics, of course; but I began to wonder whether his contribution to mutual understanding wasn't significantly greater than the contribution of academicians, as well.

As everyone knows, the humanities, and foreign languages in particular, have come under extreme existential pressure in the last decade. Secondary school language study has declined, university enrollment in foreign languages is down, academic salaries have fallen in real dollars by roughly 18% since 1970, and tenure track positions are regularly eliminated at retirement or even earlier.

The prospects for employment with any kind of degree in foreign languages have been very depressing for some time. Worse, it becomes proportionately more difficult to find a job the more advanced the degree earned is. One of the economic consequences of this situation can be seen in the fact that the number and quality of applicants for graduate study in foreign languages has deteriorated drastically in recent years, bringing on a crisis in the language departments. Not because we need to produce more M.A.s and Ph.D.s--definitely not. It is a crisis because these people are the cheap (and this, unfortunately, means dirt cheap) labor employed to teach the lower division language courses.

Rarely trained in teaching techniques, these graduate students can nevertheless be very effective in terms of enthusiasm generated. Language departments do not always recognize the "salesmanship" involved at the beginning level, but the students' reaction to the dynamics of lower division teaching is surely one key factor in their decision to continue their studies in language or to concentrate elsewhere.

As the situation grows worse the circumstances may cause consternation among established research faculty who, in some cases, may be very reluctant themselves to teach beginning language courses. Ultimately, however, university administrations are not going to tolerate an upper division program able to attract only two or three students to each class. Somehow, more students have got to be found for the upper divison courses.

The list of internal woes and problems confronted by humanities and language programs could go on at length, but I would like first to describe my own view as to why the study of foreign languages in this country has been a "bankruptcy" course, and secondly, to present a plan for "merger" designed to facilitate its revitalization.

In several reports published recently, including those by the Presidential Commission on Foreign Languages and International Studies (1979), the Commission on the Humanities (Lyman et al. 1980), and the MLA Commission on the Future of the Profession (Demetz et al. 1982), one thing which repeatedly emerges from the commentary is a kind of us/them posture. Whose fault is it that language study is floundering? The "them" side points to such factors as the general economic situation; insensitive administrators; society's general, deplorable failure to recognize the value of humanistic, artistic, and cultural expression; the government's short-sighted reduction of funds for the humanities; and so on. Many of these complaints originate out of the dependency on public patronage to which humanities and foreign languages are subjected, whether voluntarily or necessarily.

Let's take a little closer look at the us/them problem. To tell the truth, I really know a lot more about us than them, and it probably doesn't hurt to take a look in our own backyard as well. Let me try to put this into a context which might make practical sense to a businessman: not long ago I was sitting around after dinner with a few colleagues and the conversation turned familiarly to the way our students are prepared. "Today's students can't tell the difference between a noun and a verb"; "Let me tell you about the one who never heard of Napoleon"; "Our students are much worse than they ever used to be"; and so forth.

I suddenly realized that we might well have sounded like a group of General Motors engineers sitting around afternoon coffee talking about how "they sure don't build cars like they used to."

Here at the university, of course, _we_ are the senior engineers of education, and if our students are less well prepared, then we must certainly share the blame, just as those GM engineers would for faulty designs in their products. Nor can we blame the situation on elementary and secondary teachers, because, after all, we are the ones who train them. Part of the problem consists in the fact that, just as it is now difficult to attract talented graduate students, foreign language departments cannot afford to offer a competitive entry-level salary for Ph.D.s. The talent which once flowed into the humanities has naturally followed the trends of the marketplace and taken its skills elsewhere. To understand what sort of a disaster is striking the education industry as far as the humanities are concerned, try to imagine what shape your Chevy would be in if General Motors offered their engineers the same kind of beginning salary offered in academics.

The tendency towards creeping mediocrity which can occur from this situation then perpetuates itself until locked into a vicious circle: it is now true that many foreign language departments have shortchanged both their students and themselves by watering down the program at all levels. Language programs--under the false premise that students would be easier to attract if the courses were less demanding--have demanded less. Less language lab, less homework, less class time, less ability and hard work required for a good grade.

Instead of analyzing and upgrading current design deficiencies, outdated and second-rate finished products (graduates) with a reduced price tag keep coming off the line. Consequently, foreign language study is all too rapidly becoming the discount store of higher education. Moreover, it is on the verge of bankruptcy unless it faces up to a crisis of logical deduction which it has assiduously avoided: go where the market is.

I would summarize the first cause of bankruptcy, then, as follows: reacting to a rapidly declining market we have downgraded the quality of the product hoping to sell it more cheaply--a tactic which has failed in terms of enrollment--and we have generally refused to expand into new markets where demand appears to be quite promising.

As eloquently as the Commission on the Humanities presented the case for finding new ways to integrate humanities into the mainstream of science and technology, the study still reveals in places an isolationist attitude commonly held by humanists: "The importance of humanities," it states, "cannot be quantified nor. . .reduced to enrollments and budgets (Lyman et al. 1980: 8). This point need no longer even be debated because the reality of the situation now is, in fact, that enrollments do determine departmental budgets more than ever before. Individual career advancement is in no way linked with the individual's contribution to increasing enrollment as it would be in a normal business environment. Of course universities are not organized like businesses: we are not oriented towards efficiency nor necessarily towards concrete results in terms of specific goals and objectives.

In some cases, therefore, our existing structure inhibits our ability to compete effectively for students, now that we have entered into a competitive situation whether we wanted to or not. The Spanish, French, and German departments compete with each other for the dwindling number of students interested in foreign languages; but, more importantly, we are in direct competition with business school, engineering, and computer science departments for the high quality students necessary for a successful program. We need to recognize this fact and act upon it.

Now let's take a quick look at what we actually do and do not teach in order to help us understand our competitive disadvantage. In the language departments we are primarily concerned with producing literary analysts. The undergraduate programs are usually designed to develop the potential for advanced study in this field. The vocabulary and texts used generally lead into literature. There is nothing wrong with this, particularly since most students with high language aptitudes are already literature conscious. However, at the advanced levels these people are then trained to interact with a closed group of professional specialists who analyze literature for each other.

Little effort is made to establish a line of communication to other elements of society who might benefit from the interpretations, for instance by applying ethical values gained from this analysis to the overall social structure, or to individuals whose jobs require them to observe (if only in passing) certain ethical standards: businessmen, politicians. In fact, according to the Commission on the Humanities, the field pointedly rejects any responsibility in the decision-making process (Lyman 1980: 18).

We seldom teach anyone how to write well, how to teach effectively, how to speak persuasively, or how to apply critical thinking to other things besides literature. Students come either with these skills or without them. In other words, we do not actually engage in teaching students how to communicate effectively, even though, as language instructors, we ought to be considered the elite in the field of communications. Maybe one of the reasons we do not teach these skills in foreign languages is that we have a very low rate of success in developing acceptable proficiency in our students. We all know that it is a myth to believe that anybody can become really proficient in two years of language study. The most we can do, realistically, is to prepare them to develop proficiency while living abroad.

The second cause for bankruptcy, then, can be attributed to a failure to achieve our own objectives, a failure to recognize and exploit the potential wide range of skills and applications inherently associated with language learning and communication. This is compounded by a traditional and truly unwarranted antagonism between humanities and business, technology and science. The self-inflicted isolationism and antifunctionalism of the humanities constitutes a monumental failure to attempt infusing humanistic values and thought precisely into areas where they would do the most good, such as international business and international relations.

Our chicken salesman had a three-pronged competitive edge seldom enjoyed by American businessmen: he spoke the language, which gave him an enormous advantage over other Americans (I'm sure the Japanese and German chicken salesmen spoke Russian too) who rely on the global use of English. He also had a reasonable understanding of and sensitivity to the cultural context of his actions. And he was trying to put together a good deal for both buyer and seller.

There really is no country where the people are not impressed by a foreigner making a genuine effort to understand and communicate within that country's cultural and linguistic context. Conversely, an equal aversion is often felt where no such effort is made. Much of the alarming anti-Americanism is not only residue from perceived political blundering; it can also be attributed to cultural blundering, that is, a fundamental failure to communicate.

International trade is responsible for roughly one out of every eight U.S. manufacturing jobs. Some 6000 American companies have overseas operations and another 25,000 are engaged in the exporting of goods and services. Each billion dollars of exported goods creates about 30,000 jobs. Worldwide economic interdependency has become an established policy, and international trade has seen numerous joint ventures on foreign soil similar to the one about to be undertaken domestically by GM and Toyota. Many countries require U.S. firms to enter into a joint venture agreement, insuring local employment, in order to gain access to their market. The number of Foreign Trade Zones has tripled in the last decade and Import/Export Management Companies have popped up all over the place. Recent legislation has encouraged the creation of Export Trading Companies to facilitate opening foreign markets to small business.

The need for improved U.S. competitiveness internationally has resulted in a sharply increased demand for well educated, articulate, culturally sophisticated and ethically trained young men and women who can interact effectively in the world market by building long-term, mutually beneficial business ties and exchanges.

Just as the global strategies of business have now clearly recognized the need for people well educated in liberal arts and with strong cultural perception skills, so can humanities and foreign language departments, through increased involvement in business, develop a new role and emerge as practical instruments steering business away from perceived exploitation into long-lasting friendships with the world community.

By accident I can give you a very current example of the potential which exists. On my flight into Tulsa I met the Director of Manufacturing for the largest firm in Stillwater, a subsidiary of Brunswick Corp. During the course of our conversation he offered me a ride on into Stillwater, an unusual and folksy thing for a stranger to do. It made me glad to know there are still a few places left in the world where this kind of thing can happen. I asked him about his company's involvement in international trade and here are some of the things he told me:

--The company contracted to obtain German-made components for an item which they were assembling and marketing. The instructions were in German and the translations were inadequate. They wound up having to pay for a group of German engineers to come in on a temporary basis and explain the operation and functions to their own engineers.

--When trade to China opened they were one of the first companies to go in with a joint venture proposal. When they were ready to close the deal they discovered that their interpreter for Chinese was completely useless because he could not handle the complex financial terminology necessary for the contract, nor the language required to clarify the legalities involved in the transfer of technology.

--A similar event took place in India and the company wound up having to settle for a licensing agreement instead of a joint venture, which would have been much more to their advantage and kept them involved in things like quality control as well.

--Their joint ventures with Japan were much less problematical because the Japanese were so highly sophisticated in English.

--They have a Foreign Trade Zone operating in Mexico.

--Like other large corporations, they have a development fund which could be a contributing source of support for the kind of program I am going to suggest.

II. Merger

My proposal for a merger--or a joint venture--between foreign language study and other academic disciplines, primarily business, would include the development of options for a second track of language training at the upper division undergraduate level, and the development of a Masters in International Business similar to those at the American Graduate School of International Management (Thunderbird School) and at the University of South Carolina. This program would have the following mission:

--To provide, for the expanding areas of international business and relations, competent professionals skilled in languages, knowledgeable in historical and current affairs, and sensitive to cultural and value differences.

The program subscribes to the concept that international business is a going concern seeking to establish and cultivate mutually beneficial transactions between countries on a long-term basis. The professional attitude and communication skills of the graduate should help overcome widespread negative attitudes towards the "ugly American" abroad, and improve U.S. competitiveness in the world market.

The program should revitalize the study of foreign languages and cultures in U.S. educational institutions by developing a new track of language teaching skills aimed at the practical application of communication skills within the above context.

Students selecting this program will be able to perceive the acquisition of foreign languages as a marketable skill, and <u>traditional literary disciplines should experience an increase through spinoff from heightened enrollments in the new areas.</u>

The elements of such a program, which might be called a "Center for Applied International Studies," are as follows:

1. Support and Funding.

The first order of business is to present a proposal soliciting funds for a pilot program. This support should be sought primarily in the private sector, probably with contributing funds from foundations and federal and state sources. It may well be useless at this point to seek support from university administrations until a strong commitment from other sources is in place. The same holds true for the area of greatest resistance: the departments of languages themselves. Outside funds can provide an incentive to adapt, and it may often be the case that such a move could make the difference between survival and elimination or reduction of the department.

2. Interdepartmental Cooperation.

Clearly a productive liaison needs to be established with the schools of business, both at the undergraduate and M.B.A. levels. Other departments contributing key courses could include Economics, History, Law, Engineering, Political Science, Fine Arts, International Relations, Computer Science.

3. Curriculum Development and Skills Acquisition.

Language departments will have to adapt to expanded objectives by retooling or hiring for skills in such areas as public and social speaking in a foreign language, commercial writing, technical writing, and other topics not presently taught. An initial portion of any funding will have to be used as an incentive to encourage faculty to acquire needed skills during, say, summer training sessions.

A language textbook may have to be written for a coordinated two-year program. This textbook would include, if possible, an intensive first year course meeting five days per week and requiring language lab.

The second year textbooks would provide the students with the option of working within the traditional and established structure of foreign language study concentrating on literature. In addition, I would propose that textbooks be developed for three other options beginning with a series of two-hour courses at the intermediate or initial level. The techniques employed should not deteriorate into an exercise in passive vocabulary building but, instead, must concentrate on developing the student's ability to use the language in his or her chosen area. This may mean continued lab work and less overall vocabulary. These electives would include a) business, with attention given to commercial writing skills, public speaking, and oral presentation of selected business reports and topics (highly simplified summaries at this stage); b) high tech industry, which would include simple introductions to computers, electronics, and possibly industrial machinery and optics in the target language, with an emphasis on writing technical reports, summarizing technical reports orally, and spoken clarification of selected topics; c) international relations, which would concentrate on presentation of the language of politics, economics, law, and current events. Public speaking and journalistic writing could be developed, with oral summaries of articles from news magazines, papers, and professional journals and periodicals. Students will need to commit either to a summer abroad or a summer immersion course at some point. Students would select an appropriate combination from this group, and all would still be required to take a two-hour grammar review.

The suggested target languages, to be phased in as is appropriate, include German, Spanish, French, Mandarin Chinese, Japanese, Russian, Arabic, and Portuguese. Also included would be English as a second language.

Offering ESL is a key aspect of the graduate portion of this program. It will provide an initial pool of students and develop a base of foreign nationals seeking M.B.A.s who can make key contributions to the acquisition of skills needed to carry out the program. Their value in terms of networking and further recruitment, as well as in placement and the creation of an international atmosphere, cannot be underestimated. I seriously doubt that the program could be successful without the inclusion of English as a second language.

4. Internship

The other key aspect of the program is a one-year internship with a multinational or domestic firm on foreign soil. The internship can and probably should be preceded by a summer language session, reinforced by a family live-in arrangement. I would project this internship for the fourth or fifth year. The internships will also provide a networking foundation for future support and placement after graduation.

Moreover, these interns can enter the following year as T.A.s, providing the expertise, at last, which we will have only partially developed in our summer training sessions. We may even have to import skilled personnel in the beginning, if only on a temporary basis.

I have sketched a working draft of a proposed curriculum for a five-stage program targeted to German/Business. If the M.I.B. is to have similar credibility as an M.B.A., a sixth year obviously is also required. This curriculum assumes a continuity between undergraduate and graduate level programs. I have not allowed for the obvious need to adapt the language programs for students entering the M.I.B. program from elsewhere with a B.A. in hand; nor are other university requirements included. (* indicates courses offered by German departments.)

I. *First Year German (intensive) with Language Lab
Modern European History
Accounting and General Business Practices
International Relations
Computer Science

II. *German Grammar Review (includes informal conversation and writing)
   *Intro. Business German
   *Intro. German of International Relations
    Marketing
    Finance
    Accounting
    Business Management and Policy

IIa. Summer Abroad
     Option for Junior Year Abroad

III. *Intermediate Business German (letters, reports, speaking, analyses)
     *Intro. German Literature and Philosophy
      Fine Arts: European Painting and Music
      European Business Practices and Management
      Foreign Tax Laws and Business Regulations
      Export Marketing
      International Finance and Trade

IV. Internship in Foreign Country
    Regular short reports on general experience (in German)
    Business analysis of company operations (German with English translations)

V. T.A. for German Business Practice and selected topics
   *German Literature and Politics
   *Advanced Public Speaking in German
   *Advanced Business Composition in German
    Foreign Industry and Management
    Export Management and International Trade
    Economics and Trade with Socialist Countries
    Environmental Constraints: Legal and Cultural

See also chart on following page.

(At the conclusion of this talk Christiane Keck and Barbara Kienbaum responded with information on current developments in Business German across the country and indicated that a great deal of material for the proposed curriculum is well on the way to being developed. Objections were raised about beginning too early with Business German and the broad scope of the project was questioned. The Panel Discussion held by Keck and Kienbaum the following day discussed "hands on" methods and presented an extensive selection of materials developed for teaching Business German. During that discussion the important distinction--very relevant for this proposal--was made to clarify that foreign language departments could not teach Business in German but could and should only teach students how to use German in a business environment.)

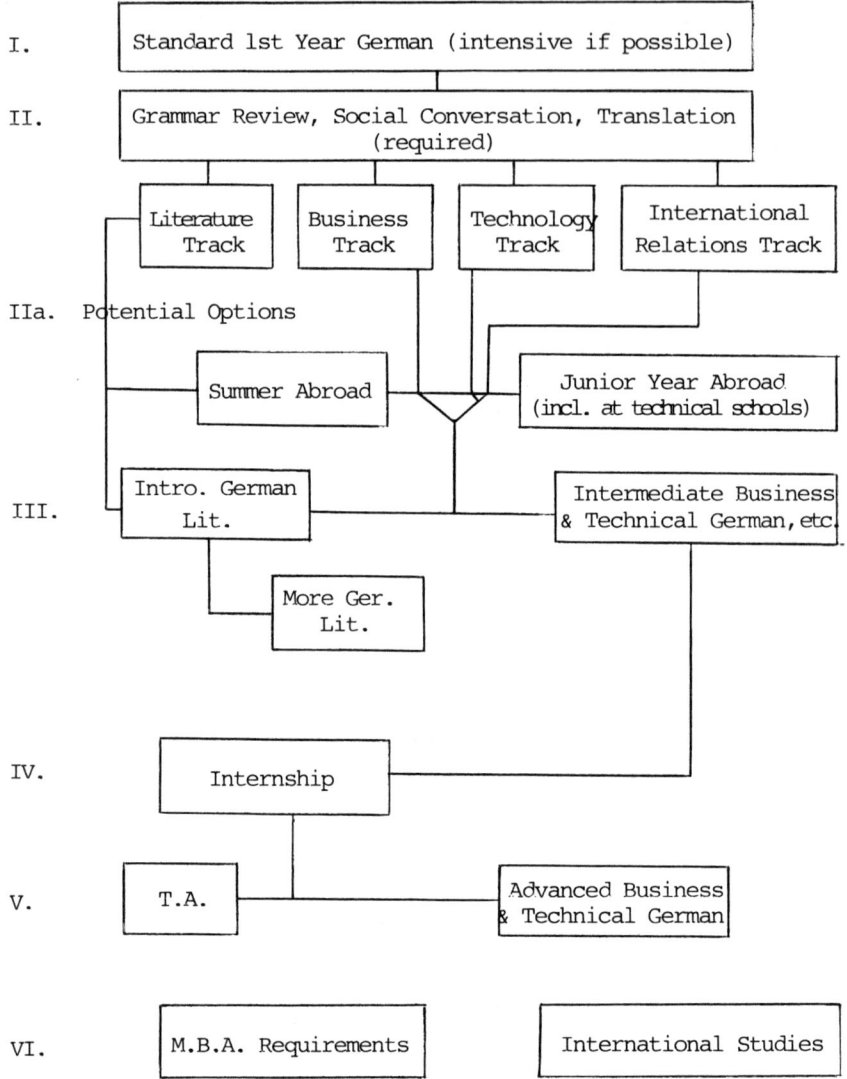

REFERENCES

Demetz, Peter (chair) et al. "Report of the Commission on the Future of the Profession, Spring, 1982," PMLA, 97 (1982), 940-956.

Lyman, Richard W. (chair) et al. The Humanities in American Life. Report of the Commission on the Humanities. Berkeley, Los Angeles, London: Univ. of California Press, 1980.

President's Commission on Foreign Languages and International Studies. Strength Through Wisdom. A Critique of U.S. Capability. Washington, D.C.: U.S. Gov't Printing Office, 1979.

A SURVEY OF THE FOREIGN LANGUAGE NEEDS AND USE OF TEXAS BUSINESS

Elaine K. Horwitz and Gloria Contreras
University of Texas at Austin

Global education is the lifelong growth in understanding, through study and participation, of the world community and the interdependency of its people and systems--social, cultural, racial, economic, linguistic, technological, and ecological (Michigan State Department of Education 1977). The President's Commission on Foreign Languages and International Studies (1970), while not specifically mentioning global education, recommended the strengthening of foreign language and area studies in accordance with the principles of the above stated definition. Increasingly, professional educators of all subject areas and levels are committing themselves to global (or international) education and foreign language study, the most recent being the American Association of Colleges of Teacher Education through its position statement A Global Perspective for Teacher Education (1983).

The introduction of a global perspective into the school curriculum opens new challenges to educators of varying subject areas and levels of instruction. In the case of foreign language education, for example, there is a need for applied language study with new objectives and methods. One obvious application of foreign language study is to the field of business. However, American business has been slow to recognize a need for foreign language skills. In 1978, Inman conducted a survey of 267 large American companies to determine their needs for personnel with proficiency in a foreign language. Her findings showed that the companies did not perceive a great need for foreign language proficiency. Only 17% of the companies reported that Americans speak foreign languages in the United States in an international situation, and only 35.7% do so abroad. If a need to conduct business in a foreign language arose, the companies generally use non-U.S. national employees, or interpreters hired by one of the parties involved. More commonly, business abroad was conducted in English. Inman concluded, "U.S. corporations doing business abroad rely primarily on English as the business language and the means of communication" (Inman 1978: viii).

Before the study of foreign languages can be applied to business, it is necessary to determine how foreign languages are used in business settings. Inman found a gap between educators' beliefs about the need for foreign languages and business reports of actual use. In order to prepare foreign language students for employment in the private sector, our new curricula must be based on accurate usage data.

This paper reports on a survey of the foreign language needs and use of Texas business. The survey questionnaire was a modification of the Inman instrument to allow replication of her results. The businesses surveyed are part of an ongoing collaboration between private industry and the Social Studies Education program at the University of Texas at Austin. Specifically, the companies are internship sites for the Institute on Free Enterprise. This program allows in-service teachers to spend a month with a participating company for purposes of studying economic concepts and principles from a business perspective.

The decision to use this set of businesses was based on several criteria:

1) We hoped that the already established relationship with the companies would insure a good response rate. Previous surveys of the foreign language needs of American business have suffered from low rates of return.

2) We felt that since these businesses have an ongoing relationship with a university social studies education program, they might be particularly sensitive to the importance of foreign languages and cultural understanding in the economic arena.

3) We thought that business in Texas might be sensitive to foreign language concerns because of the state's multilingual, multicultural heritage.

4) Texas has experienced unprecedented economic growth. The Texas 2000 Commission (1982) anticipates continued growth, especially in international trade.

5) Finally, and most importantly, we as Texas educators are interested in developing curricula which will meet the needs of our state.

The five page questionnaire was mailed to the forty-four companies participating in the 1982 Economic Education Institute. Twenty completed surveys were returned, and three additional firms returned detailed letters describing their use of foreign languages but did not complete the questionnaire. The numerical results reported here will be confined to the twenty completed surveys. The sample includes eight companies in the petrochemical industry (three oilfield equipment firms, four oil companies, and one petrochemical firm), three in electronics, three in engineering, two in construction, two in energy/utility, one in steel, and one diversified. The companies cover a wide range in both size and revenues. While Inman's sample companies averaged between 1000 and 50,000 employees and between $100 million and $10 billion in revenues, 25% of our respondents are on the lower range of this scale. Six companies have between 100 and 1000 employees and four companies have revenues in the $10-100 million category. 86% of our participants report that most (at least 60%) of their business is domestic; this figure was approximately 65% in the Inman study. Three companies in our sample report that 60% of their business is foreign.

We first asked the companies where they are conducting foreign business. The greatest amount of international business for this sample is being done in Western Europe, followed by Central and South America and Mexico, the Middle East, Canada, Africa, and the Far East. In addition, two companies each report commerce with Eastern Europe and the U.S.S.R. These findings are similar to those reported by Inman with the exception of the reversed rankings for the Middle East and Canada, which might result from the higher proportion of oil-related industry in our sample.

English was the language most commonly used for business dealings abroad, followed by French and Spanish, German and Arabic, and Portuguese and Norwegian. Chinese, Dutch, Japanese, Italian, and Indonesian were also cited by one company each.

Of primary importance to our study is the use of foreign languages by business personnel. The companies were asked to name their personnel "who need a second language for their job activities." Table 1 lists the job categories indicated and the number of companies specifying each.

Job Category	Number of Companies Indicating a Need	Percentage of All Responding Companies
Sales	8	40
Supervisory	6	30
Technical	6	30
Administrative	5	25
Middle management	5	25
Other	4	20
Clerical	2	10
Instruction	2	10
Public relations	2	10

Table 1: Job Categories Needing Foreign Language Proficiency

Additionally we asked if there were any personnel "for whom a knowledge of a second language is considered useful but not necessary." Table 2 shows the job categories and the number of companies indicating them.

Job Category	Number of Companies Indicating Usefulness	Percentage of All Responding Companies
Management	5	25
Sales	3	15
Supervisory	3	15
Service	3	15
Customer contact	3	15
Administrative asst.	3	15
Marketing	2	10
Personnel	2	10
Secretarial	2	10

Table 2: Job Categories For Which Knowledge of a Foreign Language is Considered Useful

Although the companies indicate that personnel in a wide range of job categories need or could use foreign language skills, personnel policies do not show a commensurate appreciation of them. Only two of the responding companies claim to offer higher compensation or special consideration for employees who use foreign language skills on the job. Four of the twenty responding companies said that promotion opportunities were greater for individuals with foreign language proficiency. Thus the vast majority of the businesses do not reward these abilities. The question of initial hirings was not posed; it remains to be determined whether individuals with foreign language ability are given preference over monolingual applicants with comparable backgrounds. However, only a substantial minority of the companies indicate that foreign languages are used by their employees for transactions with non-English speaking clients. Nine companies (45% of the sample) state that transactions in the U.S. with non-English speaking clients are handled by U.S. nationals who speak the foreign language and seven companies (35%) report that U.S. nationals use the foreign language when dealing with non-English speakers abroad. Four companies concede that some international aspects of their business are hampered by their foreign language deficiencies.

The companies were next asked about their translation and interpreting needs. Table 3 presents the ranked order of languages for which translation and interpretation are necessary. Additionally, we asked the companies to name the types of documents which they commonly have translated and the types of situations for which interpreters are required. Tables 4 and 5 present these results.

Language	Companies Naming This as the Most Commonly Translated Language	Companies with a Translation Need	Companies Naming This as the Most Commonly Interpreted Language	Companies with an Interpreting Need
Spanish	7	9	7	9
French	3	6	3	6
Arabic	3	6	3	6
German	2	5	2	6
Portuguese	2	2	2	2
Asian	1	4	1	4
Oriental	1	2	1	2
Russian	1	1	1	1
Greek	0	1	0	0
Persian	0	0	0	0
Other	1	2	1	2

Table 3: Translation and Interpreting Needs

The majority (50% or more) of the translating and interpreting is performed by in-house employees whose responsibilities are in nonlanguage areas. Private individuals and agencies are also used in these areas. Two companies indicate that some of their translation and interpreting is performed by company employees whose major responsibilities is to deal with foreign language matters. Three companies state that translation and interpreting is provided by the other party involved.

	From Foreign Language to English		From English to Foreign Language	
	# of Companies	% of Companies	# of Companies	% of Companies
Correspondence	6	30	3	15
Financial reports	3	15	2	10
Promotional literature (advertisements)	3	15	4	20
Journals, professional articles	2	10	2	10
Brochures, manuals	4	20	3	15
Instructional materials	3	15	2	10
Other	1	5	2	10
Have no requirements	3	15	4	20

Table 4: Types of Documents Which Require Translation

Situations	# of Companies	% of Companies
Professional, technical subjects	6	30
Top level negotiations	5	25
Social, conversational	4	20
Daily operations	2	10

Table 5: Situations for Which Interpretors are Necessary

The next question dealt with language training provided to employees. Seven companies provide instruction to employees either in-house or by contract. Language training takes place in Norway, the U.S., the United Arab Emirates, Indonesia, and Japan, in the following languages: English, French, German, Japanese, Spanish, and Portuguese. Two companies provide the training in-house and five by contract.

Finally, the companies were asked about their future plans. Five companies are planning new overseas expansions. Areas mentioned were Holland, Norway, Europe, and the Middle East. The companies unanimously agree that their future need for foreign languages will not decrease. One third of the companies expect their need for foreign languages to increase while two thirds expect that their need will remain constant. The companies expecting an increased need volunteered several comments. "Foreign languages (Spanish) are needed in the U.S. for social use and for dealing with expatriate employees." "The number of foreign workers is rising and U.S. education in foreign language is poor." "English is needed for foreign managers. It is not a must but is helpful."

An Economic Perspective: Implications of the Trade Deficit for Education

In the first part of this paper we have shown a contract between professional educators and their business counterparts with respect to the perceived need for foreign language skills in today's world. While educators believe that global interdependence is no longer just a cliche and that foreign language and international education are critical to the school curriculum, research from a business perspective shows that the perceived need for foreign languages to conduct business is not increasing at the same rate. There are, however, a few businesses in our sample which value and make great use of foreign languages. One respondent commented:

> The U.S. college and school system totally ignores the fact that the U.S. is not the center of every activity in the world anymore. Therefore, we need to require students to learn at least one foreign language in order to get out of high school, and another language in college.

The next section of this paper will present an analysis of the economic cost of a monolingual business policy, to help educators bring a stronger case for foreign languages to the business community.

The Globe as a Single Market Place. The swing in the U.S. merchandise trade balance from a $9 billion surplus in 1975 to an enormous $200 billion deficit in 1983, is largely the result of 1) the growing U.S. dependence on high-cost foreign oil, 2) the rising U.S. import demand, and 3) a depressed world demand for U.S. exports as a result of the relatively slower economic recovery of major U.S. trading partners. Even though a multitude of other factors are involved, these three forces are primarily responsible for the U.S. trade balance having moved so deeply into deficit in such a short span of time (Emrich 1978).

According to Reich (1983), the underlying problems of the U.S. economy lie in the very structure of American industry, and not in the rhetorical scapegoats of excessive regulation, government deficits, inadequate investment, or greedy labor unions. America's relative decline, he asserts, is rooted in changes in the world market. In the 1960s, he explains, only a small portion of American-made goods were exported; likewise, only a small amount of foreign products entered the U.S. Today, however, this situation has changed dramatically.

The importance of foreign competition is revealed by the fact that by 1980 more than 70% of all the goods produced in the U.S. were actively competing with foreign-made goods. That is, America has become part of the world market, but American producers have not fared well in this new contest. Indeed, Reich notes that "Goods are being made wherever they can be made the cheapest, regardless of national boundaries. And the most efficient places for much mass production are coming to be the Third World countries."

Another well known economist, Lester Thurow, a frequent Newsweek columnist, has resounded the same message. Accordingly, Americans who have never been export oriented must learn to be competitive in international markets, for without exports, a country cannot pay for the imports necessary to maintain its standard of living. Thurow (1982) suggests that U.S. companies will have to design products expressly for foreign markets, "and their employees may have to learn foreign languages to make certain they understand what is needed."

That the majority of U.S. manufacturers still shows little activity in overseas markets is revealed by the following fact: The Commerce Department has estimated that about half of U.S. exports of manufactured goods are made by only 100 companies, and that 80% are made by only 250 companies (Emrich 1978). Presumably, too many manufacturers look on foreign markets merely as an add-on to domestic operations, that is, a place to unload excess production.

The indifference toward exporting on the part of major portions of American industries stands in sharp contrast to the strong commitment to exporting among other trading nations. Other economies with more limited domestic growth opportunities constantly push outward in an attempt to capture the world economies-of-scale. For example, Latin American markets are no longer dominated by the U.S. Rather, it appears that Japan is outhustling American industry in its once "private preserve."

In conclusion, the ranks of U.S. competitors have steadily increased while the U.S. attitude toward exporting has remained relatively lax. However, the recent trade deficits appear to have driven home the point that the U.S. must export more. American industry must redefine its own attitudes toward the global market and begin to match the effort of its competitors with a strong export commitment of its own.

Exports and American jobs. In his State of the Union Message, President Reagan (1983) recognized that America's economic well-being is inextricably linked to the world economy. He pointed out that one out of every five jobs in the U.S. depends on trade and proposed a strategy in the field of international trade ". . .that increases the openness of our trading system and is fairer to America's farmers and workers. . ." Thus, exports mean jobs as well as the earnings necessary to import the commodities that a country cannot produce for itself (30% of oil consumption) or is inefficient in producing (consumer electronics) (Thurow 1982).

America's industrial inefficiency is particularly dramatic in capital intensive, high volume industries (automobile and industrial and agricultural machinery industries). Drucker's (1968: 68) observation made over fifteen years ago partly explains the decline:

> What the Japanese realized twenty years ago was that they had to make sure their productive resources were going to tomorrow's rather than into yesterday's work.... The Japanese have, therefore, systematically projected the trends of the world economy onto their economic policy, both domestic and international.

In short, in an era of technological change, Japan shifted its industrial base toward products and processes that required skilled workers; for high volume, standardized production facilities can be established anywhere; however, production processes that depend on skilled labor must stay where the skilled labor is (Reich 1983).

Industrialized countries, then, are moving into precision manufactured, custom tailored, and technology driven product categories that depend on sophisticated skills, skills that are frequently developed within teams. The traditional separate business functions that include design, engineering, purchasing, manufacturing, distribution, marketing, and sales must be merged into a highly integrated system that can respond quickly to new opportunities. Essentially, flexible systems of production have replaced high volume, standardized production. However, this does not mean abandonment of older industries; rather, the older industries of steel, automobiles, chemicals, and textiles are the gateways through which new products and processes emerge (Reich 1983).

For the U.S. the shift to flexible-system production has been difficult and painful, for this transition requires a basic restructuring of business, labor, and government of such magnitude that it has met resistance because of the threat it poses to vested economic interests and established values. The result, Reich posits, is that the U.S. has forfeited world industrial leadership to Japan and resorted to "paper entrepreneuralism." This, in short, means paper profits and is both cause and consequence of America's faltering economy.

Implications of a World Market for Education. If paper enterpreneuralism is indeed the root cause of America's recent economic decline, the possible implications for schools are a matter of some importance because we have come to place a premium on the manipulation of symbols to the exclusion of other sorts of skills. Reich identifies these as how to collaborate with others, to work in teams, to solve concrete problems, and to speak foreign languages in view of the newly competitive world economy. He points out, for example, that in Japan 65% of all seats on the boards of Japanese manufacturing companies are occupied by people trained as engineers. Roughly the same percentage of American counterparts are trained in law, finance, and accountancy. Thus, Japanese problems are viewed as questions of engineering or science, requiring technical solutions, while American problems are apt to be seen as questions of law or finance, able to be dodged "through clever manipulation of rules or number."

Consequently we offer two recommendations for bringing about more effective communication between business and education in respect to applied language study. First of all, the foregoing study has shown that American industry is going to have to commit itself to being competitive in international markets. Ideally, employees will learn foreign languages in order to design products expressly for foreign markets. Indeed there is a need for case studies of American business firms that already have a commitment to international markets and systematically use foreign language skills in their marketing research efforts. According to our survey, for example, several business firms reported a higher salary scale or special form of compensation made to those employees who use foreign language skills on the job, and several indicated an increasing need for foreign languages to conduct business. Follow-up case studies of such "model" companies are needed.

Secondly, students of foreign languages at both the high school and college levels would benefit from a field-based internship or practicum in a

business firm designed to ascertain the applied use of specific foreign languages. Business firms, on the other hand, could learn from the foreign language students the nuances involved in marketing to certain foreign populations. Many companies, for example, have assumed erroneously that simply translating their advertisements into foreign languages will make their products sell.

Related to this business/foreign language school exchange is curriculum development of an "applied" nature, and consideration of the effect of curricular materials on the achievement and attitude of foreign language education students at various levels of schooling.

It is hoped that American industry will meet foreign competition head on and look to education, training, and retraining as fundamental to our success and productivity as a nation.

REFERENCES

American Association of Colleges for Teacher Education. A Global Perspective for Teacher Education. Washington, D.C.: AACTE, 1983.

Drucker, Peter F. The Age of Discontinuity: Guidelines to our Changing Society. New York: Harper and Row, 1968.

Emrich, Thomas D. Imports, Exports and Jobs: An Economic Perspective on the Trade Deficit, Employment and Protectionism. New York: American Importers Association, 1978.

Inman, Marianne E. An Investigation of the Foreign Language Needs of U.S. Corporations Doing Business Abroad. Unpublished doctoral dissertation, The University of Texas at Austin, 1978.

Michigan State Department of Education. Global Education Guidelines. Lansing, Michigan: Michigan State Department of Education, 1977. (ERIC Document Reproduction Service No. Ed 159 106)

Reagan, Ronald. We Have a Long Way to Go, State of the Union Message. The New York Times, 26 January 1983, p. 10Y.

Reich, Robert B. "The Next American Frontier," The Atlantic Monthly, March 1983, p. 43.

Texas Past and Future: A Survey. Texas 2000 Project. Austin, Texas: Office of the Governor, 1982.

Thurow, Lester C. "A Strong Dollar's Price," Newsweek, 29 November 1982, p. 89.

BUSINESS GERMAN: A DEVELOPING DISCIPLINE

Christiane E. Keck
Purdue University

Since the mid-seventies, a new dimension has emerged in our foreign language course offerings and curricula. The last few years have seen a flurry of activity in the area of Business German, French, and Spanish. Programs at various colleges and universities differ greatly in this new field, ranging from one course in the language department, to an interface with the business school, to a whole program of concentration for undergraduates. A few universities even offer a graduate degree in International Studies. According to the New York Times (6 April 1983, p. 41), a study comparing the international course offerings of eleven leading graduate business schools, including Harvard, Northwestern, Stanford, the University of Virginia, the University of Pennsylvania, and the University of Chicago, revealed that "all the graduate schools of business report large enrollments in international courses, and a growing demand for them." Foreign language departments can capitalize on this new emphasis on the international scene. But in practical terms, this means that some professors, trained in the traditional areas of language, literature, and linguistics, must "retool." As was noted in the Times article, the push comes in part from the students, who are eager to learn something practical and marketable. Students of business are beginning to enroll in foreign language programs which offer more than just the traditional literature courses.

Just as Scientific German for reading knowledge has long been a viable part of the German curriculum, offering the scientist a practical tool, so business language gives a valuable learning experience to students preparing for a career in business. This is not to say that most of the students, who show an interest in international courses or who study Business German, plan to work abroad or in export areas of major international companies. They will, however, be dealing increasingly with foreign firms in the U.S. as well as overseas. Students today show a growing awareness of the importance of international understanding and a greater sensitivity to the existing cultural differences among the peoples of the world. Future managers will almost certainly be increasingly involved with multinational companies and international trade, and that means involvement with language and culture.

In learning Business German all four skills--reading, writing, listening and speaking--must be stressed. An up-to-date look at the customs, culture, and business practices of the German speaking world is also an essential ingredient. It becomes readily apparent that teaching such a course challenges the instructor far more than teaching the more traditional language course usually does. It takes an enormous amount of time to read daily and weekly newspapers and magazines in order to keep the information in the courses current.

One very desirable and integral part of the education process for the student in business language is the internship. Ideally, after completing a course or two of Business German, the most qualified students should be given an opportunity to go abroad and to work in a firm as a "Praktikant." The advantages of such an experience should be obvious. Not only is the student exposed to direct, hands on, highly supervised work in a foreign setting, but in addition undergoes a total immersion process in the language and culture of the foreign country. Financially, the internship does not garner the student a profit, but it practically always covers the basic expenses of travel, food, and housing. With the current rise of unemployment in Europe, and even in Germany, placing students as interns in companies abroad is becoming increasingly more difficult. This makes it more complicated, then, for professors just beginning to look into internship opportunities abroad for their students. Most of us already involved in such efforts cannot make arrangements for students from other universities, but the University of Cincinnati and Eastern Michigan University have programs reaching beyond their own campus (see Schaub 1983).

While internships abroad are an ideal learning experience for the business language student, there is also great merit in placing students in firms located in the U.S. with international divisions or import/export departments. These "local" internships are much easier to arrange, since they do not involve applications for a student visa or an "Aufenthaltserlaubnis." Firms located in the U.S. actually welcome the intelligent, willing student who works with enthusiasm at a minimal cost to the firm. Universities located in or near large cities, and particularly universities located in the southeast, where so many German companies have recently established branches, have greater opportunities for placing Business German students than colleges in small towns removed from such industrial centers. One of the most successful ways to obtain intern positions for students, I have found, is by inviting executives of various companies into the classroom for a lecture about their particular jobs in their firms. Executives like to be invited to campus, and students benefit enormously from hearing their points of view. These contacts often result in a few internship offers and occasionally even in a permanent position for a student (see Keck 1983).

Now, how does a very traditional German department go about organizing such a course or begin a program of Business German. Since 1975, the Goethe Institute has generously sponsored a number of intensive seminars for German professors around the country. Three very useful works, published by the Goethe Institute Atlanta, were a direct result of these seminars: Wirtschaftssprache Deutsch, Summer 1981; Bibliography for Business German, Fall 1981; and Wirtschaftsdiplom Deutsch, Spring 1982. This practical information on Business German curriculum building, course descriptions, and available textbook lists was gathered together, organized and written up by the various seminar participants. Gradually there emerged out of these seminars a core group of professors, committed to working in and disseminating information about this new area to the profession through workshops, papers, and articles. We have now established a national committee on Business German, a standing committee of the American Association of Teachers of German. Slowly, too, we are seeing the formation of a whole network of persons actively engaged in Business German programs. National, regional, state, and local meetings now regularly include Business German on their professional conference programs.

In an attempt to document for the advanced student a certain body of knowledge which could be meaningful to future employers, we are now working toward the establishment of a recognized "Wirtschaftsdiplom Deutsch." Actively involved in this project are the Goethe Institute,the Carl Duisberg Society, the German-American Chamber of Commerce and the members of the AATG Standing Committee of Business German. A pilot advanced Business German Examination is being tested this spring and fall in the Business German courses given by the professors on the Committee. The examination will test the four skills: reading, writing, listening and speaking. It is designed for the advanced student, who has completed at least one or two Business German courses. Passing the examination will then result in the granting of the "Wirtschaftsdiplom Deutsch." Such an exam already exists for Business French students and is administered by the Chambre de Commerce in Paris. This endeavor to establish the "Diplom" will greatly aid Business German teachers, in giving them some guidance as to content and direction of their courses. It will also document a certain proficiency achieved by students, who must acquire the knowledge and language skills needed to pass the examination. This reward to the students can then enhance their career opportunities.

REFERENCES

Keck, Christiane E. "Teaching Business Language Courses: Curriculum and Career Opportunities." ADFL Bulletin, vol. 14, no. 3 (March 1983), pp. 54-57.

Schaub, Ray. "Language Training for International Business at Eastern Michigan University." ADFL Bulletin, vol. 14, no. 3 (March 1983), pp. 51-53.

A PRACTICAL APPROACH TO BUSINESS GERMAN

Barbara E. Kienbaum
Purdue University Calumet

An ever increasing number of German departments charge their faculty with the responsibility for developing a Business German course to be included in the curriculum. The chances that an economist is in the department are remote. Usually it is a junior faculty member, a traditional Germanist by training, who is given the formidable task of starting such a course. What is there then to do but to research the available texts, order some books, give library and bookstore their orders and anticipate with mixed feelings the beginning of the semester? Unfortunately, even a superficial survey of the existing texts gives the investigator the distinct impression that they would not be suitable for class purposes: they are terribly dull, out of date, or not at all geared to an American college audience.

It is my purpose to suggest an alternative. Why not collect readily available material, select the material into a chosen number of topics which are to be covered in the course, develop key vocabulary, and create exercises suitable for a specific classroom. The prerequisite, of course, is that the instructor do some extensive preparation prior to the beginning of the course. The advantages, however, of using authentic materials in a business language course are numerous. The material is up-to-date, it is personally selected, and it is not artificial; selected and edited for students, it addresses the native language audience and it uses the environment our language student aims to be functional in. With those considerations in mind the German Business course becomes an excellent testing ground for the communicative method with the functional/notional approach to language learning.

The greatest aid in the beginning process of resource development is the Bibliography for Business German compiled by A. Galt, J. Frey, and H. Braun, (published by the Goethe Institute Atlanta, Fall 1981). Not only does this bibliography list books, texts, and dictionaries suitable for Business German but also periodicals, magazines, newspapers, brochures, and handouts, all tremendous tools for someone starting a German Business course. Additionally, it lists addresses of such places as the Deutscher Gewerkschaftsbund, Bundesanstalt für Arbeit, Bundesministerium der Finanzen, Bundeministerium für Wirtschaft, as well as the addresses of the various German-American chambers of commerce who publish the United States-German Economic Survey, German-American Trade News, Amerika Handel, and two weekly newsletters, the German Business Weekly and Kurzbrief aus U.S.A. Almost all organizations have printed materials available for class use, covering such topics as banking (Zahlungsverkehr), labor, transportation, investments, the stockmarket, etc. One postcard to the Posttechnische Zentralamt, Schulberatung VW 15-5, Postfach 1180, 6100 Darmstadt, netted a whole stack of overhead transparencies, plus numerous handouts and brochures, all explaining the different methods of payment in the Federal Republic. Internationes Kennedy-Allee 91-103, 5300 Bonn 2 is a government organization which is extremely helpful and generous in providing, all free of charge, materials for use in specific classes.

Every state in West Germany has a Wirtschaftsförderungsbüro; after writing to the office of the Saarland, Römerbrücke 22, 6600 Saarbrücken, I received 36 slides about the Saarland, a booklet with statistical economic information and a cassette describing the economic climate of the Saar; needless to say, all are extremely useful materials when the topics Standort and Infrastructure are covered.

After one amasses a wealth of information and materials, it becomes necessary to divide it into topical headings much like different chapters one would have in a traditional textbook. Following are a series of suggested topic or theme headings. Individual teachers can add, delete, or otherwise supplement this list to reflect their own interests and inclinations: Wirtschaftsgeographie; Wirtschaftliche Grundbegriffe; Industrieunternehmen in der BRD; Standortwahl; Das Finanz- und Steuerwesen; Bankbetrieb und Investition; Mitbestimmung: Rolle des Arbeitnehmers und Arbeitgebers; Sozialleitungen in der BRD, einem demokratischen und sozialen Rechtsstaat; Medien und Werbung; Minoritäten: Soziale Probleme im Wirtschafts- und Sozialbereich; Europäische Wirtschaftsgemeinschaften: EWG COMECON; Stellungssuche in der BRD.

It is one thing to collect raw material, another to prepare oneself for the task of teaching such a course. To acquire some general background information on the economic systems of both Germanies and their role in world trade, and a familiarization with the whole nomenclature of Betriebswirtschaftslehre and Volkswirtschaft, I recommend the following: <u>Wirtschaft und Gesellschaft in der Bundesrepublik Deutschland,</u> by Dieter Menyesch and Henrick Uterwedde, (Heidelberg: Julius Groos, 1982), written for the non-specialist, such as a foreign language teacher who has to explain the German economic system; and another helpful book, since it explains the two German economic systems and their differences, <u>Deutsche Wirtschaft nach 1945,</u> by Gert Leptin, (Uni-Taschenbücher, vol. 878, 1980). For information on the geography of economics, population distribution, concentration of industry, transportation, and communication methods (etc.) I suggest the <u>Fischer Informations Atlas, BRD, Karten, Grafiken, Texte und Tabellen</u> (Fischer Taschenbuch, 1982). Additional statistical information is available from the Statistische Bundesamt, Gustav-Stresemann-Ring II, 6200 Wiesbaden 1. An informative look at the cultural aspects and implication of the German business world is <u>Meeting German Business,</u> 2nd ed., compiled and edited by Irmgard Burmeister (Atlantik-Brücke, 1977).

To keep abreast of the current events in the business world at home and abroad it is necessary for the instructor or the department to subscribe to several newspapers and magazines. The most important one for teacher and students is the Wirtschaftswoche, published weekly in Dusseldorf. Also very good for background reading is Der Spiegel, a weekly from Hamburg, which publishes an annual summary dealing with business and economics under the title Der Spiegel: Unternehmen, Märkte, Manager (available by writing to Spiegel Verlag, Postfach 110220, 2000 Hamburg 11). A costly but nonetheless very important tool for gaining information are several daily newspapers such as the Frankfurter Allgemeine or the Süddeutsche Zeitung. Affordable is the U. S. edition of the weekly Die Zeit; a one year subscription costs at this writing $37.00.

Being immersed in this material will not make an economist out of a Germanist, but it certainly will reduce the anxiety level when one is chosen to teach Business German. After a certain time one can even grow comfortable with the idea and start to develop strategies to make the course exciting.

After the instructor has decided what topics will be covered in the German Business course and has selected the majority of the text materials, his or her next task is to edit, that is to shorten the texts, in order to insure that only the most precise and up-to-date information will be used. The chosen material should also contain a sufficient amount of target vocabulary. The instructor should help the students with the most difficult portions of the text, not by giving translations but by decoding texts, using free association with key words, emphasizing cognates, recalling the general subject matter, and keeping in mind that not all text portions have to be totally comprehended. In fact, to pursue total comprehension of the text would be too time-consuming and hinder the learning process considerably. The exercises should reflect this teaching approach by testing only the comprehension of key information and key vocabulary.

A MODEL: PURDUE CALUMET'S FOREIGN LANGUAGE INTERNATIONAL STUDIES PROGRAM

Arlene J. Russell
Purdue University Calumet

Purdue University Calumet's Foreign Language International Studies program provides students with intensive written and oral practice in French, German, or Spanish, with emphasis on communication within the appropriate cultural setting. The program also includes instruction in the basic principles of international business, management, foreign affairs, and social and economic issues. Emphasis is interdisciplinary, involving areas of history, political science, economics, and other coursework complementary to the foreign language/business combination. A key component of the International Studies program is the internship, by which cooperating companies provide students with the opportunity to observe, learn, and practice aspects of international business procedures.

The overall objectives of the program, therefore, are six:

1. instruction in basic grammatical principles, using contrastive grammatical structures;

2. practice in oral language skills with emphasis on real communication within the appropriate cultural setting;

3. practice in written language skills for grammatical correctness and accuracy of expression;

4. knowledge of the culture of the people whose language is studied, awareness of self through contrastive studies in culture and ethnicity;

5. awareness of the economic, political, and social situation of the country where the language is used;

6. instruction in basic principles of international finance, banking, transportation and management.

Several steps were taken in the development of the International Studies program. Companies with international departments located in Indiana and in the Chicago area responded to a questionnaire proposing an undergraduate curriculum to prepare students with a business/language combination. Additionally, a three-month survey of job opportunities as listed in the Chicago Tribune revealed 40 to 50 jobs per week that specifically required or recommended a foreign language background or competency. The program was then redesigned to prepare a graduate to enter the job market in an international field or to continue graduate study.

The foreign language faculty needed to prepare to teach the commercial language courses; they participated in training sessions, workshops and conferences at the regional and national levels. Faculty members are now active in the writing of commercial language textbooks, the pursuit of pedagogical methodology, the presenting of papers and workshops, the gathering of authentic materials, and the organizing of regular export seminars on campus for student participation.

The International Studies program, although a career oriented course of studies, is a foreign language major within the School of Humanities, Education, and Social Sciences. It therefore provides the students with a strong liberal arts foundation. Students complete 57 semester hours of general undergraduate requirements in addition to their major requirements. Twelve of the 57 hours are in science and mathematics; the remaining 45 hours are in humanities and social sciences. Students choose electives to total 126 semester hours needed for graduation with the bachelor's degree. Students in the program are urged to take courses in business data processing, business writing, and advanced math. Additionally, in order to strengthen their business background, many students are opting to minor in management, accounting, finance, labor or marketing.

The existing program requires 45 semester hours in the major: 21 semester hours in intermediate and advanced courses in the foreign language, 12 hours in economics, and 12 hours in history and political science. The 21 hours in the foreign language are communicative skills/culture oriented courses: nine hours of conversation and composition, six hours of commercial language and practicum, three hours of civilization/culture, and an additional three hours of a language elective. A principles of economics course precedes the 12-hour economics component which consists of microeconomics, macroeconomics, and areas of international economics. The 12-hour history and political science component comprises courses in the history of the country of the language studied and appropriate courses in international relations, U.S. foreign policy, international law, and organization.

The language practicum in business, a three-credit course, consists of on-the-job training in international corporations, industry, commerce, or government where the foreign language is used. The practicum is designed to add a dimension of practical experience to the student's academically acquired knowledge. There is a three-part requirement to the practicum: prefield work, field work, and postfield work. The prefield work involves two weeks of class instruction for which the student does preliminary reading related to the company and prepares an outline of a paper that will be based on the internship experience. The field work consists of a 12-week observation/training/performance period during which the student works a minimum of six hours a week under the company supervisor as approved by the director of internships. The student keeps a log of each week's experience and meets with the instructor to review the internship activities. The postfield segment closes the practicum with two weeks of class instruction during which the student writes a final project paper about the experience gained in the field. The instructor issues a course grade based on the student's written paper and the evaluations provided by both the student's field supervisor and the director of internships.

The Department of Foreign Languages and Literatures is seeking to insure the quality of its program. We propose to limit access to the required (and very much sought after) practicum to the abler student. The student must meet certain prerequisites to be considered for placement in an internship position: completion of all language skills courses and the commercial course with a B or better, a B or better G.P.A., approval of the director of internships, and successful completion of foreign language proficiency exams administered by outside agencies.

The first internship in Fall 1979 provided eight students with field experiences in different business establishments. As part of their on-site internship duties, students prepared export documentation, translated correspondence, used the Telex, made telephone calls to foreign countries, did market analyses, estimated the cost of commodities overseas, and prepared letters of credit and packing lists. In short, these students performed many of the duties involved in the export departments of international companies. The companies themselves were diverse: pharmaceutical products, sales and services, manufacturers of steel tubing, international transportation. Several students worked in a courtroom setting, interpreting for a judge and the non-English speakers in his court. More recent internships saw students placed with international freight forwarders, a chemical company, a supplier of photographic lighting equipment, and a foreign exchange house. Students used language communication skills in a variety of ways: responding to phone orders, translating correspondence, taping, using Telex, preparing documentation, converting currencies, interpreting, working with supervisors in the target language, and preparing correspondence. Each practicum experience is unique and involves duties set out by the company supervisor and approved by the director of internships.

Since the program's inception in Spring 1980, Purdue Calumet's Foreign Language International Studies majors have increased from eight to thirty-four. The continuously increasing number of majors and the many inquiries from persons seeking this program of studies give testimony to the need and desirability of the program. The cooperating companies that offer internship experiences and their favorable evaluation of our students' performance further attest to the program's relevancy.

FUNCTIONAL FL FOR THE NON-FL SPECIALIST:
Curriculum Design and Instructional Strategies for an Entry Level FL Program Geared to the Workaday Needs of a Targeted Group of Non FL Professionals

Sidney Pellissier
Purdue University

Designing the syllabus for a specialized Foreign Language (FL) training program is both challenging and problematic; this paper discusses, from a frankly pragmatic and hopefully practical point of view, some ways in which the challenges may be met and the problems resolved when one faces the task of teaching a FL to learners who intend to use the FL on the job. The particular bias of this discussion is that the FL will be taught and learned as a means rather than as an end in itself: the learner's goal will be to acquire a level of skills in the FL which will allow him or her to use the language as a functional tool in applied settings, i.e., outside the confines of the classroom.

A clarification of terminology is in order. The term functional is used here both in a general sense and in a restricted, technical sense. Functional in general terms connotes that which is useful, that which accomplishes the work for which it was intended, that which gets the job done. In its restricted, technical sense the term refers to the categories of communicative function as set forth by D. A. Wilkins in Notional Syllabuses, and subsequently much discussed in pedagogical literature as the "functional/notional" or "notional/functional" approach to FL instruction. Wilkins argues convincingly that FL instruction has concentrated more on the use of language to describe and to report than it has on the use of language as a vehicle for getting things done. He feels that FL teachers have unwisely substituted grammatical categories for categories of communicative function, perhaps on the false assumption that the two are fully synonymous. However, such is not the case: categories of grammar and categories of communicative function are related only in limited ways. For example, it is erroneous to assume that the grammatical category imperative equals the communicative function command because the imperative is only one choice among several for a speaker who wishes to make something happen via a command. It would be more germane to the FL learner's needs to learn communicative functions such as advise, advocate, persuade, suggest, recommend, urge, propose, because direct commands are often not the way we get other people to do as we wish.

My objective in this paper is to propose guidelines for organizing and teaching functional FL at entry level to a group of learners who need to acquire the FL for use in the workaday world. First, I will describe a specific functional French intensive program which I designed and conducted at Purdue University. Then, I will provide examples of selected instructional software which was specially developed for the program, and mention some teaching strategies which were adopted. Finally, I will propose general practical guidelines which may be helpful to those interested in syllabus design and materials development for specialized applied language programs.

During the 1979-80 academic year a special French course, funded by Title XII Institutional Strengthening Grant monies, was designed for Purdue faculty and graduate students who would subsequently be assigned to overseas duties in Francophone West and Central Africa. Participants in the program were scientists, agronomists, agricultural, and technical specialists who needed to learn enough French to qualify for an FSI-2 rating in order to meet linguistic proficiency standards set by U.S.A.I.D. for on-site consultant work in Francophone African nations.

The functional French training program consisted of 300 contact hours of instruction, spread over a two-semester period (2 hrs/day X 5 days/week X 2 15-week semesters = 300 hours total). Instruction was provided by a staff of four: three French language instructors and one Africanist. The curriculum of the program comprised the following components, weighted as indicated:

>   General African Culture and Civilization   (10%)
>   Basics of French Language   (45%)
>   Pronunciation (Fr. phonetics)   (5%)
>   Reading   (20%)
>   1. Francophone African topics
>   2. Professional literature (reports, articles, documents)
>   Conversation   (20%)
>   1. Social discourse
>   2. Job related discourse

Courses were scheduled so that there would be nine hours per week of French language instruction conducted in contact language for the most part, and one hour per week of civilization taught in English. One of the French language instructors provided tutoring on an ad hoc basis for participants who missed class due to conflicting professional obligations (conferences, consulting trips); this tutor/instructor also helped the staff to develop individualized instructional materials. The other two language instructors alternated in the classroom to maximize efficiency and to minimize boredom. Participants attended two consecutive hours of class per weekday, and were taught daily by two instructors. Twelve participants completed the two-semester program; there were as many as twenty-two participants in the group at various times during the two semesters; however, some of them left early to go to work in Africa, others terminated when they found it too difficult to fulfill their professional obligations while participating in an intensive FL program. All participants continued to work full-time while concurrently attending French classes.

The General African Culture and Civilization consisted of a one-hour weekly lecture or lecture/discussion on a broad range of topics such as African history, geography, religion, languages, art, architecture, life styles, government. Approximately half of this course was devoted to French West African topics, because that was the target area where most participants would eventually be sent. The African culture lectures were presented in English by Professor R. Dumett of the Purdue History Department, however the language instructors developed adjunct teaching materials in French designed to help the participants assimilate the cultural information while they practiced using French.

Basics of French Language was a fairly conventional grammatical syllabus, adapted to the needs of the participants. A broad range of grammatical categories had to be taught because once on the job, participants would have to be able to read scientific and governmental documents. Since it was known that the participants would have little need to write French, superficial attention was given to such features of the language as agreement of past participles or literary tenses. Grammatical categories most frequently used in oral communication were emphasized and taught for active mastery. Insofar as practical (and logical), specialized lexical items related to things scientific, agricultural, and/or African were utilized in the grammar component of the course, which was taught in the contact language, although participants read explanations of the grammar in English.

The reading component of the program comprised two broad subject areas: 1) texts related to Francophone African culture and civilization; and 2) texts related to professional concerns. The first group of readings contained both "manufactured texts" (simplified French prose specially written for the program) and authentic materials from a variety of sources (periodicals, books, reference works) which were graded according to level of linguistic difficulty, slightly edited and glossed initially in English only, subsequently in French and English, and finally in French only. The second group of texts, those related to professional concerns, were all authentic materials: reports, government documents, articles. Initially, these texts were glossed (in English and/or French, whichever way seemed most efficient), but toward the end of the training program participants were given the opportunity to work with unedited, unglossed authentic materials so that they could gain experience using general and technical dictionaries. The following excerpts illustrate the type of reading materials developed for the program. "L'Afrique" is a "manufactured text" which was introduced at the beginning of the second week of instruction:

L'AFRIQUE, texte n° 1

L'Afrique est un énorme continent caractérisé par la diversité de ses peuples et de sa topographie. Plus de 235 millions d'habitants habitent sur une superficie de plus de 30.300.000 km^2. (Comparaisons: l'Afrique est 54 fois plus grande que la France, et elle est 3 fois plus grande que les Etats-Unis qui mésurent 9.347.680 km^2 y compris les 50 états, le district fédéral de Columbia et ses territoires extérieures.) (. . .)

Reading Worksheet

The following exercises require educated guessing. They are intended to help you approach the unknown (French) from the vantage of what you know about English and/or other Romance languages, and to begin to develop a "feel" for French.

1. Cite cognates and near cognates in the text. (Which words look exactly like English words or somewhat like English words?)

2. Lines 2-3 of text: Predict the effect of the word "plus" in relation to the number "235 millions" ... in relation to the number "30.300.000 km^2." Observation: the use of punctuation in French multiple digit numbers.

3. Cite English word(s) which probably belong to the same family as the French words "habitants" and "habitent." "Habitants" and "habitent" are both plural. Which letters at the end of these words indicate plurality? Which word is a verb? Which one is a noun? If you had to look up the word in a dictionary, how would it be spelled?

4. Line 3: Given the following information about French nouns which describe common geometrical shapes, predict how a Frenchman would read the "2" in "30.300.000 km^2":
carré / rectangle / cercle / triangle / cube / sphère

5. Line 4: Relying on context, predict a plausible meaning for the word "fois."

6. Line 3: Relying on context, which of the following English words is least like "superficie" in the French sentence?
a) superficies b) area c) surface d) superficial

7. Line 3: The word "sur" is a preposition when it stands alone. Also, it may be used as a prefix to certain words. Are you inclined to group it with a family of words meaning "off/under/less" or a family meaning "on/over/more"?

(. . .)

(Pellissier 1979.)

Note that the learner is encouraged to decode in an inductive manner. This text was presented as a sight reading, distributed in class and read at the time of distribution by students who had no dictionary or time to prepare the reading. My intent here was to teach the student how to approach a FL text when the reader's object is to retrieve information and how to rely on his/her knowledge of English as a tool for reading French. Such an exercise fosters confidence, promotes educated guessing and eases the learner into the difficult task of reading a FL.

Pellissier

The text entitled "Toujours exploitées" is an authentic text of medium difficulty, on a civilization topic; glossing for the text is entirely in French:

TOUJOURS EXPLOITEES

Les femmes, qui représentent la moitié de la population mondiale, accomplissent les deux tiers des heures de travail, mais ne détiennent qu'un dixième du revenu et un centième de la propriété du monde.

Dans les pays en voie de développement, les rurales produisent 50% de la nourriture, mais la petite culture vivrière dont elles ont souvent l'apanage ne bénéficie pas des programmes d'aide au développement agricole.
(. . .)

Jeune Afrique, 976 (19 septembre 1979), p. 69.

GLOSSAIRE
1	la moitié	Cinquante est la moitié de cent (50%)
2	mondial(e)	adjectif basé sur le nom: monde
		la population mondiale - la population de la planète
	accomplir	faire
	tiers	Trente-trois est le tiers de cent (33.3%)
		Soixante-six est les deux tiers de cent (66.6%)
	détiennent	de l'infinitif détenir - posséder
3	dixième	Le dixième de cent est dix (10%)
	centième	Le centième de cent est un (1%)
	propriété	le terrain, les maisons, etc.
4	pays	Le Mexique est un pays. L'Afrique est un continent.
	en voie de développement	Il y a des pays développés (par example: les Etats-Unis) et il y a des pays sous-développés (par exemple: le Mali). Dans un pays sous-développé où il y a des efforts pour changer et moderniser le pays, on dit que c'est un pays en voie de développement (en route vers le développement).

(. . .)

(Pellissier 1979).

Note that words and phrases of the text are defined in French via either: 1) synonyms or similar phrases which are cognates or near cognates of English; 2) identification of their grammatical function; or 3) "demonstration/definitions" which illustrate the meaning of a term to be defined by using it in a different context whose sense will be more immediately apparent. The learner's task is to extrapolate meaning of the term as used in the "demonstration/definition" and then apply that meaning to the term as used in the original text. Whenever appropriate, cultural information was included in the glosses. For example, the definition of "en voie de développement" = developING ≠ UNDERdeveloped clues the learner to an important philosophical/cultural difference in West African and North American point of view: citizens of a third world country may view their nation not as UNDERdeveloped (a negative appraisal) but rather as in the process of growth and development (a positive value judgement).

Some readings were wholly devoted to sociocultural or anthropological topics, such as excerpts from Jacques Maquet's discussion of "Négritude" in Africanité traditionelle et moderne, or entire research project reports such as Danièle Poitou's documentation of a study of juvenile delinquency in Niger (Approche sociologique de la jeunesse délinquante au Niger) conducted under the auspices of the C.N.R.S., the French National Center of Scientific Research. The Maquet text was bilingually glossed; Poitou's study was given to the students with no glossary support. Students were to decode the text using either a French/English or a French/French dictionary as a research tool, and answer content questions in English.

The conversation component of the Functional French Intensive program consisted of sixty hours of instruction equally divided between social discourse (conversation for general, everyday purposes) and job-related discourse (conversation for the workaday setting). Rather than follow either a situational syllabus (one in which you might find dialogues entitled "At the train station" or "In the barber shop") or a grammatical syllabus (one in which the morphological and syntactic content of utterances is determined by a hierarchical arrangement of grammar), conversation materials were presented in an eclectic manner similar in spirit and intent to Wilkins' idea of a notional syllabus. That is, students were taught how to express selected categories of a communicative function such as agreement and disagreement:

CONVERSATION

How to AGREE with a statement someone makes
1. Je suis d'accord.   I agree. (neutral statement of opinion)
2. Cela est vrai.   That's true. (slightly stronger; implies value judgement)
3. Absolument.*   Absolutely.   (strongest)
   Tout à fait.*   Completely.   (strongest)

*Use these adverbial expressions alone or add them after the verb in 1 and 2 to intensify your expression of agreement.

How to DISAGREE with a statement someone makes
1. Je ne suis pas d'accord.   I disagree. (neutral)
2. Ce n'est pas vrai.   That's untrue. (stronger)
3. C'est faux.   That's false. (stronger still)
4. C'est complètement faux.   That's dead wrong. (strongest; shows indignation)

Note that the utterances are relatively short and that students are presented with a range of nuance from neutral to strong. Some of the conversational materials were arranged topically, according to the predictable types of conversations an American agricultural consultant might be likely to hold in social settings: talking about one's educational background, one's previous foreign assignments, one's immediate family. Participants were taught such phrases as

TOPIC: Your family

How to refer to your SPOUSE
<u>Ma femme</u> est née en Floride
<u>Mon mari</u> m'aide un peu
   avec le ménage

<u>My wife</u> was born in Florida.
<u>My husband</u> helps me do
   some of the housework.

How to explain your MARITAL STATUS
Je suis célibataire.   I am single.
      fiancé(e)   engaged
      marié(e)   married
      divorcé(e)   divorced
      veuf   a widower
      veuve   a widow

How to state whether your PARENTS are alive
<u>Ma mère</u> habite près de
   Chicago avec une de
   mes soeurs.
<u>Mon père</u> est à la retraite.
Oui, <u>mes parents</u> sont en vie.
Ma mère est morte il y a 3 ans;
   mon père est mort pendant la
   guerre.

My mother lives near
   Chicago with one of
   my sisters.
My father is retired.
Yes, my parents are alive.
My mother died 3 years ago;
   My father died during the
   war.

Such materials were, of course, intended as illustrative examples and not for rote memorization. Instead, the learner was encouraged to tailor these utterances to reflect authentic personal information.

Each unit of conversation was conducted in two phases. Initially, the instructor verified by question and response that each participant could indeed say the French utterances intelligibly and accurately. The second phase was to assign the participants to small groups in which they would role play, according to prescribed scenarios such as the following:

      X, Y and Z are at a social gathering. X introduces
      Y and Z, who tell one another where each works,
      where each went to college. Y asks about X's family.
      All three are married or divorced; they speak about
      their children. X finds an excuse to terminate the
      conversation.

No dialogues were prefabricated for the learners; all were done as a creative act of application in simulated--but "real"--contexts.

In an effort to individualize the conversational component of the training program, participants were given the option to learn to say in French whatever they most wanted to be able to express. Both in the interest of economy of staff time, and to keep the exercise manageable from the learner's perspective, students were asked to write in English five things (phrases or sentences) they would like to say in French. The instructor would then write a French translation and record the five French items on an audio cassette. Each student was directed to practice the material as a self-instructional activity using the written translation and the cassette. Once a student successfully learned the five items, he/she would be given the option to repeat the exercise with new items. This procedure not only proved to be popular among the participants, it also gave some important cues to the instructors about the sort of language the students wanted to learn. Many of our decisions about what to teach in conversation were a direct reflection of the sort of information requested by students on the five-things-I-want-to-say cue sheets.

In order to determine what sort of job-related discourse to include in the conversation component of the training program, the needs of the participants had to be assessed through questionnaires and interviews. Our first step was to ask a series of questions in English to be answered in English, about the participant's job. Using the completed questionnaires we were able to determine areas of professional interest common to all participants. Because none of the language instructors had had formal training in agronomy, agroeconomics, nutrition, or soil conservation (areas of specialization of the participants), we had to rely upon the learners to supply English lists of high frequency lexical items used in the workaday setting. Using the completed questionnaires we were able to compile workable French vocabulary lists, with the aid of technical dictionaries. Because there were some topics of common interest to all participants (energy sources, conservation; agricultural processes such as planting, fertilization, crop rotation), we developed some conversation units intended for the group as a whole. Individualized listings were created for vocabulary items related to the unique needs of each participant. Our strategy in the classroom was to have the participants explain their work to one another in French; another technique was for the language instructors to "interview" participants individually or in small groups, in an effort to have the students explain in French the nature of their professional endeavors.

Before concluding with a brief list of guidelines for the design of a functional FL course of instruction, I am going to request the reader to think of himself or herself as a tailor who must take measurements, create or adapt a design, and then use craft and artistry to produce a quality garment. This is the very sort of mental set required for specialized FL curriculum design. Here are the broad guidelines which I propose:

1. Carefully assess the learner population: whom will you teach? (what age group? what FL background? what general educational level? what occupational or professional objectives?) 2. Use the learners as resource persons: find out from them what they perceive their needs to be. 3. Keep the needs of the learners as your primary focus when you design the course: why do the learners want to acquire the FL? Axiom: The more specific the answer to the question WHY?, the easier your task of selection, organization and presentation of course materials. 4. Adopt the attitude that what the learners want to accomplish through the FL (what they want to do with it) is more important to them than is the language per se. FL study is a noble discipline and sine qua non of a liberal education. Many learners, however, have more pragmatic reasons for wanting to know a FL. Identify what those reasons are. 5. Assign priorities to the receptive and communicative skills to be taught: will listening, reading, speaking, writing be weighted equally in your syllabus? If not, establish a ranking and teach according to plan. 6. Teach communication skills: focus more on teaching students how to give and receive messages than on the manipulation of grammatical elements. And remember that language is contingent to cultural setting. It is equally important to know how a foreigner thinks as it is to know his language, if one hopes to communicate effectively in the FL. Set practical, attainable goals for the learner, keeping in mind the duration of the course and the amount of time the learner can devote to out-of-class preparation. 8. Use culturally authentic software as directly related as possible to the learner's occupational interest. 9. Use your knowledge, skills, and creativity as a teacher in the same way a tailor uses his or her knowledge, skills, and creativity: take the measurements before you make the suit; make sure the garment satisfies the client's needs and your own standards of quality construction; tailor it to fit by making necessary adjustments to flatter the client's profile; construct it artfully, and above all, make it <u>functional</u>.

THE "CONTEXTUAL APPROACH": AN INNOVATIVE
METHODOLOGY FOR ATTRACTING SCIENCE MAJORS
TO OUR LANGUAGE PROGRAMS

Kevin J. Mc Kenna
University of Utah

For a decade now Russian language programs have been seriously affected by the trend among our university students to abandon liberal arts studies in favor of career enhancing courses in engineering, mathematics, and the hard sciences. Although enrollments in German, French, and Spanish have not declined as severely--in part because increased opportunity for European travel continues to attract student to these languages--these areas too have felt the sting of a development whose intensity and long-range prospects indicate that the halcyon days of the '60s and early '70s are not destined to reappear for some time.

Yet the trend toward business, sciences, and engineering need not significantly reduce our Russian language programs. While the reality of studying in or even visiting Russia has diminished because of severe reduction of federal and private financial aid programs, there nevertheless is an important and sizeable group of students whose need to study Russian remains constant. I have in mind those students who contemplate careers in mathematics and the hard sciences as well as certain of the social sciences such as psychology, history, anthropology, and linguistics.

This continued need among many of our science students to study Russian derives from its position as the second most frequently used language in scientific and technical articles. By the late '60s Japan and most of the countries of Western Europe had realized that their scientific journals achieved a larger circulation if published in English. This development never materialized in the Soviet Union, where almost all scientific papers appear entirely in Russian.

Having determined an untapped source for infusing our Russian language enrollment with new, promising students eager to undertake a goal-oriented study of Russian, we face the task of responding properly to their specific needs and interests. In the past our response has been less an attempt to meet the needs of this group than to make their needs conform to our existing grammar/translation and audiolingual approaches. Rather than focusing more narrowly on the specific desideratum of reading comprehension, many of our programs have channeled these students into a two-year overview of listening, speaking, reading, and writing skills. Unfortunately, even the best of these students often find themselves little more able to comprehend articles in their chosen disciplines than when they first undertook their study of Russian.

Even those courses designated as "Scientific Russian" or "Russian Reading" have often failed to enable students to read Russian articles in their major fields. Although these courses properly dispense with speaking, listening, and writing formats, they traditionally have failed to employ a methodology suitable to the single skill of reading. Rather, they perpetuate much of the traditional grammar/translation and transformational/ generative approaches which subject the student to a heavy dose of morphological endings and devote overwhelming attention to the minutiae of grammatical rules and their exceptions. What has been lacking in these so-called "single skill" courses is careful consideration of the nature of expository prose. Seeking to convey information in the most precise and direct manner, expository prose simplifies the task of reading comprehension by limiting itself primarily to third person singular and plural verbal forms. Its mode of conveying meaning is well suited to Russian with its heavy reliance on redundant relationships between prefixes, prepositions, and verbal endings. Thus the student can dispense with the onerous and not particularly productive task of memorizing an often ambiguous and detailed system of nominal and adjectival paradigms.

Of the five available textbooks which undertake the single skill task of teaching Russian reading comprehension, only one departs from the traditional grammar/translation approach. On the basis of a six-year experience in using three of these textbooks at a number of research institutes in the Boulder/Denver scientific community, I am thoroughly convinced of the efficacy of a "contextual methodology" to Russian reading, as utilized in the Howard Daugherty, Dale Plank textbook A Contextual Approach to Russian.

A bit of background information is in order here. I did not use this particular textbook during the first three years that I taught some ninety-two scientists at the National Center for Atmospheric Research, U. S. Geological Survey, and National Bureau of Standards. The two textbooks which I used during this period, 1973-76, were Beresford's Complete Course for Scientists and Dewey & Mersereau's Reading Modern Russian. I found the main obstacle in the grammar/translation approach of these textbooks to be their implicit contention that morphological case endings function as the primary tool in decoding Russian sentences. Unfortunately, the authors who advance this technique fail to take into account the fact that the various case endings in Russian constitute only one of the levels of meaning in a text; and, because of the multiplicity and repetitiveness of some of these endings, they represent the most difficult and ambiguous level of meaning. The ending a, for example, can convey nominative singular, nominative plural, and genitive singular information. Final и appears in four different cases. Availing themselves of this particular approach, my students often succeeded in identifying the declensional forms, but ultimately failed to recognize the proverbial forest for all its inflectional limbs.

Results of a survey I conducted at the end of three years in using this grammar/translation approach are particularly telling. Of 92 students who took one to two years of Russian reading classes, only 25 were able to apply their aptitude to the reading of scholarly papers in their given area of scientific research. They claimed that the main obstacles impeding their reading comprehension were: 1) vocabulary limitations, and 2) the complex system of case endings.

Taking their observations into account, I decided to employ a new reading methodology which had been used experimentally at the University of Colorado. Unlike the vast majority of traditional grammar approaches, A Contextual Approach to Russian utilizes a systematic approach to phrase and sentence structure, focusing on the far more informative aspects of "functional" grammar rather than the "formal" with its time consuming memorization of declensional paradigms and detailed attention to the subtle points of grammatical rules. This is not to suggest that the contextual methodology attaches no significance to morphological endings in their various declensional and conjugational paradigms. Rather, it provides a far more expedient alternative to the excessive attention traditionally devoted to retention and generation of the various inflections. Because of their "functional" importance in describing syntactic relationships (governing and governed nouns and noun phrases), the nominative and genitive cases receive considerable emphasis in the contextual approach, in terms of the student's passive recognition of their role in noun phrase relationships. The authors dwell less on the frequently unreliable inflectional information, and give more attention to "grammatical words"--prepositions, conjunctions, interrogatives, and emphatic words--which, as the redundant counterparts to noun and adjective inflections, impart far less ambiguous information. Of the grammatical words, prepositions receive the most attention since they are so highly identifiable and thus helpful in the partitioning of a text into its noun and verb phrase components.

The textbook for A Contextual Approach to Russian consists of three parts: 1) "Introductory Lessons" (36 minichapters accompanied by two appendices), 2) "Context and the Russian Sentence," and 3) "A Basic Russian Root List." Since Part Two primarily addresses the issue of the formation of sentences in spoken Russian, I used only Parts One and Three in my classes. The "Introductory Lessons" form the main part of the text and can be covered in little more than a semester, an important advantage to the hard science or social science major who cannot afford to spend one and a half to two years mastering Russian grammar. Maintaining a thematic continuity in Soviet geography and related readings, these lessons progress from an introduction of nouns and noun phrases to the presentation of a systematic reading strategy designed to facilitate understanding of stylistically neutral texts in Russian.

The "Introductory Lessons" are divided into mini-units capable of being treated in individual class sessions. The first five lessons present the Russian alphabet and spelling conventions. Lessons 6 through 11 introduce the student to the simple noun phrase and to the notion of how compound noun phrases in Russian are generated by prepositional or genitive relationships. Lessons 12 through 17 cover the conjugation (past and nonpast tenses), structure, and derivational, participial, and nominal features of verbs, as well as introducing the frequently redundant aspects of directional and locational prefixes and prepositions. The remaining lessons expand on previous material (for example, participles, lexical morphology) and introduce a selection of new topics such as short-form and comparative adjectives, impersonal constructions, particles, adverbs, and essential functions of the various cases. At all times the authors carefully tailor their presentation to suit only the task at hand, the goal of reading comprehension. Since passive understanding of the function of the various grammatical considerations is the point here, the student's learning experience is not retarded by constant memorization and generation of a multitude of paradigms, functions, and exceptions. Also, the textbook's mini-unit format is organized in such a way that, beginning from Lesson 10, grammatical discussion is integrated into totally ungraded, thematic reading selections which serve to explicate the theoretical presentation of grammar topics.

While the presentation of "functional" grammar topics is at once practical and linguistically sound, what distinguishes this approach from other reading methodologies is its thoroughgoing presentation of a consistent strategy to reading comprehension. At all times students are encouraged to utilize both "external" and "internal" contexts. By the former is meant the students' pre-existent aptitude or knowledge of a given subject matter. That is, they are taught how to adapt many of the same information generating techniques they automatically use, when reading English language materials, to the task of reading in Russian. Understandably, a student with some background in parapsychology will have an easier time reading scholarly papers in this discipline than he would in reading articles on platetectonics. Ironically, in practice, the utilization of this seemingly natural process progresses rather slowly. Foreign language students often feel that they must understand each and every word before they can comprehend a given thought or idea in a sentence or paragraph. A large part of the instructor's job, therefore, is helping them realize that the issue is to understand the meaning of the sentence or paragraph, proceeding from information which is known or accessible to that which is unknown--a task often accomplished irrespective of a failure to understand some or even many of the individual words.

Presentation of the various types of "internal context" is the essential goal of <u>A Contextual Approach to Russian</u>. While there exist many levels of internal context, the most general application derives from principles of composition in expository writing, such as exposition from the general to the particular and the use of syntactic parallelism and contrast of words and phrases. Another aspect of internal context is consideration of how the topic/message divisions of a sentence relate to the grammatical divisions of subject and predicate. While these two types of structure sometimes coincide, this is not always the case in Russian, where the topic of one part of the sentence introduces its message, which itself often becomes the topic of the following sentence. A proper understanding of this topic/ message dichotomy enables students to reduce any verbose, multiphrase sentence to its two constituent parts, its topic and its message, as represented in either the subject or predicate parts of the sentence.

In pursuing the essential contextual strategy of working from known or more accessible information to that which is unknown or less accessible, the students learn to follow a series of information-expanding steps. After they have skimmed a given sentence several times to glean whatever surface context is provided by cognates, familiar terms, or rhetorical features of syntactic construction (parallelism, contrast, etc.), they proceed to isolate the verb and subject noun. The number and gender information (for past tense verb forms) assists them in locating the subject noun. They then place the two words together and translate their function or meaning, if possible, and proceed to ask and identify the relative questions and answers which they generate. The subject-noun or noun-phrase, plus its predicate, function as the "kernel" of a given sentence, and typically, the remaining prepositional noun phrases gradually reveal their meaning in an examination of their adverbial relationships to either the subject-noun or the verb. Longer sentences in Russian, containing two or more clauses, can likewise be "partitioned" into their respective syntactic kernels.

While Part One of A Contextual Approach to Russian focuses primarily on an analysis of sentence structure, Part Three ("A Basic Russian Root List") operates as a handy companion with its careful attention to lexical analysis. The authors shrewdly make the most of the students' ability to derive overall meaning from constituent parts of a sentence, or, in this case, a word. To assist the students in this endeavor, they stress a passive yet helpful recognition of key semantic fields represented by word roots. The acquisition and retention of vocabulary has long been a major stumbling block for students of Russian, and our recourse to word glosses or individual word memorization has had little or no success in addressing the problem. The productive power of deriving meaning for some ten to twenty words on the basis of a single root, however, holds great promise. Instrumental, of course, is the role played by prefixes as they subtly impart a host of shades of meaning to a given root. Thus, throughout the course of instruction, the student is not allowed to use a dictionary, but is instructed to derive meaning on the basis of a twofold analysis of sentence and word structure. Not all words are subjected to lexical analysis: preference is given to those whose subject-noun or predicate roles make them likely candidates. Also, lexical analysis of individual words must await the more important treatment of overall sentence structures.

The results I have had with the contextual approach over the course of three years at scientific institutes in Boulder, Colorado, have been striking. Whereas only 27% of my students using the traditional grammar/translation approach felt themselves able to read scientific papers written in Russian, an amazing 76% of the students from these same institutes who learned the contextual method continue to use their Russian today.

Unfortunately, it has been more difficult to compile a statistical analysis of the number of college students who continue to use their Russian for reading purposes. One of the main problems is that few of them maintain contact following graduation. However, over the course of several years in employing the contextual approach with college students, I have been able to make a number of observations.

First of all, because of the inductive nature of this approach, our best students have been those who are very comfortable with thinking in the abstract, as one must do when transforming concepts into words. Those students who expect word-for-word decoding from Russian into English have not fared well with this approach.

Secondly, a certain degree of familiarity with one's native grammar is a definite asset in employing this approach. The student must feel comfortable with notions of subject and predicate noun phrases, past passive participles as predicates, syntactic inversions of SVO and OVS sentence constructions, and the like. While this comment applies to the traditional language student as well, I find its functional importance even greater in working with the contextual approach.

Lastly, a certain level of sophistication in the field in which one is reading proves very helpful, giving students more confidence in using "anticipation" of concepts as part of their reading strategy. For larger classes, composed of students with mixed backgrounds in the hard and social sciences, I have found selected readings from Pravda to work well, since current events articles presuppose a certain amount of context.

Our task now is to apply this systematic, single skill approach in specially designated reading courses. I find that some time is required before students are prepared to accept a course which enables them to read materials in their special disciplines within only four to six months. For a language like Russian, whose teaching practices rarely have imparted reading facility even after four years of coursework, this is a major accomplishment. My experience thus far has shown best results to be obtained from graduate level and fourth-year students, presumably because they apply a more mature attitude toward their studies, and have had greater opportunity to acquire a certain amount of expertise or familiarity with the specific disciplines in which they will be reading. I can see how this particular approach benefits students in the social and political sciences by their reading of current events articles in Pravda or other Russian media. Already, for example, my first and second quarter classes are submitting translated political cartoons and commentaries from Pravda to our school newspaper. In time I hope to be able to break down the traditional reluctance to take Russian reading courses, a situation which has resulted from three decades of our inattention to the real needs of this particular group of students. We may have been able to overlook the science students in the '60s, but if many of our programs are to survive through the '80s, this must not be the case.

FOREIGN LANGUAGE INSTRUCTION FOR SINGERS

Signe Denbow
Oklahoma State University

Although "applied language study" is most often concerned with preparing students for the international business world, I would like to discuss quite another practical application of language instruction: that of singing. First, I will discuss the types of foreign language requirements for singers at American colleges and universities; next, the French course for singers which I taught recently at the University of Michigan; and finally, the issues which arose when I taught this course, and which must be addressed by any instructor who plans to teach a foreign language course for singers.

The need for specialized courses in foreign languages for singers is far from new, yet a preliminary survey of offerings and requirements at various colleges and universities which have highly esteemed programs in voice shows no concensus on how best to fulfill this need. Most colleges and universities offer voice lessons, and the students enrolled cannot limit their repertoire to English, but must include musical works from German, French, and Italian as well. In a rigorous undergraduate or graduate program in voice, students simply do not have the time to study each of these languages for two years in order to obtain a moderate degree of proficiency. Nor is the tyical elementary foreign language class suited to their needs.

What are the foreign language goals of the voice student? They appear to be twofold: one, an ability to sing with correct diction in the target language when presented with a text, and two, the ability to read lyrics in the target language. These two skills are not generally taught in the framework of a single class.

The different approaches toward reaching these goals are reflected in the variation of foreign language degree requirements for voice majors among universities throughout the country. They seem to fall into three categories: first, schools which require either one year or one semester of elementary language study in French, Italian, and German, or in only one or two of these languages; secondly, schools which offer and/or require special classes in diction for singers in these three languages, offered either in the appropriate language department or the music department; thirdly, schools which recognize the shortcomings of the above two, and require a mixture, that is, a course in diction for singers in the target language or languages, as well as a course in language skills.

I would like to discuss the pros and cons of each of these approaches. In the first, students who attend an elementary foreign language course acquire some degree of proficiency in the four traditional language skills: listening comprehension, speaking, reading comprehension, and writing. In addition, they gain valuable knowledge about the culture of the country or countries where the language is spoken. However, their proficiency in these four skills, and the amount they learn about the culture is, necessarily, very basic. Moreover, the singers have spent one semester or one year learning rudimentary language skills which they do not need, those of writing, listening comprehension, and speaking. Singers may never need to write in Italian, understand a radio broadcast in German, or order food in a French restaurant. The only skill that they have acquired which is of immediate use to them is reading comprehension. In addition, they have learned a little about the culture. Both of these aspects of language learning are requisite to the interpretation of song. However, they have not learned singing diction, which is quite different from everyday speech. Also, they have probably not mastered adequately the reading techniques necessary for a real understanding of the stylized dialogue of an opera score, or the poetry of an art song.

The second category (schools which require courses in the foreign language diction alone) solves the problem of teaching the voice student correct lyric diction. It does leave open the question of who should teach such a course, a voice instructor or a language teacher. The ideal instructor needs to know the target language, needs to have a solid background in phonetics, needs to know the correct singing pronunciation, and needs to know the technicalities and the art of singing. Thus, some schools opt for a musician to teach this course, whereas others prefer a language teacher. Aside from the question of who is to teach a diction course, the major drawback of such a course is that the student learns only diction, and cannot read a word in the target language.

Unlike instrumental music, vocal music has two elements, a musical text and a literary text. As Pierre Bernac explains in his book <u>The Interpretation of French Song</u>, "In instrumental music, when the composer indicates on his score <u>expressivo</u>, (with expression), he cannot specify the kind of expression he means. He therefore relies on the emotion that his music arouses in the interpretation; but in vocal music the expression is clarified by specific poetic texts" (1970: 3). Therefore, it can safely be said that in order to interpret vocal music, the singer <u>must</u> understand the lyrics. Lyrics have a dual role in vocal music, as in poetry: aesthetic and semantic. That is, the sounds which are emitted upon reciting or singing the words are part of the musicality, and their meaning is the basis of the interpretation expressed by the singer, and of the emotion aroused in the listener. I do not mean to imply that the vocalist's interpretation rests solely upon the meaning of the lyrics, but merely that the semantic component is a major consideration along with the music itself.

The third approach (that of a dual requirement in lyric diction and elementary language skills) attempts to compensate for the inadequacies of each of the first two categories by requiring a combination of them. Among universities adopting this approach (according to their catalogues) are Indiana University and the Eastman School of Music. The advantages of this arrangement for the voice students are now obvious; they study both the lyric diction and the essentials of grammar of the target language. However, do these two requirements satisfy the voice student's foreign language goals? The disadvantage again seems to lie in the elementary language class requirement. Voice students do not need an active knowledge of a foreign language, nor is listening comprehension a primary concern. What they do need is a course on reading comprehension alone, with an emphasis on poetry, instead of the standard elementary language course. Many colleges do offer courses in reading through translation, but the emphasis is generally on technical reading, for doctoral candidates.

My introduction to this specialized area of language study came about in the fall of 1981, when I had the opportunity to teach a course in the Romance Language Department at the University of Michigan entitled "French for Singers." Courses are offered at the University of Michigan in French, German, and Italian for singers, taught by language instructors. I tried to assess the needs of the voice student and to devise a curriculum accordingly. The guidelines given by the Voice Department were that the course should include lyric diction and reading comprehension.

These guidelines have been interpreted loosely according to the interests and backgrounds of the instructors. I was the second French instructor to teach the course, and I used as a musical text a book entitled 30 Songs of Gabriel Fauré, which are classics included in most singers' training and repertoire. I diverged from the course outline of my predecessor by focusing solely on diction and reading comprehension, and in my approach to teaching these skills. The class met four times a week for one semester, and in it I covered the following subject matter: the fundamentals of French phonetics as needed for singing, the International Phonetic Alphabet (I.P.A.), the relationship between French orthography and pronunciation, production of the correct sounds in speech and in song, the fundamentals of French grammar necessary for reading French by translation, and basic poetic vocabulary used in poetry and drama. This seems to be an enormous amount of material for a one-semester course, and could easily be the basis for a two-semester course. However, at the end of the semester my students had acquired a functional ability in reading French lyrics, and had mastered lyric diction.

The class was designed for students who had no previous French or foreign language background. As it turned out, my students varied from first-semester freshmen to doctoral candidates. Some had studied French previously, others had not. Some had taken courses in German or Italian for singers and were familiar with I.P.A. symbols and phonetic principles, whereas others had no notion of phonetics. Some students were highly literate, others were not; some had an excellent background in grammar, others had only the vaguest notion of sentence structure. What did they have in common? They were all first and foremost performers, and none of them had ever taken a class in French for singers. With this motley group, it is obvious that much instruction had to be done on an individual basis. The class was limited to fifteen students (I had eleven) and given the time constraints and voluminous material to be covered, I was fearful that the class size would be a major drawback. For lack of a good text with supplementary tapes for individual practice in a laboratory, most practice had to be done in class. The two factors which I had not taken into account were the intense motivation of the students to learn the correct pronunciation of a written text, and their musical ability: that is, their "ear" for sounds. Thus, relatively little time had to be spent in class on pronunciation practice, which allowed time for instruction in the fundamentals of French phonetics and in the application of theory to the written French word and sentence.

The I.P.A. is a useful tool for singers to learn, since they will be able to prepare a text for performance by transcribing it into I.P.A. symbols. Also, several books contain I.P.A. transcriptions of the lyrics of classic songs and arias, and dictionaries can be consulted for pronunciation purposes as a last resort. I add the cautionary note "as a last resort" because the dictionary reflects spoken pronunciation, and not singing pronunciation.

In French, the obvious differences between the two are in the pronunciations of r and mute e. In the classical tradition of French singing, the r is never uvular or velar, but is instead flapped or trilled. The problem of when to pronounce a "mute" e in speech is of little concern to the singer, because the music dictates whether or not an e will be sung. Less obvious distinctions between spoken and sung French occur in the mid-vowel range, particularly open versus closed o. For example, the word for 'dawn' which occurs frequently in poetry and thus vocal music, is pronounced in spoken French with a closed o in the first syllable, aurore / orɔr / (perhaps to avoid confusion with horreur 'horror' / ɔrœr / ?). In sung French, however, this o is opened: / ɔrɔrə /.

Another aspect of pronunciation which can be omitted entirely in a course for singers is that of intonation. This is possible because pitch, stress, and accent are supplied by the music.

In my course, I tried to divide class time equally between the two goals of lyric diction and reading comprehension. I first taught the I.P.A. symbols used for French orthography, followed by the effects of syllabification on vowel shape within a word and across word boundaries, and of course liaison and linking. Students pronuced and transcribed letters, syllables, words, phrases, sentences, and eventually whole poems into I.P.A. symbols from the anthology of songs of Fauré.

The reading component of the course proved to be much more difficult. Again, the lack of an appropriate text in reading through translation for singers was a drawback, and there were no inherent strengths in the voice students to make up for the lack of a good textbook on reading, unlike the strengths which overcame the difficulties due to a lack of tapes for lyric diction practice. For a grammar textbook, I used one which is designed to teach students to read French by translation. The problems which arose came both from the text and from the student's academic preparation. This textbook is intended for graduate students who must pass reading proficiency exams in French. Consequently, many of the readings and much of the vocabulary is very technical. It also presupposes a rudimentary knowledge of English grammar, which the arts and sciences student usually possesses. However, a singer may or may not know parts of speech, or the names of verb tenses.

Grammatical terminology can be taught easily when necessary for the understanding of a foreign language text, but it does require more time. As a result, we were not able to cover all of the grammar presented in this textbook on reading French, but I tried to stress those aspects which seemed fundamental to comprehension, such as verb tense recognition. Instead of the readings in the books, I substituted poems from the songs of Fauré, readings in French about Fauré and nineteenth-century French music, and other lyrics. The vocabulary which I emphasized was that found in the poems of the Fauré book.

The students were evaluated on the basis of weekly quizzes, a midterm, a paper, and final exam. These tests concentrated on both the phonetic and the reading comprehension components of the course. They included items of symbol/sound association, followed by phonetic transcriptions of written French, as well as phrases, verb tenses, and sentences to be translated into English. The midterm had a speaking component, in which students were given a poem and asked to read it with an orthoepic pronunciation. For the oral component of the final, the students sang a song of Fauré which they had earlier selected. The "paper" was actually a preparation of the song selected, and had several sections. In it, the students transcribed the lyrics into I.P.A. symbols; translated them rather literally into English (many flowery translations are available); researched the author and looked up literary and musical criticism of the song, when possible; analyzed the poem, and the emotions it evoked. They then compared these emotions to those that the music aroused; and they justified their interpretation, in terms of the music and the lyrics. Since I am a French instructor and not a musician, I left the musical interpretation up to the students, but I wanted them to show me that their interpretation was based on an understanding of the text, so that they would not sing a sad poignant poem in a lilting manner, or merely imitate a favorite recording. I believe that by the end of the course, the students had a good basis from which to continue an independent study of French song.

I would now like to discuss some of the issues which arose from my experience in teaching this course. The range of the foreign language backgrounds of my students brought to mind the idea of coordinating, to some extent, the various language classes for singers. Once students have mastered the I.P.A. symbols for one language, it is fairly easy to learn the few others necessary for additional Indo-European languages. They may find the introduction of I.P.A. symbols and the discussion of sound production in the beginning weeks of each new language class quite dull. The first day of class, they are ready to start practicing the sounds of the target language, and associating them with orthography. Perhaps there should be a prerequisite course on phonetics, even within the framework of an English diction class, in order to avoid repetition of subject matter. This would also allow more time to be spent on applied phonetics in the foreign language class.

Another issue which was raised in the course of the semester was whether or not the pronunciation rules of spoken standard French should be taught. Often in contemporary music, words and phrases are spoken or even shouted. Is the traditional, orthoepic pronunciation really appropriate for this style of music? There is also the question of appropriate diction for folk songs. To give an example in American English, would it not be absurd to sing a spiritual with the "correct" diction used in Handel's Messiah? Moreover, might not some of our voice students be preparing for a career in musical theater, where a modern spoken pronunciation is called for? In my class, I presented an outline of standard contemporary spoken French pronunciation, originally to simply explain why I sometimes pronounced words differently from the way I taught them, during lapses in my concentration on lyric diction. Whether or not this is a useful component of a class for singers, I do not claim to know, but the question arose, and must be answered by those in the music profession.

Another matter to be dealt with by the instructor is the fine line between pronunciation and interpretation. If a voice instructor is teaching this class, he or she will of course be well aware of this, whereas a language instructor may not be. Often sounds must be altered in order to produce the desired tone. For instance, high front vowels are more difficult to sing on the higher notes of one's range. Therefore, the vowel color may be altered. Both French and German have the high front rounded vowel phoneme /y/, and language teachers have a generally uncomprising attitude in their insistence on the correct pronunciation of this sound, to insure comprehension on the part of the listener. However in singing, and particularly on high notes, the quality of the desired musical sound must take precedence. Where does clarity of diction end and musical interpretation begin? How much leeway can be taken with the pronunciation before audience comprehension is lost?

Roland Barthes has discussed this problem of interpretation of song in an article entitled "L'Art vocal bourgeois". He criticizes a dramatic rendering of songs of Fauré in a recording by the renowned baritone Gérard Souzay. He claims that Souzay "ne se contente ni du simple contenu sémantique de ces mots, ni de la ligne musicale qui les soutient: il lui faut encore dramatiser la phonétique de l'affreux, suspendre puis faire exploser la double fricative, déchaîner le malheur dans l'épaisseur même des lettres; nul ne peut ignorer qu'il s'agit d'affres particulièrement terribles. Malheureusement ce pléonasme d'intentions étouffe et le mot et la musique, et principalement leur jonction, qui est l'objet même de l'art vocal" (1957: 169). This issue of musical interpretation versus diction is one of great debate, and any lyric diction instructor must be aware of it. The foreign language instructor can provide his or her impression of the point where audience comprehension ends, but ultimately, the interpretation must be left to the singer.

I would like to be able to conclude with an outline of the ideal foreign language class for singers, the qualifications for the ideal instructor, the contents of such an ideal course. However, it does seem evident that each college or university must decide for itself, according to its standards and needs, what type of foreign language courses it wishes to offer its voice students; and all "ideals" are hampered by the dearth of specialized courses and materials in foreign language study which cater to the needs of the singer. I hope, in any case, to have signalled some crucial issues and some possible directions.

REFERENCES

Barthes, Roland. Mythologies. Paris: Editions du Seuil, 1957.

Bernac, Pierre. The Interpretation of French Song. New York: W. W. Norton and Company, 1970.

A NEW CURRICULUM DESIGN IN "JAPANESE FOR TRAVEL INDUSTRY MANAGEMENT MAJORS"

Kyoko Hijirida
University of Hawaii

The School of Travel Industry Management (TIM) at the University of Hawaii has no language requirement, nor does it count regular foreign language courses toward a TIM degree. Regular courses are time consuming and offer a general orientation to the foreign language with little direct relevance to the tourism-oriented student. To respond to the students' needs for more specific, tourism-related foreign language instruction, UH language departments implemented new experimental courses in the fall semester of 1982 and in the spring of 1983. The languages involved are Spanish, French, Chinese, and Japanese. The title of the new courses in Japanese is "Introduction to Japanese for Travel Industry Management Majors" (3-3 credits). They were designed to provide the language skills and cultural awareness necessary for effective communication with Japanese visitors.

These courses were proposed through the cooperative effort of the UH administration, the faculty of the School of TIM and the language departments. This joint undertaking acknowledges the need for specialized language skills and cultural awareness in the tourist industry, an area that plays a key role in the Hawaiian economy. It is, I feel, the responsibility of the foreign language departments to accommodate the needs of the students in the professional schools. The rationale for offering such specific courses is the cost effectiveness of the foreign language study and relevancy to the students' needs.

This paper will discuss various aspects of the curriculum designs of the Japanese courses for specific purposes. Points to be covered include the concept of the course, needs assessment, course objectives, language and culture content, and the text design. An "eclectic" teaching methodology, incorporating elements of the comprehension approach, including the total physical response approach, will also be discussed.

COURSE CONCEPT

The course content can be thought of as combining three areas: Japanese language, culture, and the specific area, in this case TIM. This concept can be illustrated as follows:

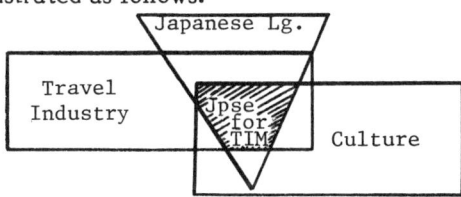

The shaded area in the model represents the integration of language, culture, and business for international business personnel in order that they may be better prepared for the business world.

Traditionally, curricula have reflected culture, business, and the foreign language itself as separate domains. It has become apparent that this is not a very functional approach, particularly not for language study programs designed for Travel Industry majors. Rather, elements of culture must be integrated into the Japanese language curriculum, and instructional materials which would help students communicate effectively in the business field need to be developed.

In designing this course, I used Hilda Taba's curriculum theory as a theoretical framework. Taba (1962: 12) suggests that systematic curriculum development should follow these steps:

1. Diagnosis of needs.

2. Formulation of objectives.

3. Selection and organization of content.

4. Selection and organization of learning experience.

5. Determination of what to evaluate and the ways and means of evaluation.

DIAGNOSIS OF NEEDS

The assessment of needs was conducted by examining literature. In addition, people in Hawaii's hotels and restaurants were interviewed in order to identify needs or problems in communication and cultural understanding between employees and Japanese tourists in various situations. Some of the cultural problems mentioned were due to the differences in social customs and such related areas as tipping and the 4% sales tax. Local tourism personnel said Japanese visitors:

--were confused by the 4% state sales tax,
--either forgot to tip or tipped unnecessarily,
--were not accustomed to having to wait to be seated by a hostess,
--wore night wear in public areas of the hotels,
--were polite at times and yet rude at others.

Statistics provided by Hawaii Visitors Bureau showed a steady influx of Japanese visitors to Hawaii over the past years. There were 690,400 visitors from Japan in 1981, representing 17.5% of the total of visitors to Hawaii (Hawaii Visitors Bureau 1981). Statistics also indicated that Japanese visitors on the average spent about three times more in total expenditures, and almost nine times more in purchasing souvenirs, than did visitors from the U.S. mainland (State of Hawaii Data Book, 1981).

One of the reasons for this is the Japanese practice senbetsu, giving friends or relatives a gift when they leave for a trip. This gift (usually in the form of money) places an obligation on the traveler to return with appropriate souvenirs for those who gave him/her gifts before he/she left. Thus shopping is a very important concern for Japanese tourists. Giri and on, or "social obligations and a sense of debt of gratitude," also play an important role in the gift-buying custom. For the traveler, it is a good opportunity to repay his social obligation or debt of gratitude to his relatives, colleagues, or superiors by bringing gifts from the place he visited. It is still felt that locally produced souvenirs are the most appropriate. The Japanese tourist certainly does not want to return home with "made in Japan" products as souvenirs. This is an important consideration for gift shop owners in Hawaii.

Because of these social customs, the Japanese tourist always buys souvenirs when travelling. Travel and souvenir buying cannot be separated for the Japanese. This type of cultural study has been included in order to understand some of the behavioral characteristics of the Japanese.

The instructor also observed actual Japanese hotel management operations. By staying at Japan's hotels and inns, a comparison of accommodations and services to tourists could be made. From various studies, an outline of the needs for language skills as well as cultural information emerged, which included business protocol, holidays, types of trips, history of omiyage (gift) buying customs, tipping and reservations, Japanese cuisine, hotel accommodations and services, and so on.

GOALS AND OBJECTIVES

This is a basic course designed for Travel Industry Management students with no prior knowledge of Japanese. It enables them to communicate and interact effectively as managers, shop owners, or service personnel. It focuses on oral/aural skills. Classes will meet four times weekly for 50 minutes each session. Lab drill is also required.

After two semesters (120 hours of classroom time plus additional lab time) the students should be able to carry on simple conversations in working and social situations and should have a basic knowledge of sentence structure, competence in listening comprehension, and an understanding of basic Japanese cultural patterns, thus fostering an understanding of and empathy for the Japanese people and their behavioral characteristics.

Skill levels to be achieved include:

Listening — ability to comprehend simple conversations, spoken at the native speaker's normal rate, on Travel Industry Management related topics;

Speaking — ability to engage in social and functional conversations in situations such as hotels and restaurants; ability to make

	personal inquiries or telephone calls and to assist foreign visitors;
Reading	recognition of the writing system, including <u>hiragana</u>, <u>katakana</u>, and <u>kanzi</u>, which frequently occur in signs as well as in elementary level texts;
Cultural	ability to understand reasons for behavioral characteristics of tourists in terms of social customs, ways of thinking, and values; ability to demonstrate an awareness of cultural nuances in the language and in normal behavior; ability to demonstrate an awareness of how social variables like age, sex, class, education, and occupation affect language use.

NEW TEXT DESIGN AND CONTENT

The main purpose of these newly proposed courses was to aid Travel Industry Management majors in developing communicative skills and intercultural capabilities required for effective interaction with Japanese visitors in tourism-related businesses such as hotels, restaurants, and souvenir shops.

This kind of TIM language study is substantially different from regular core courses in its content and objectives. Whereas the regular language course is designed to provide students with a general background in the language skills of reading, writing, listening, and speaking, the new courses include material specifically suited to students of Travel Industry Management. It focuses mainly on communication in Japanese within the more specific scope of travel industry related topics, providing more specialized vocabulary, conversational ability, developing empathetic understanding of the characteristic Japanese patterns of behavior and interpersonal skills to enable effective communication with Japanese-speaking people while on the job.

The biggest problem involved in the implementation of this course was the unavailability of a textbook integrating linguistic and socio-cultural elements with the TIM vocabulary. The University granted an Educational Improvement Fund to the instructor so that she could develop new text materials. Administration and faculty members of the School of Travel Industry Management were extremely helpful to the language instructor in determining the course content. The projected textbook includes such lessons as "Greeting and Introductions," "Shopping," "Eating and Drinking," "At the Hotel," "Telephoning," "Personal Interaction with Japanese Tourists," etc.

Selection of language and cultural elements was based on needs diagnosed and assessed at the beginning. Some of the questions considered during this process were:

--What skills should the students possess at the end of the course?

—What vocabulary should be functional for certain job situations?

—What situations should be included as classroom activities?

Answers to these questions were generated from needs assessed previously. To make each lesson coherent and to assure a systematic process of language learning, the material for each lesson was arranged in the following sequence: useful expressions, conversation, vocabulary, explanation, drills, exercises, simulation and skits, and cultural exploration.

The content of each lesson can be viewed as a learning experience and can be rearranged in the instructional process. Language learning is a series of phases that needs to be explored with maximum effectiveness. In this course, the teaching/learning process has been defined as a particular and continuing activity involving a number of steps or operations. The process is conceived as continuing and more or less sequential in the sense that each activity forms a logical base for the next. At the same time, the process is cyclical, progressing in a spiral movement, achieving small objectives at each stage. The following is the schematic learning process for each lesson of the classroom instruction.

Presentation ⟶ Explanation ⟶ Drill ⟶ Application ⟶ Evaluation
                                              (Simulation)

The application stage was especially emphasized by providing various simulated job-related situations for role playing and skit activities. Impromptu presentations were encouraged by providing a card listing a situation and a direction, as in the following situations involving two people:

1. You meet your friend on the street. Greet him/her and strike up a short conversation.

2. You are introduced to a business person by one of your associates. Both of you exchange your business cards (meishi) and converse for a while. Remember, the meishi is serving as the medium.

3. Make up a list of Hawaiian souvenirs and prices to go with them. With one student playing the role of customer and the other the role of sales clerk, simulate sales transactions in a souvenir shop.

4. You have made reservations at a hotel and wish to check in. The man at the front desk asks you how long you will stay, tells you where your room is, and gives you your key.

5. You would like to exchange some currency at your hotel. Ask if you can do that, and what the current rate of exchange is. Ask for 10,000 Japanese yen. The man at the front desk will tell you what the rate is, and how many dollars you can have.

6. You are ready to check out of your hotel. Tell the man at the front desk that you would like to check out, give him your key, and ask him how much you should pay. Then ask him where you can call a taxi.

The role playing, simulation and skit activities mentioned above were also included as a part of the evaluation of the students' performance, in addition to the written quizzes. Communicative competence, cultural understanding, and grammatical knowledge were evaluated, since these areas were claimed as objectives of the course. As a final project, the class produced video taped skits as group efforts in which they acted out job situations in hotel and in restaurants. They demonstrated in this production their capability to achieve on-the-job communication, even though it was in the limited scope of one semester.

TEACHING STRATEGIES

The basic position taken in teaching this course was "eclecticism," with the belief that a good teacher is well informed of various teaching approaches and strategies, and of the strengths and weaknesses of each approach. The methodology adopted incorporated elements of the comprehension approach, including the Total Physical Response strategy. The Learnables (International Linguistics Corporation) materials were also used as supplementary materials in the Language Lab. Experiential learning strategy was especially effective in conducting the class for "Interaction with Tourists from Japan." The class members went out to the Waikiki area where they could readily meet tourists, after they learned a "personal touch" approach to the tourists using greetings, phrases, and sentences such as Hawaii wa hajimete desu ka? "Is this your first visit to Hawaii?" or Hawaii wa ikaga desu ka? "How do you like Hawaii?" etc. The class held feedback sessions after their experiential learning opportunities.

CONCLUSION

At the end of the semester, three different sets of evaluations were taken. One was students' written comments about the course taken near the end of the term, another was the departmental evaluation form for language courses, which is designed to measure effectiveness of teaching materials, teaching performance and teacher competence, and last was an evaluation form made by the Travel Industry Management Department.

The students' general reaction was very positive and the teacher was encouraged to continue to improve and develop the course. The main factors contributing to the high degree of the students' satisfaction, according to the data, were the course's "relevancy" and "communicative skills" development activities. Instead of waiting for two semesters as was originally scheduled, the School of Travel Industry Management, after one semester's experimentation, has decided to keep these Chinese, Japanese, French, and Spanish Language courses as humanities electives for its majors.

Although the objective-specific curriculum has an inherent weakness in that the material covered is limited, its existence within the overall language program, especially for professional school students, is still justifiable because of its high relevancy for a particular group of students. Cost effectiveness and relevancy are important factors in today's academic community; this is because the public, as well as the legislature, is placing more and more stress on the accountability of the academic community for the high cost of education.

REFERENCES

Asher, James. Learning Another Language Through Actions: The Complete Teacher's Guidebook. California: Sky Oaks Productions, 1982.

State of Hawaii. Data Book: A Statistical Abstract, 1981. Hawaii: Department of Planning and Economic Development, 1981.

Taba, Hilda. Curriculum Development: Theory and Practice. New York: Harcourt, Brace and World, 1962.

THE PLACE OF THE TRANSLATION LABORATORY
IN THE UNIVERSITY CURRICULUM

Gertrud Graubart Champe
The University of Iowa

During the first day of the Applied Language Study Conference, two important themes were language instruction for purposes other than educating scholars in language and literature, and the several forms that such instruction might take. The University of Iowa is presently experimenting with language education of this kind. This is being done, in part, through the cooperation of the foreign language departments and the Translation Laboratory.

The Translation Laboratory is an instructional unit within the College of Liberal Arts. It was designed and implemented over a five-year planning period by Professor Jacques Bourgeacq of the Department of French and Italian, who is now the Laboratory's director. The determination to work toward the creation of a laboratory where advanced students could obtain practical training in translation, under competent supervision, arose out of a number of related observations and considerations.

By 1977, it was becoming very difficult, in all conscience, to support most students in the choice of foreign languages and literatures as a sole field of concentration. Even in the case of outstanding students, justifiably looking forward to a career in research and teaching, the giving of wholehearted support seemed a chancy business. Therefore, it often became the practice to suggest that students choose a second field of concentration. But what field? And then what?

At the same time, it became clear that there was a mild groundswell in translation activity in our part of the Midwest. State government and industry, trying to increase export potential, began opening European offices, producing brochures, inviting the visits of foreign delegations. It seemed likely that university students and faculty could somehow play a productive part in this activity.

The first step toward the eventual training of translators was the establishment of upper division courses in the translation of preponderantly nonliterary texts. Such courses were instituted in the Departments of French and Italian, Spanish and Portuguese, German, and Russian. (The Department of Asian Languages and Literatures will consider taking this step when it has developed a course of language study for nonmajors.) Texts from commerce, technology, law, the natural and the human sciences are the primary teaching material in these courses. The tone and nature of the instruction are far from mechanical; there is frequent discussion of comparative stylistics, of cultural traits embodied in the language under discussion, and of contrasts between the literary and workaday registers of the language.

For the last three years, it has been possible to earn a bachelor's degree in Applied French and Applied German. In the Department of Spanish and Portuguese, it is possible to choose courses which lead to the same concentration, but without particular notation on the student's record. In all three departments, a student choosing to concentrate in applied language is required to study the literature and culture of that language with some thoroughness.

By the spring of 1982, there was an increase in the number of statements concerning the need for language competence in business, industry, government, and science. Returning from a trade mission to France, the governor of Iowa formed a commission to examine and strengthen the teaching of foreign language in the state. The time had come to put the Translation Laboratory into operation. With generous financial and administrative support from the University, the Translation Laboratory began its active existence in July, 1982.

Language students present themselves to the Laboratory when they have completed their department's offerings in special language and translation courses. In addition to the usual language majors, we also work with bilingual English speakers, native speakers of languages other than English, and with properly qualified students whose expertise is in fields other than foreign language. Practicum credit, granted by a language department, is arranged on an individual basis. Wherever appropriate, arrangements are also made to designate a student's work in the Laboratory as a Cooperative Education position.

The Laboratory works with students on the premise that the best experience comes from collaboration in a real commission. Therefore, a significant task for the Laboratory staff is to obtain assignments from clients on and off campus. These assignments are carried out for normal translating, interpreting and consulting fees, with a considerable reduction in rates for clients within the university community. During the first eight months of our existence, we have been engaged in such things as: translating personal and academic documents into English at the request of the Office of Foreign Admissions; translating conference talks, articles and abstracts into foreign languages; sending out consecutive interpreters for foreign visitors; translating advertising copy; working with firms to translate operating manuals, specification sheets and informational pamphlets; training corporate personnel to act as hosts to foreign visitors; helping copy writers produce texts less ambiguous for translators to work with.

When a commission is received, the task is assigned to the most suitable student, who is then given a deadline. Students consult freely with Laboratory staff or outside advisors (usually faculty members in the content area of the text under consideration). When the work is returned by the student, it is reviewed by a member of the Laboratory staff and any other outside advisor that might seem appropriate. With only the rarest exceptions, students translate into their native language. They are paid for their work in proportion to the independence with which they carry it out.

At the moment, almost everything that happens at the Translation Laboratory is happening for the first time. As a result, we are ready and willing to revise methods and expectations if experience tells us that we should. The basic principle, however, remains to produce excellent work while giving students the best possible guidance and experience. The burden for maintaining this principle rests largely on the shoulders of the director and the coordinator of the Laboratory. Between them they offer native to strong command of French, Spanish, German, and Russian. The director of the Laboratory is a specialist in comparative stylistics and Business French, and the coordinator has a strong background in science, which proves useful almost daily. It barely needs to be added that both are devotees of accuracy in letter as well as in spirit.

The eventual goal of the Translation Laboratory is to become self supporting. In addition to working toward an increased flow of commissions, we stay informed of possibilities for outside funding. This fall the Translation Laboratory applied for federal funding under a program which seeks to integrate upper division language study with professional study. The work of pulling together the grant proposal has had a by-product of permanent value: an increase of discussion and cooperation between the Laboratory and the departments of foreign language on the one hand, and professional schools and programs on the other hand. A new course, team taught by faculty of the Department of French and Italian and professional schools is being developed. Several other lines of long-range planning have also resulted.

With the advice and cooperation of the language departments, the Translation Laboratory plans to study other translator training programs in the United States and abroad, hoping to learn of methods and emphases that can be applied at this university. One facet of translator training in which we are particularly interested, and which we hope to strengthen as soon as possible, concerns the necessity for a translator to have one or two fields of content specialization. The majority of our translators to date have been students of languages and literature who find themselves at a severe disadvantage when confronting a text in any other field. Since a good translator is far from being merely a dictionary technologist, we are already doing a good deal to encourage students to:

-spend time learning specialized vocabulary;

-become acquainted with the professional literature;

-work up a familiarity with major trends and questions in one or two fields from which translations might come.

It is our hope that after we have visited other institutions and discussed our concerns with colleagues at The University of Iowa, we will be able to develop structured methods for introducing our student translators to this kind of research.

Should the day come when the Translation Laboratory is not only self supporting but also producing a surplus of funds, the plans (dreams?) are to sponsor research assistantships, visiting lecturers, and exchanges of students and faculty with other institutions. We will also be particularly interested in supporting the translation and publication of scholarly and literary works of merit, as determined not only by us but also by our colleagues.

I hope that this sketch of what is happening at the Translation Laboratory, and what is anticipated, gives a clear impression of the strong support being offered by administration and colleagues to the advanced study of language for a wide range of purposes; it is certainly meant to. We have also had a great deal of support and advice in conducting our dealings with the world of clients from the Duke Translation Service at Duke University in Durham, North Carolina.

There is one more topic, prominently under discussion at this Applied Language Conference, which must be considered in the present outline: the relation of language teaching to the proposition that the study of languages is a branch of the humanities. The old, original definition of liberal studies, which stated rather clearly that such things are not meant to provide a man with the means of making a living, is seldom voiced directly in public these days, but its influence has not altogether died. Now, while there is indeed a metaphorical truth hidden in this conception even today, it can only be stated after much clarification and elaboration. But it is possible, and necessary, to have much fruitful discussion of the nature and purpose of the humanities without broaching this line of thought, a pleasing puzzle for a long winter evening.

We believe very strongly that the kind of teaching which is going on at the Translation Laboratory is at the very heart of a broadly and vigorously defined humanistic view of life. Both director and coordinator are happily engaged in literary research. But we believe that in addition to knowing and cherishing and teaching what _has_ been done, we must also observe, analyse, and present to our students what _is being_ done. Whether they are concentrating on a tourist leaflet, an advertisement or a medical case history, our translators are being taught to consider two languages side by side as collections of neutral and affective expressions, as systems which impose rank ordering on the environment by the way they assign names to objects and phenomena, in short, as the bearers of cultural values.

Translators must consider the differences among several style levels of the two languages with which they are working, and so must be familiar with the literary language. Occasionally a translator must resolve a complex cultural problem such as translating a meditation on an Old Testament verse for a predominantly Buddhist audience. Frequently translators who have had training chiefly in the arts, literature, and the human sciences must come to grips with material from the natural sciences and technology, areas which our liberally educated young must learn to contemplate knowledgeably and analytically.

Professor Joseph F. Byrnes reminded us to good purpose on Saturday morning that "...the world is so full of a number of things...." A student using the Translation Laboratory to the fullest labors with words to transfer the immediacy of this fullness from one language to another. In so doing, he observes, analyses, conflates and muses, weaving the thread of humanist thought into the fabric of everyday life.

APPLYING ORAL AND TRANSLATION SKILLS IN THE HIGH SCHOOL

Cida S. Chase
Oklahoma State University

When one contemplates the topic of applying the oral and translation skills that students have acquired in their high school foreign language program, it is imperative to consider the motivational problems that high school teachers encounter today. Let us examine the devices that would encourage an adolescent to want to become proficient in oral and translation skills.

In 1980 Senator Paul E. Tsongas of Massachusetts addressed the ACTFL annual meeting in Boston and made some significant remarks. "If Americans," he said, " are the can-do types, what can we do with a foreign language? Most Americans will look at a proposition calling for an investment of their time and money in pretty hard terms. Where's the payoff? If I take German for five years in school, what do I get back?" (Tsongas 1981). This is precisely the frame of mind found in high school students and their parents. The arguments that we are offering today do not convince young people of the need to become highly proficient in a foreign language. Teachers may relate to their students multiple anecdotes in which a distressful situation originates because of the enormous lack of foreign languages skills in most Americans. They tell stories like the one about the brave Russian who sought political asylum at the U.S. Embassy in Kabul and was not able to find anyone there who spoke Russian (Lurie 1982: 414). Needless to say, the poor man ran back to the Russians with whom he could at least communicate. This is certainly a tragic event. However, it would be difficult for a high school student even to conceive of how much we could have learned about the situation in Afghanistan from this man had someone been able to communicate with him at the U.S. Embassy in Kabul.

Anecdotes depicting translation errors can be pathetically laughable, occasionally downright obscene. One can recall how "Body by Fisher," describing a General Motors product, turned out "Corpse by Fisher" in Flemish, and that did not produce sales. Along the same line, Schweppes Tonic Water was advertised in Italy as "bathroom water." And one of the most remarkable flops of the Colgate-Palmolive Company was trying to encourage the French to buy "Cue toothpaste." The advertisement did not have translation errors, but Cue seemed to be a rather pornographic book in France at the time, and I leave to your imagination what must have happened with the pronunciation of that word (Lurie 1982: 417).

All these anecdotes are amusing, but are they effective in encouraging students to master a foreign language? They are too far removed from the students' immediate reality. Even if teachers appeal to the special fascination that faraway places have for Americans, and how much more gracefully received is an American who speaks the language of the country where he or she is a guest, it is still not enough. For more effective publicity, one can provide factual statistics that may encourage youngsters to think about their future. One might quote Joel Honigberb, President of the Overseas Sales and Marketing Association: "There are only about 1000 college students who graduate each year with majors in international trade, a field which we call geotrade. There are jobs for at least 200,000 geotrade experts" (Lurie 1982: 418).

However, long-range goals are difficult to visualize for most high school students. Their mentality does not allow them to put a great deal of effort into something, if it is not clear to them what they can get out of it hic et nunc. It then becomes necessary for teachers to give them an immediate cause for becoming very proficient in oral and translation skills.

Let us imagine that a statewide booklet were produced featuring the names of those excellent students who have reached a desirable level of proficiency in a foreign language, and could therefore serve as on the spot emergency interpreters. These students could assist officials in their respective communities until the arrival of a more highly trained individual. Their names would appear in a useful publication to be distributed to all important institutions of the state: hospitals, highway patrol department, fire departments, police departments, sheriff departments, courts, schools, churches, community service agencies, health and human service agencies, utility companies, driver's license examiners, tag agencies, and so forth.

This booklet would be a source of immediate pride to all those students and their parents. However there arises the question of financing the production of such a publication. It would have to be reviewed and enlarged at least every two years, an endeavor that certainly would exhaust the small treasuries of foreign language teachers' organizations. As a matter of fact, teacher organizations would not have to spend a single penny if an effort were made to examine the directories of state foundations and grant giving agencies, which annually award generous amounts of money to support certain "popular" areas, including higher education, health, welfare and community service, and precollegiate education.

Let me cite a few possible sources of funding from my own state's Directory of Oklahoma Foundations (Broce 1982):

1) Cordelia Lunceford Beatty Testamentary Trust
   Box 514, c/o James R. Rodgers, Trustee
   Blackwell, OK   74601

   Financial Data
   Assets, $781,534
   Expenditures, $54,990, including $36,615
   for ten grants

Areas of Grant Activities
    Community Welfare: $26,340
    Precollegiate Education: $10,275

Foundation Manager
    James R. Rodgers
    Box 514
    Blackwell, Oklahoma 74601

2) Boudreau Foundation
    618 Philtower Building
    Tulsa, OK 74103

   Financial Data
       Assets, $9,235; gifts received, $30,000
       Expenditures, $37,605, including $37,570
       for twenty-nine grants

   Areas of Grant Activities
       Community Welfare: $3,650
       Higher Education: $770
       Precollegiate Education: $1,500
       Health: $1,350

   Foundation Manager
       A. F. Boudreau, Jr.
       618 Philtower Building
       Tulsa, Oklahoma 74103

3) Broadhurst Foundation
    5350 East 46th, Suite 116
    Tulsa, Oklahoma 74135
    Founded in 1951 in Oklahoma

   Financial Data
   (1979)   Assets, $4,279,353
            Expenditures, $408,043, including $398,959
            for sixty-four grants

   Area of Grant Activities
       Community Welfare: $23,250
       Higher Education: $189,125
       Precollegiate Education: $500
       Health: $5,350

   Foundation Manager
       William Broadhurst
       5350 East 46th Street
       Tulsa, Oklahoma 74135

4) Drummond Family Foundation
P. O. Box A
305 West Lille Boulevard
Madill, Oklahoma 73446

Financial Data
(1979)   Assets, $479,675
Expenditures, $205,778, including $198,526
for four grants

Areas of Grant Activities
Community Welfare: $181,351
Higher Education: $1,000
Precollegiate Education: $1,175
Health: $15,000

Foundation Manager
Myril T. Adamson, Trustee
305 West Lille Boulevard
Madill, Oklahoma 73446

Alfred A. Drummond
Box 597
Madill, Oklahoma 73446

James A. Drummond
Box 597
Madill, Oklahoma 73446

5) Sylvanus G. Felix Foundation
5924-N West Hefner Road
P. O. Box 20609
Oklahoma City, Oklahoma 73156
Telephone number: (405) 721-5822
Founded in 1952 in Oklahoma

Financial Data
(1979)   Assets, $230,062
Expenditures, $243,565, including $236,725
for seven grants

Areas of Grant Activities
Community Welfare: $5,300
Higher Education: $226,425
Precollegiate Education: $2,500
Health: $2,500

Foundation Manager
> Charles S. Felix, President
> P. O. Box 20609
> Oklahoma City, Oklahoma 73156

Proposal Submission Information
> Proposals not required; request deadline October 31; no grants made to individuals; gifts not restricted to Oklahoma or local community, but they receive preference

6) First National Foundation, Inc.
> P. O. Box 25189
> Oklahoma City, Oklahoma 73125
> Telephone number: (405) 272-4186
> Founded in 1954 in Oklahoma

Financial Data
(1979) Assets, $1,207,295; gifts received $309,891
Expenditures, $199,943, including $199,706 for eighty-seven grants

Areas of Grant Activities
> Community Welfare: $63,979
> Higher Education: $26,584
> Precollegiate Education: $3,100
> Health: $81,953

Foundation Managers
> Dale Mitchell
> Drake Keith
> David Pollarhide
> All at First National Building
> Oklahoma City, Oklahoma 73125

Proposal Submission Information
> Proposal not required; quarterly deadlines--January 15, April 15, July 15, October 15; no grants made to individuals; gifts restricted to Oklahoma, but not local community, though it receives preference

7) Herbert and Roseline Gussman Foundation
> 3200 First National Tower
> Tulsa, Oklahoma 74103
> Founded in 1961 in Oklahoma

Financial Data
(1979) Assets, $1,238,093; gifts received, $130,000
Expenditures, $47,780 for seventy-six grants

Areas of Grant Activities
  Community Welfare: $7,445
  Higher Education: $12,150
  Precollegiate Education: $2,580
  Health: $6,325

Foundation Manager
  Herbert Gussman
  3200 First National Tower
  Tulsa, Oklahoma 74103

Similar data are available for every state.

In addition to local foundations, foreign language textbook companies could be approached for aid in financing a project of this nature.

The wealth of positive implications that the production of this booklet could have are endless. High school evening courses could be generated for those adults who, for a fee, would be able to become proficient enough in a foreign language to be included in the state booklet. Furthermore, high school students could be motivated to assist in these evening courses and receive some remuneration. This endeavor would allow further practice for the young students plus provide a very healthy activity for them in the evenings; nocturnal mischief and negative adolescent behavior are a major concern to every community in the nation.

If we are able to bring this project to success in Oklahoma, we will help other states institute it by publishing, through the Oklahoma Foreign Language Teachers' Association, a step-by-step listing of the procedures required to produce a similar program. If the project does come to approach this grander scale, a national foundation could be approached, such as the Reader's Digest Foundation, which funds programs offering adolescent youth a variety of character building experiences (see Lewis 1981). Foreign language teachers will be able to motivate their students to excel in their foreign language studies when they are able to convince them that the linguistic skills they are acquiring are relevant to them as individuals, and to their immediate reality.

REFERENCES

Broce, Thomas E. Directory of Oklahoma Foundations. 2nd ed. Norman: Univ. of Oklahoma Press, 1982.

Lewis, Marianna O. (ed.). The Foundation Directory. 8th ed. New York: The Foundation Center, 1981.

Lurie, Joseph. "America...Globally Blind, Deaf and Dumb." Foreign Language Annals, 15 (Dec. 1982), 413-421.

Tsongas, Paul E. "Foreign Languages and America's Interest." Foreign Language Annals, 14 (Apr. 1981), 115-119.

PART TWO:

FROM THE WORLD TO THE CLASSROOM

SOME AQUARIAN OBJECTIVES IN APPLIED LANGUAGE STUDY

Richard L. Frautschi
The Pennsylvania State University

If some of you are puzzled by the first adjective in the title of my paper, let me assure you that I did not select it because of an addiction to astrology, or because today, 18 February, marks the end of the period for those born under the sign of the Water Bearer. Rather, let me explain the circumstances which led me to the term and to the relationship which the sign of Aquarius may connote for certain objectives in applied language study today.

Last September my secretary informed me that she was taking her sister to a Toronto physician to seek relief from a cancer which New York specialists had declared untreatable. Upon her return she described a complex nutritional therapy which sounded remarkably similar to one described to me by a colleague and friend in Texas who was given a similar diagnosis. In both cases, I am happy to report, the seemingly unorthodox treatment has worked.

To get on with my story, as a Christmas present last December my wife gave me a book by Marilyn Ferguson entitled The Aquarian Conspiracy, Personal and Social Transformation in the 1980s. Ms. Ferguson describes a covert network of shakers and movers who are quietly challenging what is commonly referred to as the Establishment, be it cultural, scientific, governmental, corporate, or educational. While iconoclasm has never been my forte, the shocking discovery of effective medical therapies which are not commonly known (I am not talking about quack panaceas such as laetrile) and the Ferguson theme of clandestine forces for beneficial personal and social change--the confluence of the two incidents has prompted me to read recent literature related to applied study in an "Aquarian" perspective.

Some of you familiar with the rhetoric of enunciation theory may be wondering what criteria I intend to use in a distinction between Aquarian and non-Aquarian objectives. For the purposes of the present argument, let us try to distinguish between those speakers whose objectives are presented as deontic pronouncements versus those, the Aquarians, who are prepared to interact with their receivers. To borrow from the nomenclature of information science, the objectives posed by the Aquarians are "user friendly." In some of the sources which I would like to share with you, I hope that you will detect, as I did, a tone of indifference, if not hostility, toward the language consumer. In others you may note a sense of concern for the well-being of each addressee.

According to Louis G. Kelly (1969), language teaching has been in existence for twenty-five centuries. And yet it is a subject about which much has been written, but little actually discovered. At least that is my prevailing impression gleaned from recent statements in the popular press and in new directions of language acquisition research. Let me begin with present objectives of foreign language (L2) teaching as perceived in the context of American secondary and postsecondary education. Let me then suggest some new objectives of L2 acquisition, focusing primarily on the teacher and on the language student. In both instances I will shape my comments according to the attitude--sensitive or insensitive--toward the language consumer, whether the nation or public at large, the language teacher, or the individual learner. Among the sources I hope that you will recognize the Aquarians, those whose objectives emphatically favor the user.

Let us start with the image of our profession as we find it in the national media today. We are quite familiar with the "scandalous" level of monolingualism and monoculturalism reported by the 1979 President's Commission of Foreign Language and International Studies and by Representative Paul Simon in his The Tongue-Tied American (1980). Such indictments of our presumed national insularity continue to appear. For example, let me call to your attention an article by Joseph Lurie in the December 1982 issue of Foreign Language Annals, whose title speaks for itself: "America . . . Globally Blind, Deaf and Dumb. A Shocking Report of Our Incompetence Through Ignorance in Dealing with Other Countries." From all sides a politicized educational media is bombarding the profession and the general public with the embarrassing "facts" about our national incompetence in language abilities. For example, only one of fifty native-born Americans is fluent in a second language, whereas one of five Japanese speaks a second language. There are more teachers of English in the Soviet Union than there are students of Russian in the United States. Of the mere fifteen percent of U.S. high school students who pursue a foreign language, only one out of fifteen studies it for more than two years. Such deficiencies, we are told, threaten our national security and our international economic interests. The increasingly conspicuous luxury of isolationism prevents us from becoming citizens of the world. Rose Hayden, Executive Director of the National Council of Foreign Languages and International Studies, reports from data supplied by the Task Force on National Manpower Targets, that the nation faces a critical shortfall of foreign area experts, persons "who know the language, culture, politics and economics of a given region." Only Western Europe and the United Kingdom show an approximate match between supply and demand, with the greatest deficiency anticipated in Sub-Saharan Africa (see Basic Skills in the U. S. Work Force, Center for Public Resources, 680 Fifth Avenue, New York, NY 10019; and Humanities, 3.6 1982 , 10.)

We know that corrective legislation has been proposed. Witness the Bureau of Language Services (H. R. 5738), introduced by Representative Leon Pannetta and coauthored by Representative Simon. The bill would improve the quality of translation and interpretation services available to the U.S. diplomat. Yet, according to ADFL Updates (September, 1982, p. 1),

"Mail favoring this bill has not yet been sufficiently great to convince the subcommittee to consider the bill." More successful has been Senate Bill 1193, sponsored by Senator Pell, to provide funding for increased foreign exchanges monitored by the International Communication Agency. Another bill, Representative Simon's National Security and Economic Growth through the Foreign Language Improvement Act (H.R. 3231 and S. 1817), remains in the committee. The 97th Congress however did establish an Office of Undersecretary of Travel and Tourism, with a Tourism Policy Council, and it has also approved pay raises, educational incentives, and the creation of a linguistic reserve for the intelligence communities.

At present, the American Defense and Education Act (H.R. 6674 and S. 2663), a bill proposed by Senator Gary Hart and Representative Carl Perkins, seeks incentive funding to encourage local school districts to remodel curricula, including performance objectives in mathematics, science, foreign languages, communications skills, and technology. The American Defense Education Act (S. 2663 and H.R. 6674) again addresses curricular revision in an interdependent world. Representative Gonzales has introduced a bill (H.R. 1448) to establish a National Commission for the Utilization and Expansion of Language Resources. Both the twenty-one member Joint National Council on Languages and the Council for Languages and Other International Studies are lobbying for these measures, sounding a new level of political activism for language educators (see Northeast Conference Newsletter, 13 (1983), 14.)

While some Washington observers find reason for optimism in the number of bills before the 98th Congress which address our national linguistic shortcomings, the reluctance of Congress to provide generous funding may have other causes. First, why does Congress want to appropriate more tax dollars when the nation already spends more on education than any other country in the world? Some 7.7% of our GNP goes for education, versus 4.4% for Sweden, the second highest. Also, the U.S. has the world's highest student retention rate, a phenomenon which Frederick Rudolph at the 1980 Wingspread Conference claimed acts as a safety valve for keeping the young out of the labor market and in what he calls a mood of "sweet reasonableness."

Futhermore, Congress is not alone in its skepticism. The purpose of foreign language acquisition remains distressingly unclear to educators themselves. In a study of attitudes of secondary school superintendents toward language study in 1979, De Felippis (1979) found that only 38% of high school administrators saw a direct relationship between foreign language study and the total school curriculum. Three years later, Koppel (1982) reports little improvement. As major colleges and universities reinstate foreign language requirements, we may anticipate continued attitudinal modification toward language study at the secondary level. Yet, as Herron (1982) reminds us, in the 1920s foreign languages became electives for gifted college-bound students. The aging myth of elitism, rather than the fresh realities of the market, may also contribute to congressional reluctance to open the purse.

The problem is compounded by the dismal achievement levels of American students when compared with their international peers. During the sixties and early seventies, in standardized tests ranging from reading comprehension to chemistry, U.S. students never scored first or second place. The American mean scores were closer to Thailand's. It now appears that low achievement was linked to homework levels which also declined (Lerner 1982). Although SAT scores are now on the rise, the failure of corporate academia to assure minimal competency in basic skills such as reading, writing, mathematics, and science is confirmed by a recent study from the privately funded Center for Public Resources. The report, <u>Basic Skills in the U.S. Work Force</u>, concludes that there is "...a significant gap between business and educators' perceptions as to the adequacy of job skills among young people." Many companies report deficiencies in basic skills in a majority of job categories. By contrast, school officials insist that the majority of graduates entering the job market is adequately prepared for employment. Both sides agree that companies would need to be more precise in defining job preparation requirements, in assisting with the development of curriculum, and <u>even in participating in classroom instruction</u> (Teltsch 1983; my underlines). Business, faced with stiffer economic competition from other nations and with the purchase of expensive technology, expects job applicants to be able to handle more comprehensive tasks. Yet, according to the same report, 80% of the schools surveyed said that graduates read well enough for employment, 66% claimed writing ability was adequate, and 79% that graduates had an adequate knowledge of mathematics.

The failure of American academia to produce marketable "basic" skills (I will return to foreign languages in the curriculum in a moment) is not a unique phenomenon. For example, falling college attendance rates in Australia (an 18% drop from 1975 to 1981) are tied with high unemployment (20%). Job prospects for college graduates there are bleak. Starting salaries for college grads and non-grads are about equal (see <u>Chronicle of Higher Education</u>, 8 February 1983, 23.) Similar declines can be found in Europe.

If we can assume that falling enrollments apply particularly to students in liberal studies rather than in technical fields, such as computer science, engineering, and even business administration, we can pinpoint a double problem. On the one hand, students have abandoned "basic" subjects such as mathematics, communication, and letters because they promise no economic future. Yet businessmen fume that their employees are functionally underprepared in the "basics."

In view of the less than brilliant record of academia to assure quality of achievement in the '60s and '70s, we can begin to understand the reluctance of Congress to rush funding to omnibus proposals for general education. May I remind you of the one dissenting voice in the President's Commission of Foreign Language and International Studies, former Senator Millicent Fenwick, who chastised the Commission for not insisting on quality or proficiency controls for the millions of dollars in block grants recommended for L2 training.

If the less than positive results of American student achievement tests in mathematical and verbal skills during the sixties and seventies are being rationalized today by what can be euphemistically called "social factors," the burden of the proof is now squarely on U.S. educators to reinterpret the purpose of their product. We have the same problem as General Motors, Ford or Chrysler: improve the effectiveness of the product for the consumer, or go bankrupt. If we are observing a national groundswell of renewed interest in "basic" subjects, there is by no means unanimity in regard to goals or procedures. One gray area of great concern to all language teachers in the 1980s is the relationship of L2 study to the total curriculum, primary, secondary, and postsecondary. Will L2 acquisition retain its traditional aura of an elitist luxury, an indicator of intellectual refinement and spiritual elevation, or will it be understood as having a more fundamental role in cognitive development?

Were we to address such a question to the National Endowment for the Humanities, I suspect that we would find, in the light of current funding priorities, that L2 training is subsumed under general or liberal studies at the secondary level, where it appears to be intertwined in mysterious ways with both communicative and cultural development. At the postsecondary level, L2 acquisition is ill-considered by NEH, if not taboo, with the occasional exception of funds to promote professional linkages between postsecondary and secondary instructors. You and I can solicit NEH for funds to study L2 authors who have a patina of high culture. Yet we cannot solicit NEH for funds to address fundamental problems in L2 acquisition, because literacy without culture is merely communication. Apparently the Endowment perceives the mission of the humanities as one of intellectual refinement and spiritual elevation. Teaching American students to say "please pass the pepper" in Japanese or Hausa has no redeeming humanistic value. Such concerns are the purview of other Washington agencies.

And yet, what do we find behind the ideological facade of high culture? The present Chair of NEH, William J. Bennett, published an article in the <u>Wall Street Journal</u> on 31 December 1982 entitled "The Shattered Humanities." Mr. Bennett bemoans the loss of "rigorous modes of inquiry in organized fields of knowledge." The Humanities, he claims, have become a "jumble of indiscriminate offerings, providing neither the educational institution nor the student with what Flannery O'Connor called 'the promise of the whole.' " Bennett laments the loss of requirements, the disconnected and eccentric areas of inquiry, what he calls the competition for complete unintelligibility. He offers no remedy, other than an implication that his office will continue to support research about "great works, important bodies of knowledge and powerful methods of inquiry." Although one may infer that he excludes foreign language study as an important body of knowledge or powerful method of inquiry, he shows sensitivity to certain consumer needs: "Students want to know where educated people stand on matters of enduring importance: courage, fidelity, friendship, honor, love, justice, goodness, ambiguity, time, power, faith."

The relationship between concern for universal values, as articulated in Mr. Bennett's humanism for the people, and the role of foreign languages in the "total" curriculum is broached more directly by William Brewster, Professor of Spanish at Memphis State, in a recent op-ed piece appearing in the Chronicle of Higher Education: "The Truisms, Cliches and Shibboleths of Foreign Language Requirements" (12 January 1983). The low esteem for foreign languages perceived as an ahumanistic field of study, and so articulated by NEH, is caught by Brewster in his opening phrase: "The very practicability of foreign language study renders it eminently illiberal" (underlines mine). Historically, foreign languages are nonacademic subjects, like fencing or voice, outside of what used to be the quadrivium and trivium. Brewster's pessimistic position is that reinstatement of foreign language requirements, as they used to exist, will provoke a revival of anti-foreign language sentiment. Language teachers are wrong to claim that their courses teach culture. They do not, says Brewster; verb conjugations always win out. Language teachers are also wrong to claim that language study is a broadening experience. It would be more effective, counters Brewster, to require world geography or a non-European language such as Japanese or Chinese. Language teachers are further misguided in their claims to assure competency. Look at the poor acquisition levels of the golden sixties. And finally, Americans, according to Brewster, do not have the personal motivation or socioeconomic incentives necessary to learn another language.

As foreign language teachers we may be chagrined by such fervent negativism. Yet what do we find in the way of an official "correction"? Let me share with you a recent public statement by Richard Brod, head of foreign language operations at the Modern Language Association. In his response (CHE, 9 February 1983), Brod chides Brewster for beating a dead horse. Language requirements are now more subtle. The eighty or so colleges and universities restoring the requirement recently have done so as a "no-nonsense mandate to produce graduates with working competence in a language." Proficiency rather than seat time is the new watchword.

However, in an article by Brod, "Language Study and Global Civics," published in Humanities (December 1982, pp. 6-7), an organ of NEH, we find a less pragmatic tone, if not a curious echo of sentiments voiced by Chairman Bennett. According to Brod, present-day L2 study suffers from "fragmentation and confusion of expectations," an attitude reminiscent of Bennett's "shattered humanities." Again, as a revisionist, Brod seeks a holist solution: "No greater challenge faces the language field today than that of defining feasible and desirable outcomes of study." The mandate of a general education language course is fourfold: (1) a measurable capacity to use L2, (2) awareness of language in its universals and particulars, (3) knowledge of facts and generalizations about the cultures where the particular language is spoken, (4) awareness of culture as a universal phenomenon, including cultural parity, and racial, ethnic and linguistic diversity in American society as well as global society. In essence, Brod is suggesting that an expanded language/culture program can legitimately take its place as "a core discipline of the Humanities" as well as "the keystone of Global Civics--the education necessary for responsible citizenship in an interdependent, interactive world." Brod's vision, which juxtaposes L2 learning with linguistics, cultural anthropology, world geography, and political science, would at first glance appear to offer a view of the Humanities outside the ethical concerns of Mr. Bennett. Yet, with the use of the term "civics," an allusion to secondary-level curricula, can we infer that college-level L2 courses may forego the heavy emphasis on awareness of the global village? If so, then Brod's position is essentially in line with present NEH policy in which high culture is reserved for the universities, whereas support for language acquisition research belongs to the Department of Education, if not the private sector.

The issue of foreign language instruction within a broader curricular design, then, has become a matter of national debate in the United States. We can anticipate a period of trial and error (perhaps of <u>Sturm</u> <u>und</u> <u>Drang</u>) analogous to the classic skirmishes between "ancients" and "moderns," as schools and colleges review the role of L2 in their programs.

But I have promised to explain my use of the adjective Aquarian. Let me attempt to do so by giving some examples of Aquarian enterprise in three areas of foreign language delivery: curricular marketing, teacher training, and student counseling. When I look back at foreign language classes as they were taught over thirty years ago, and at what is currently being done, I find virtually no difference. Students still register for small, presumably sequential units of second language. Dropout rates remain high. Acquisition levels the opposite. Student/teacher ratios are constant. Yes, there are new textbooks, more than ever, with fresher layouts. But the pluperfect subjunctive never arrives until the last chapter. Although I enjoy my chosen profession, I confess my amazement at the absence of change. Today my car comes equipped with front wheel drive. My quick frozen dinners are heated by microwave. My television set has become a private movie theatre. Yet the classrooms in which I teach remain without soundproofing. The seats are still uncomfortable. I continue to meet my French 2 students every Monday/Wednesday/Friday for fifty minutes.

Despite a quantum increase in the number of publications related to language acquisition (the <u>ACTFL Bibliography</u> alone runs to several thousand items annually), the content and form of L2 delivery has remained virtually static for several decades. One reason for our seeming reluctance to abandon familiar patterns is an intuitive conviction that what we are doing in the classroom is not bad. Stated otherwise, our professional associations are not telling us that TPR, Silent Way, or Suggestopedia offer a guaranteed increase in our effectiveness as foreign language teachers.

But what would be our sentiments if such were the case: a methodology and content sequence certified by the new national lobbyist group

JNCL-CLOTIS? Would our tradition of tenured autonomy, of cautious eclecticism and no accountability other than lack of extreme student dissatisfaction, would such professional manners and mores tolerate an imposed pedagogy? Perhaps my question is impertinent, perhaps seditious. A Czarist foreign language program, indeed!

Then again, what if your students and my students begin to whisper that they have heard of a wonderful foreign language program at College X (or International High School Y) which produces an active vocabulary of 2000 words in six weeks, and without a trace of accent? Will we then be prepared to switch or fight? Will our deans give us a bonus? And what will we do in our spare time at the end of the six weeks?

We sincerely think that we practice what Hector Hammerly (1982) has described as an "enlightened eclecticism." He states: "Good teachers have always engaged in synthesis...resisting the pressures to follow blindly this or that trend and at the same time willing to incorporate into their teaching the good things that any trend has to offer." But in our heart of hearts can we say with certainty that we are applying right now, today, the very best, the most effective methods and materials of which we are aware? These are uncomfortable questions because they impact directly on our individual teaching styles and also on our professional mores.

As Thomas Scovel has wisely stated, "truth has many shells." There exist a number of lines of inquiry which address the issue of effective nonprimary language acquisition and its relationship to human cognition. As such, the process of language learning is holistic and can never be approached from a unidirectional perspective. The proverbial glass of water is both half empty and half full. We do know that cognition has its social, situational, psychological, and neurological dimensions. Some researchers, the Aquarians to whom I alluded at the beginning of my paper, are on the threshold of new dimensions in second language research. They are raising fundamental questions about language learning. Let me share a few of them with you.

First, what is a <u>natural learning order</u>? There appears to be mounting evidence that mental processing involves unconscious "filters" and "organizers" and conscious "monitors." Also, learning errors in L2 appear to be minimally attributable to crossovers from L1. Again, error correction, the papers, exams and workbooks which we have so patiently redpenciled, is of dubious effectiveness. And finally, we underestimate the learner's contribution to the learning process. You may have heard the wistful remark by a student: "The geranium died on the window sill, but the teacher went right on talking." If these problems are of interest, may I recommend a new book by Aquarians Heidi Dulay, Marina Burt, and Stephen Krashen, <u>Language Two</u> (1982).

Let us turn to other issues. As mentioned at the beginning of this paper, foreign languages were originally accepted into the curriculum as mental gymnastics. At present, language classes are sometimes classified in curricula as a communicative skill, sometimes as cultural or humanistic by nature. In general, the lower the course, the more skill oriented, the higher, the more humanistic. The distinction, however, has eroded to a point where learning objectives are being warped by curricular convenience.

Let me illustrate with a vignette from my own institution. Some students in the College of Engineering would like to take elementary French so that they can spend a junior year at a French technical institute. The Engineering curriculum is so tightly structured that it cannot include a foreign language without extending studies by a semester or more. Yet, when the Engineering College requested that available humanities requirements be expanded to foreign languages, both the humanities and foreign language departments objected, claiming that substituting elementary language for humanities was illiberal. It seems a pity that twelve credits of basic French leading to a year of study in a francophone institution must be pitted against the sacrifice of twelve credits of history, literature, or philosophy. Is the glass of water half empty or half full? One solution which has been suggested is to require both humanities and foreign language of all students at the university.

A less academic form of social reality is the useful distinction of R. Cooper (1981) between language acquisition and "language spread," the difference between the discretionary learning of a foreign language, whether at home or in a host country, and the imposed acquisition of a lingua franca. In a social situation of language acquisition, the status quo in American education (except for Hispanics), rare talent leads to even rarer mastery. Many students take courses in French, German, Spanish, Italian, and a handful of less frequently taught languages, yet few acquire significant competence. On the contrary, students who are exposed to "language spread," as witnessed in our burgeoning ESL courses, are minimally influenced by such variables as cognitive style, aptitude, attitude, and personality, the very factors which are crucial for the success of language acquisition. In ESL courses there is rarely any doubt that learning has occurred. International students in the United States must pass a TOEFL examination or acquire similar certification, particularly if they are to be permitted to function as teaching assistants. Again, in multilingual cultures, central Africa, for example, Swahili may be acquired as the lingua franca of social "solidarity" and English or French as the lingua franca of social "status." As Whiteley (1969) has noted: "It is worth remembering that the desire to learn another language springs rarely from a disinterested wish to communicate with one's fellow humans." If he is correct, then the immigrant moving from Ibadan who is a speaker of Hausa and who must learn Yoruba in order to sell his wares, will have an easier and more effective learning experience than the Anglophone in French 3, a course required for graduation.

Most of you are familiar with the psychological/neurological theory and practice of Georgi Lozanov and so-called whole-brain learning (see, for example, Lozanov and Racle, eds. [1975], and Bancroft [1978]). Yet, there remain unanswered questions about biologically determined predispositions to language study. Other than a conscious selection to learn, one can perhaps say on the basis of genetic make-up that the final product of L2 acquisition is the result of processes and developments beyond the control of the individual. You and I cannot decide to vocalize like native speakers. It may or may not happen. So, is genetic determinism compatible with the presumed ethically liberalizing goals of a foreign language requirement? What do we think about the use of drug-induced states which revive a second or third language which has been dormant for years? What about the use of hypnotism as a tool in second language acquisition research to encourage disinhibition or pronunciation ability? As we move into the neurological dimensions of language learning a host of problems and possibilities of solution emerge. Present research confirms the intuitive perception that there is a cognitive development in L1 but not in L2 acquisition. As Earl Stevick (1982) has cogently noted, learning as a formal exercise is not the same as acquisition or true proficiency, just as grammar comprehension is far removed from active usage.

Other questions: do normal bilinguals have more active right brain activity? Do teachers unintentionally communicate their expectations of what students can do even when relying on bogus tracking (the problem of special programs reserved for the gifted).[1] Do we really know what the essential contributions of formal instruction are in terms of what does the most good, when and where? In short, are there limits to cognitive development, genetic and/or environmental?

These are some of the Aquarian questions being raised by researchers in applied language study. They suggest a shift in our objectives. As teachers we want the security of language programs which provide as much of a language as our students really need for what they really want. If we can accept this as a premise, then in a user-friendly language program, proficiency becomes a means and not an end. Let us imagine, in the best of all possible anglophone worlds, a foreign language program which assures the student of continuous, interactive support. There are no grades, those monuments to <u>Sitz-fleisch</u> or to natural talent. No final examination. The instructor and instructor surrogates, such as a smart microprocessor, introduce the language according to a sequence compatible with encoding patterns acquired with language one. At every moment in the program, the instructor and the student are in full agreement about the level of acquisition, that is, fully assimilated learning. If reasonable progress in acquisition stops, whether for personal, environmental, or genetic reasons, then the student and instructor agree to termination, without tears. A record of acquisition competency is available.

Some of you may be wondering: what about standards, grades, credit hours? How can I provide individualized instruction in classes of forty students? You cannot. Nor can I. But perhaps together we can. Last summer I learned from a practicing suggestopedist at the University of Adelaide that the Japanese are experimenting with simultaneous multilanguage acquisition, using the Lozanov concern technique, but with non-Western music, and specially designed couches.[2] J. D. Guilford of S.O.I. Institute in El Segundo, California, has separated "intelligence" into 120 discrete skills. Certainly some of these have relevance to language learning. Another private concern, Innovative Sciences of Stamford, Connecticut, has developed packages of problem solving techniques, with application to strategic reasoning problems in English and mathematics. Why not apply some of these to foreign languages as well? Xavier University in New Orleans has developed a short course in reasoning for pre-med applicants. CUNY has developed special courses in thinking skills for "low achievers." The National Education Corporation operates the largest vocational training program in the country (including the Spartan School in Tulsa). As college costs soar and liberal arts students scrounge for work, the N. E. C. promises highly marketable skills in a relatively short time and at an affordable price.

Such Aquarian developments in theory and practice are occuring independently of much of academia and its professional associations and agencies. It would seem to be in our individual and collective interest to design an array of foreign language programs for specific acquisition objectives, defined by the proficiency measures under development by ACTFL and ETS,[3] and which could be marketed under accelerated time frames. Academia's failure to develop user-friendly programs, meaning a reasonable expectation of effective acquisition for a given investment of time and money, may encourage the growth of scientifically engineered programs in the private sector.

From this brief overview of current foreign language studies, I believe that it is reasonable to conclude that we can no longer identify ourselves strictly as language humanists or as language teachers. The field has acquired a complexity which exceeds the familiar labels. One way to direct the increasingly diverse and disparate advances in language study would be the creation of a national institute for cognitive and communicative studies. Such a center would collect and disseminate data. It would design pilot programs in commonly and less commonly taught languages. It would provide in-service training for language teachers in the most reliable methods. A future function of such an institute would be to develop a graduate degree training program for future language teachers drawing from the complexity of subject areas which are increasingly relevant to the task.[4] A national institute for language research and delivery would cost less than federal sums presently encumbered or projected for foreign language welfare. Alternatively, a national center for cognitive and communicative studies could be funded by Aquarians from the private sector, or even by a combination of public and private support.

Since the President's Commission in 1979, the American public has been sufficiently sensitized to an attitude not unfavorable to foreign language study. However, it will insist, and rightly so, on a quality product available under realistic expectations. If we can focus our language acquisition strategies more effectively and more honestly, then the related humanistic, political and economic concerns will, I believe, take care of themselves.

NOTES

[1] For a discussion of the so-called "Pygmalion Effect," the unconscious influence of instructor expectations, see Rosenthal and Jacobsen (1968).

[2] I am indebted to Ingrid Gassner-Roberts, Department of German, University of Adelaide, South Australia, for news of the experiment.

[3] A preliminary version is now available: ACTFL Provisional Proficiency Guidelines, n. d. [1983].

[4] The Center for Cognitive Science (University of Texas, Austin) offers a partial model of the interdisciplinary center which I am suggesting in that it brings together computer scientists, linguists, neuroscientists, philosophers and psychologists.

REFERENCES

Bancroft, W. Jane. "The Lozanov Method and its American Adaptations." Modern Language Journal, 62, 4 (1978), 167-174.

Bennett, William J. "The Shattered Humanities." The Wall Street Journal, 31 December 1982.

Brewster, William. "The Truisms, Clichés and Shibboleths of Foreign Language Requirements." Chronicle of Higher Education, 12 January 1983.

Brod, Richard. "Language Study and Global Civics." Humanities, December 1982, pp. 6-7.

Cooper, Robert L. "Language Spread as a Perspective for the Study of Second Language Acquisition." In Roger W. Andersen, ed., New Dimensions in Second Language Acquisition Research (Rowley, MA: Newbury House, 1981), 130-145.

De Felippis, D. "Views of Secondary School Superintendents on Foreign Language Study: A Support-Constraint Analysis." Foreign Language Annals, 12 (1979).

Dulay, Heidi, Marina Burt, Stephen Krashen. Language Two. New York and Oxford: Oxford University Press, 1982.

Ferguson, Marilyn. The Aquarian Conspiracy, Personal and Social Transformation in the 1980s. Los Angeles: Tarcher, 1980.

Hammerly, Hector. Synthesis in Second Language Teaching. Blaine, Wash: Second Language Publications, 1982.

Herron, Carol. "Who Should Study a Foreign Language? The Myth of Elitism." Foreign Language Annals, 15 (1982), 441-9.

Kelly, Louis G. Twenty-Five Centuries of Language Teaching. Rowley, Mass.: Newbury House, 1969.

Koppel, Irene E. "The Perceived Contribution of Foreign Languages to High Priority Educational Goals." Foreign Language Annals, 15 (1982), 435-9.

Lerner, Barbara. "American Education: How Are We Doing?" The Public Interest, Fall 1982, Easton, Penn. (Review in Wilson Quarterly, 7, 1 1983, 19-20.)

Lozanov, G., and G. Racle, eds. A Teaching Experience with the Suggestopaedic Method. Ottawa: Public Service Commission of Canada.

Lurie, Joseph. "America . . . Globally Blind, Deaf and Dumb. A Shocking Report on our Incompetence Through Ignorance in Dealing with Other Countries." Foreign Language Annals, 15 (1982), 413-21.

Rosenthal, R., and L. Jacobson. Pygmalion in the Classroom; Teacher Expectation and Pupils' Intellectual Development. New York: Holt, Rinehart and Winston, 1968.

Simon, Paul. The Tongue-Tied American. New York: Continuum, 1980.

Stevick, Earl W. Teaching and Learning Languages. Cambridge: Cambridge University Press, 1982.

Teltsch, Kathleen. "Survey Finds Young People Lack Work Skills." New York Times, 16 January 1983, p. 21.

Whiteley, Wilfred. Swahili: The Rise of a National Language. (Studies in African History, 3.) London: Methuen, 1969.

CAN COLLEGE STUDENTS ACTUALLY LEARN TO SPEAK AND UNDERSTAND FRENCH?

William L. Easterling
Armstrong State College

Being scheduled to speak on the second day of a conference has its advantages: one has heard the other speakers. One young lady I heard yesterday began by saying that she disliked presentations which were preceded by apologies, but felt she still had to make two such apologies.

I will begin by saying that I had intended to be apologetic about the practical, nonscholarly content of my presentation, but everything I have heard so far at this conference has alluded in some way to the fact that what goes on in the classroom is and must continue to be our major concern. Therefore, I will not apologize.

When businesses are farsighted enough to recognize the need for their employees to learn a second language, why do they ignore our local universities and send their people to Berlitz, which costs a fortune? Because of what goes on in the classroom, or to be more accurate, what does NOT go on in our classrooms?

I teach French in a college which used to offer a French major. Because other departments have dropped the foreign language requirement, my department has been reduced in size to the point of being unable to offer a strong major program. Therefore, with the exception of a handful of students desiring literature courses, which I teach as a voluntary overload (this is a euphemism for "without pay"), my classes are made up of beginning and intermediate students.

When I received Dr. Joseph's notice of this conference, I wrote the following:

"CAN COLLEGE STUDENTS ACTUALLY LEARN TO SPEAK AND UNDERSTAND FRENCH?

"An impressionistic assessment by a former traditionalist. After years of insisting upon treating elementary college French as a strictly academic course, taught in the traditional manner and supplemented by a language laboratory, I came to realize that, not only was I losing students, but that those students who studied French were performing at increasingly lower levels on the national standardized test used at the end of the third quarter. After serious consideration, I decided that what today's students really need and certainly want is a means of communicating in the language, rather than knowledge of the grammar, syntax, etymology, and history of the language I had been offering them. The comparative approach I had used probably helped them in their English classes, but they clearly were not learning enough French to function effectively in that language.

"My solution to this dilemma will be to change approach dramatically. I have adopted the textbook En français, by Carton and Caprio, published by Heinle and Heinle, and my intention is to make my freshman French class into a purely practical course in which I will attempt to teach a skill. The organization of the textbook into chapters which treat situations rather than points in grammar should provide the springboard I need. I hope never again to hear a student come back from France saying, "I couldn't even ask where the bathroom was." There is no way at this time to predict results, of course, but I feel sure that by December I will have a very good idea of how successful I will be. I will keep thorough records meanwhile, and at the end of the first quarter I will prepare a complete assessment of the new approach. I intend to test early and often the level of comprehension of spoken French. I am not striving simply for the parroting of a few common expressions and automatic responses to standard greetings and questions, but a genuine comprehension of the native speaker. My college gives me three quarters of the students' time, so mine is an ambitious project, the results of which I wish to share with the conference in February."

Since writing those words, I have taught the first quarter and about half the second quarter of elementary French using Carton and Caprio's text. Keeping in mind that the goal has been to teach my students to speak and understand, regardless of whether they learned any grammar or not, regardless of whether they ever got beyond the present tense, and regardless of whether they ended the three quarters with a very limited vocabulary, I have to say that the departure from a more traditional approach has been a smashing success. My students are talking, to me and to each other. The ultimate test, understanding the native speaker, has truly been child's play for most of the group. To my great good fortune, two young Frenchmen have, on separate occasions, visited my class for several days each, and my students have not shown the usual hesitancy in engaging them in conversation. One of my visitors was a very good-looking young man, and the young ladies in the class quickly dispensed with general questions and got down to the nitty-gritty: "Quel âge avez-vous? Etes-vous marié?"

I need to backtrack a moment and say for those not familiar with En français, that the grammar is there, but if the instructor does everything in class that is suggested, there is little time left to do anything other than tell the students to read the grammar at home.

As for not getting beyond the present tense, I was surprised to realize just how early the conditional tense was introduced, for example, with no fanfare whatsoever. I think the thing which impresses me most about the book is just that: the grammar is there, the verb tenses are introduced early, and at an almost alarming rate, but no fuss is made over them. Conversation is stressed from the word "go," and everything else is subordinated to the goal of making the class a time for speaking French.

As for vocabulary, there is a basic vocabulary for each dialogue, with dozens of alternate phrases presented separately. Since I have in my group of twenty-two students several who have never had one day of French before taking my class (I was <u>worried</u>), I can tell them to memorize the basic vocabulary and simply be able to recognize the alternate words. This has probably kept them from dropping the course.

Before going on, I will backtrack once more: In case anyone thinks I am trying to sell Carton and Caprio's book, being sent by Heinle and Heinle to infiltrate this conference, I will quickly say that I have found several weaknesses in the book, the most serious one being the dialogues themselves. I find them difficult to work with. After one read-through with me speaking one part and the students the other, then a second reading with the class equally divided, or one student taking the lead part and the rest of the class being "vous," I am often at a loss as to what to do next. This may well be due to my own lack of experience with the approach, which leads me to the second weakness: the instructor's manual has been all but useless to me.

One last weakness in my eyes would be those exercises in which the students are instructed to "change the following sentences to so-and-so." I thought this was the type of thing a conversational text was supposed to avoid. Whenver possible, I have altered these exercises to question-and-answer drills.

I would like to say that since undertaking the conversational approach to beginning French, so different from my past experience, I have also attended a John Rassias seminar in the Dartmouth Model, and I will probably adopt his textbook for the fall of this year and go even further into a conversational approach. (This is by way of explaining that, while I have naturally based what I have to say on my experience with Carton and Caprio's book, I am not in any way wedded to it.)

Now, what I suppose you are waiting to read, and what I have unconsciously avoided getting to, is:

What did I really do?

How did I test results?

What made the approach work?

Why did I want to tell you about it?

<u>What did I do?</u> I spoke French to my students and got them to speak French to me and to each other from the very beginning of the class. I kept explanations and "talking <u>about</u> the language" to a bare minimum. As soon as the students knew two words of the language, they were using those two words, with me and with each other. Of course, all of us do this at least a part of every class period if we can, but with this group, I have

employed the <u>live</u> question-answer approach on the average of 40 minutes out of every 50-minute class period.

Clearly, some things have been neglected. The only time I bring up grammar is when I am introducing a new lesson. I do make myself available after class. Cultural material, one of my loves, is sadly lacking, but they are TALKING, and talking in FRENCH. I did take time one day during a unit on the furniture found in a house, to tell the students (in English, for the sake of saving time) about St.-Exupéry's wonderful description of his perception of the French family, a group gathered about a round table, underneath a circle of light cast by one of those lovely, old-fashioned hanging kerosene lamps, made of porcelain and brass. I could not have brought myself NOT to mention that when the subject of the dining room came up. Of course day-to-day cultural differences can be taught, e.g., shaking hands when teaching greetings, and making sure the students notice that we always say, "Bonjour, MADAME." I did no pronunciation drill in class, relying solely on the lab for that function. Naturally, I corrected people as they spoke, unless to do so would interrupt dialogue too badly.

My firm belief all along had been that English-speaking students could not understand spoken French unless they could see the written word, and with my "experimental" group, I have steadfastly refused to give in to the temptation to write a word on the board, or worse, to translate the word. This determination to make the student understand the spoken language without a written crutch, has been serendipitous: sometimes the student I am conversing with does not understand a word, but a classmate clearly does. Then, I say, "Jean, explique-lui ce que j'ai dit." The results have been really gratifying, and obviously this little technique keeps the rest of the class listening when I am engaged in a one-to-one conversation.

<u>How did I test results?</u> To be perfectly honest, this was probably the easiest part of all. When I spend most of every class period talking to students in French and questioning them, testing is pretty much an on-going activity. Because I have been absent more than in normal years attending conferences, I have made use of my visiting native speakers of French, letting them give oral exams for me during my absence. Again, this has been the acid test. The students HAVE understood the native speakers, and test results have been gratifying. I believe that the anonymous assessments I have asked students to make of the course would bear me out in this evaluation. I have to admit that spelling errors have been numerous on written work, but then, they always were; the level of comprehension and the excitement of the students have more than made up for that lack. Grammar errors are still present, too, but in smaller numbers. It seems that using a construction over and over in class gives better results than explaining the construction over and over. Another testing technique that is new (with me, at any rate) is asking questions which make it possible for the student to show what he knows, rather than trying to show up what he does not know. E.g.: <u>Qu'est-ce que vous avez fait hier soir?</u>, as opposed to "Fill in the blank with the proper word."

What made the approach work? This may be the most difficult question to answer, and my lack of experience with the "immersion" approach, if one wishes to give it a name, has been frankly a handicap, but it HAS worked, and I can only attribute the success of my class to the fact that the students really did want to learn to speak French, and to their enthusiasm and my own.

I think I can take some credit for having recognized two problems: one inherent in the great majority of students I have taught, and one inherent in my method of teaching over the years. (Goodness knows, I should have come to some conclusions by now. I've been teaching French off and on at some level or other since around 1958.)

The first problem I have isolated, if you will forgive my sounding like a research scientist, is the one mentioned earlier, the fact that the fundamental difficulty of French for English speaking people is a HEARING problem. Most English speaking people have no trouble learning to read French, but speaking it is another matter. French is unique among the major European languages in presenting this hearing problem; at least it does not exist to such a degree with German or Spanish, for example.

There are just too many things in French that sound so much alike. I think anyone who has taught French for more than one term probably can come up with a handful of them. And then there are those pesky, all-important little words that tell the whole story: ce que, ce qui, dont, quand, and qu'on. To the student, those words just seem to disappear in the spoken sentence. I finally decided that this hearing difficulty was the students' basic problem, and my obligation was to help them overcome it. How? By talking, talking, talking to them IN FRENCH, pantomiming on occasion, but FLATLY REFUSING to write words for them or to translate. I gained the time for doing this by not explaining anything in class that the students could get by reading the text at home. I simply had to assume that my students would do their homework, and they cooperated as no group before them had ever done. When they come to class, they hear FRENCH, and they HAVE to understand it and recognize the words that they read the night before when preparing for class. Of course, a part of every preparation session has had to be listening to the tapes which accompany the textbook.

If you remember my earlier mention of enlisting the aid of a student whose face showed that he did understand what the student questioned did not, you will realize that a lot of time is NOT wasted by my refusal to write or translate. This was my former belief. I have said more than once, "Why waste five minutes trying to make a student understand a word that you could give him in a fraction of a second?" I have now come to realize that student B is forming sentences of his own in order to help student A, and keeping everybody's interest up.

The second problem I mentioned was within myself: I have heretofore had very little success in getting my students to talk. This has clearly arisen from my choice of textbooks and my own approach to teaching. I will certainly give credit here to Carton and Caprio, because their book does not just ask or suggest that students talk, it DEMANDS that they talk. It FORCES them to talk. I have been amazed at the difference this makes in the classroom. It is so much more <u>alive,</u> and I don't get that question that used to haunt me as I was going over exercises in a book: "I'm not on any number. I'm on a street corner in Paris!" But now the question never comes up, because I'm <u>not</u> on any number, and I'm as close to a street corner in Paris as some of my students may ever get, and I truly feel, for the first time in years, that I am giving them something.

Finally, <u>why did I want to tell you about it?</u> I feel myself on shaky ground here, because it may well be that many readers have far more experience than I in conducting beginning classes in the target language; but it was a new departure for me, and I have become convinced, watching language classes diminish in size and number over the years, that I, at least, was not giving my students what they wanted, and with times changing, and education becoming more and more practical and less classical, the hour has come to give American students a working knowledge of a language, so that they can indeed ask with confidence that they will understand the answer: "Où sont les toilettes, s'il vous plaît?"

STUDENT COMMENTS

"I studied Spanish for four quarters by the old method. Now, after having studied two quarters of French, I find the new method to be superior, by far, to the old one. By the previous method I was into the fourth quarter before speaking the language as well as I now speak French in the second quarter.... To be forced to speak the words, as well as construct elementary sentences, helps to imprint what has been learned."

"The French class taught in this manner has both good and bad points. This is, of course, understandable for any type of foreign language class taught by any method.
"One of its good points is that there is a chosen contact between the instructor and the student. A bond is formed between the two, which is necessary for any conduction of information. The student is also introduced to more words, phrases and expressions used by the foreign speaker.
"There are some drawbacks to this method, however. One of these occurs when the professor begins to carry on a conversation using the language, and the student cannot comprehend the meaning behind the bulk of the conversation. This does expose the student to new words, but on the other hand the student may get frustrated because of ignorance."

"The French program is effective. The book combines dialogue, grammar and idiomatic expressions in a challenging blend. However, a main drawback is the topic choice of the dialogues. 'Chez le dentiste' or 'le docteur' are superfluous."

"By simply speaking the language, and not constantly translating back to English, I feel it is much easier to pick up the meanings of entire phrases and sentences."

"The conversational approach is the best way to learn a language; it follows the natural sequence of learning. I wish there were some way to improve vocabulary; the little games seemed effective. I keep thinking of children's books which have pictures and words: the visual, the printed word, the aural reinforcing one another. The book is good, but the dictionary/vocabulary is weak. The tapes could be longer. Class is interesting. I am improving."

"Language is not helpful if when called upon to use it, one cannot make oneself understood! Thus, the 'forcible speaking program' is making me put my French to work rather than abstract myself from it."

"Never having taken French prior to this class, I have little basis for comparison. I am doing well in the class, however, and feel that I am grasping the language. The 'method' is a bit intimidating at first. It requires adherence to one's homework and a constant program of listening to the tapes. In the end, I think it will be effective and after the student has entered securely into the language, he can buttress any weaknesses and delve more deeply into grammar. This system seems somewhat haphazard but I believe it is more 'natural' (it would please Rousseau) in that it approximates the process by which an infant or an immigrant would assimilate the language."

"The textbook covers too much material too fast and it does not have a chance to penetrate. The conversational approach is good but we should spend a little more time writing since the exercises in the book cannot give enough 'feel' for the language. The words themselves are easy to learn but sentence structure is difficult due to the lack of instruction in the book. Also, we should spend more time in class on pronunciation because it is difficult to get this from the tapes which are limited."

"I have never taken a foreign language before this French course so I have no basis on which to make a comparison. I find learning French a great deal easier than I had imagined it would be. As to whether this is a result of either the book used, the instructor, or both, I am not sure."

TRADITION AND CHANGE: NEW TRENDS IN TEACHING SPANISH IN A LIBERAL ARTS ENVIRONMENT

Thomas Deveny
Western Maryland College

Western Maryland College is a small private college located in the outskirts of Baltimore. It is a school with a sense of tradition and heritage. Founded in 1867, it is the oldest coeducational college south of the Mason-Dixon line. It is a liberal arts institution, and this focus is manifested by the First Principles adopted by our faculty, which state, "....we provide a liberal arts education as an integral part of professional training so that students will be more flexible, more successful, and happier in the world of work." Western Maryland strongly believes that language instruction is a fundamental part of a liberal arts educational program, and we have a proficiency requirement of competence in a foreign language equal to one year of college study.

The goals and objectives of our language program are twofold, and thus reflect the needs of the two different groups that we teach. For the majority of students in our elementary courses, who are fulfilling their liberal arts requirement, we provide a foundation in the use of the language. We also offer a major in Spanish with courses in advanced language study, literature, and culture. Until recently the emphasis in our program, or at least in the minds and hearts of many members of the department, was on the literature segment, and as little as five years ago we spent time devising a reading list of masterpieces of Spanish and Spanish-American literature which we felt our majors should read before graduation. We began to realize, however, that fewer and fewer students were interested in pursuing graduate studies in literature. At the same time, the level of preparation of entering freshmen seemed to decline; or at least on a quantitative level, there was a drop in the number of students who came to Western Maryland with a level of fluency sufficient to allow them to test out of the elementary and intermediate levels and matriculate in upper level courses. Consequently, members of the department examined our language program and decided to make several alterations in order to meet the changing needs and backgrounds of our students.

We first addressed our attention to the lower level program. Although we have no problem in terms of enrollment in elementary classes (thanks to the one-year language requirement), less than one quarter of our students continue on to intermediate Spanish, and very few prolong their studies beyond the second year. We believed that if students could gain a greater command of the language in a shorter period of time, more of them would continue on to take advanced studies and even to major in Spanish. Consequently, our department has adopted an intensive language methodology modeled after the program at Dartmouth College. The basis of the intensive language model is an increase in the amount of contact time and exclusive use of the target language in the classroom. Under the traditional model, students met with professors for three hours per week. Under the intensive model, we have added two hours per week of drill sessions, which are conducted by "apprentice teachers." These apprentice teachers are upper level undergraduates (sophomores, juniors, and seniors). Many are Spanish majors, although the position is open to any student who has an adequate level of fluency in the language. The positions are competitive, and all candidates must attend a three-day training workshop in the fall before classes begin. During this workshop, we acquaint the candidates with the methodology of the intensive language model, and have them practice the techniques that they will use in the drill sessions throughout the year. At the end of the workshop, each candidate is judged according to language proficiency (fluency, pronunciation, and inflection), technical proficiency (cueing appropriately and consistently, catching errors, using correction techniques consistently and accurately, moving about the room, etc.), and overall demeanor (confidence, friendliness, and enthusiasm).

A key element in the success of the intensive language model is the size of the drill sessions. Although enrollment in master classes in Spanish averages approximately 23 per section, the enrollment in the drill sessions is limited to an absolute number of twelve, with an average enrollment of ten. The purpose of the drill sessions is to reinforce the material presented in class by the professor (or "master teacher," as he or she is called). The apprentice teachers do not give grammar explanations; they only lead the responses to the drills assigned to them by the master teacher. The exercises used range from simple repetition drills (specific pronunciation exercises, vocabulary for each chapter, brief dialogues) to substitution, transformation, and question/answer drills. In addition, the apprentice teachers give weekly dictations, which they grade and return to the students. Care must be exercised in the selection of a suitable textbook for the program; the text must have enough exercises of this type to be "assigned" to the apprentice teachers. Since the apprentice teachers conduct the drill sessions exclusively in Spanish, the master teacher must insure that instructions or model exercises in the target language which are both clear and simple are always provided.

In establishing an intensive program, one must keep in mind the distinction between "apprentice teachers" and graduate teaching assistants. Apprentice teachers may not have the level of fluency that is generally demanded of graduate assistants, and allowing the former to extemporize in the drill sessions can lead to situations in which there is a good deal of negative (incorrect) linguistic modeling. In addition, graduate teaching assistants are generally given relative autonomy with regard to pacing. Pacing of drill sessions must be carefully planned and explicitly stated for proper coordination of the program, since students in any given drill session will come from several different master classes. Equally rigorous coordination of the course syllabus is imperative for all master teachers.

The small size of the drill sessions, together with the intensive nature of the exercises, has allowed the Dartmouth Intensive Language Model to obtain "an average response rate during drill practice of sixty-five times per student per drill session" ("The Dartmouth Intensive Language Model," Dept. of Romance Langs., Dartmouth College). At Western Maryland College, by including simple pronunciation vocabulary drills, and counting our active use of choral responses as part of an individual's response rate, I have observed as many as 260 responses per student per drill session. Such results can only help the elementary student to internalize the grammatical structures of Spanish so that they progress from the level of mere linguistic manipulation to the level of expression of personal meaning (Rivers 1976: 14). However, this intensive model is also a great benefit to the upper level students. Since one of our goals is that our language majors graduate with a near-native level of fluency, we must provide them with opportunities to achieve this goal. Mere attendance in an upper level class dedicated to conversation (or quite often, to conversation and composition) for fifty minutes, three times per week, often causes us to fall short of this goal. Offering an undergraduate student the opportunity to work as an apprentice teacher, however, can provide him with the chance to enunciate hundreds of linguistic utterances in Spanish for each hour of drill.

Another important segment of the elementary program is the language laboratory. We have a minimum requirement of one hour of attendance per week, and in order to optimize the pedagogical value of this segment of the program, we have divided the requirement into two half-hour segments consisting of audio lab and video lab. In the audio lab, students listen to tapes which accompany the lab manual of our textbook and perform transformation, listening comprehension, and other exercises.

The video lab consists of weekly viewings of a video program entitled Zarabanda. Zarabanda is a human interest story with a touch of mystery; it follows the life of a young mechanic who leaves his small town of Piquera in Castile and goes to Segovia and Madrid. The program is produced by the BBC, and was filmed on location in Spain. In addition to the dramatized story in each episode, two professors come on screen each week to direct the students' attention to a particular grammar point that is emphasized in the dialogue and to lead drills on this materials. Thus, the viewing is not a completely passive experience; the video lab assistant leads the choral responses to these grammar drills. An added feature of the program is unscripted street scenes with Spaniards in which an interviewer asks questions about directions or prices of objects, for example, in order to provide listening comprehension practice in an everyday context that one might encounter while travelling. In addition to the videotapes, students have a Zarabanda textbook, and there are cassettes for use in the audio lab. In order to integrate the Zarabanda material with the other segments of the course, the apprentice teachers conduct pronunciation and pattern drills from the Zarabanda test, and give dictations based on the dialogue during the drill sessions. In the master classes, professors occasionally ask for oral or written summaries of the week's episode, and each quiz during the semester contains a question which pertains to the content of the dramatization.

We have undertaken a revision of our second year courses as well. Currently, the majority of our students who enroll in Intermediate Spanish do so to fulfill a liberal arts distribution requirement. Other options for fulfilling this requirement include comparative literature courses, cultural history courses, and non-Western studies. Thus, those who enroll in the intermediate level tend to be the superior students from our elementary course. On the other hand, this second year of study generally terminates the contact that most of them have with the language. Until now, intermediate has consisted of an eclectic mixture of grammar review, cultural material, and conversation. Our change in the program represents a change of perspective and of emphasis. We hope to have intermediate seen not as a culminating experience, but as one of a continuous set of building blocks in the students' progress. Thus, beginning next fall, our first semester of intermediate will become the third semester of Intensive Spanish. This course will continue to place emphasis on oral/aural work in class, with supplements of drill sessions and laboratory work. Our second semester of intermediate will become a course in advanced grammar. By providing students with a more in-depth grammar study at this level, they will be able to perform better in our later composition/conversation courses.

We have expanded the offerings in the latter area in order that our students may acquire greater fluency in speech and writing while learning more about Hispanic culture. This shift in emphasis away from literature is intended to meet the changing needs of our advanced students: the majority of the students who take upper level courses do so as minors in conjunction with a concentration in fields such as economics, business administration, or political science.

In teaching writing, we have implemented a rewrite technique advocated by Professor Claire Gaudiani of Purdue (Gaudiani 1979). With this technique, the professor encircles errors of grammar, syntax, etc., on the students' compositions, and makes appropriate comments as to organization, thought content, and style. The student must then rewrite the entire composition and incorporate the necessary improvements. This system has the advantage of providing more active experience in good writing; the first composition is seen as a rough draft, and each week the student is able to move beyond that stage to a more polished work. This helps to eliminate passive reception of the professor's remarks, which can lead to repetition of mistakes on future compositions. Another advantage of the rewrite technique is that a great deal of emphasis is placed on improvement: the final grade for each composition is based on the average of the initial grade and that of the rewrite. This method allows one to maintain rigorous standards without great prejudice to student retention.

In the aural component of this course, we now make greater use of the audio lab, and require students to spend a minimum of thirty minutes per week listening to tapes. The content of the lab material is designed to give students a better grasp of Hispanic culture and history, and consists of news broadcasts and music.

The news broadcasts are from the new tape transcription service provided by Radio Nacional de España. Each month, we receive a cassette which contains two thirty-minute programs: a summary of the month's news, entitled, "Panorama de España," and a monographic theme dedicated to topics such as a history of elections in Spain or the life of Santa Teresa de Ávila. The tapes contain not only the voices of professional newscasters, but those of a wide variety of informants ranging from King Juan Carlos and Prime Minister Felipe Gonzalez to citizens who were victims of recent flooding in Catalonia. The tremendous advantages of the tape/transcription service are that it provides professional quality recordings covering topics of current interests, and allows students who have difficulty with aural comprehension the opportunity to read along while they listen to the tapes.

The second element of the audio lab at the composition/conversation level is music. Here students listen to folk songs or to contemporary Spanish and Spanish-American artists, such as Juan Manuel Serrat and Mercedes Sosa. Here, too, we provide transcriptions of the lyrics. We thus follow the "dulce et utile" principle in providing students with more aural comprehension practice outside of the classroom while acquainting them with this fundamental and often neglected area of culture.

We reserve part of the third conversation/composition course to deal with technical vocabulary from diverse fields in which our students have an interest. This includes working with terminology from law, medicine, business, etc. Students gain further practice in these applied areas in a new one-credit translation course. They develop skills in the art of rendering texts from Spanish to English and from English to Spanish. In addition to texts of a technical nature from the aforementioned areas, we include many journalistic texts which deal with timely cultural topics. By breaking the three credit mold, we attract students who are not majors and who might not be able to fit a regular Spanish course into their load.

The other course in which we break the three credit mold is the first course in our literature series. In spite of our de-emphasis of literature,[1] we still believe that an appreciation of the literary work of art is concomitant to a liberal education. In the past, we often became frustrated during the so-called survey courses because of the difficulty of giving students a sense of historical development of styles and genres while at the same time attempting to teach the terminology and methodology of a "comentario de texto." Consequently, we have created a course in textual analysis as a prerequisite to our survey and period courses. This is a four credit course which is team taught: one member of the department teaches the three-hour theoretical segment in English to Spanish, French, and German students; the fourth credit consists of the practical application of the theories--doing exercises in "comentarios de texto"--and is taught in each of the target languages by members of respective sections of the department.

The theoretical section begins with discussions of how language works: the structure of signs, the difference between speech and written texts, etc. In the domain of literature, we address such questions as "What is literature?," "How does figurative language operate?," "How does representation in poetic language differ from representation in 'ordinary' speech?" In this course, students gain a greater sensitivity to the literary work of art as well as a knowledge of strategies for interpreting literary texts; consequently, we are able to enhance the quality of our advanced offerings in literature.

In spite of the creation of new courses, upgrading of old courses, and implementation of the intensive language model, we recognize that it is necessary to further supplement regular classroom activities in order for students to achieve a goal of near-native fluency. Providing opportunities for study abroad is an excellent means for students to achieve this goal, but it is difficult for a small liberal arts school to maintain viable programs abroad for its students. Consequently, Western Maryland College has become a member of a consortium of schools headed by Central College of Iowa which maintains programs in Germany, France, and Spain. For those students who do not wish to spend a full year or a semester abroad, we offer a three-week study tour of Spain during our January term.

On campus, we have renewed our commitment to the concept of language houses with the reinauguration this year of the Spanish house. While more modest a program than in years gone by (we no longer import a house person from Spain), it provides the truly motivated student with an extraordinary opportunity to use the language outside the classroom. We have also recommitted ourselves to assist with activities of the Spanish Club, such as arranging to show Hispanic films.

Like many small liberal arts schools, we face challenging years ahead. Our success--or perhaps our survival--in the future rests with the strength of the academic programs in each of our individual departments. In Foreign Languages, we have undertaken a revision of our entire program in order to provide the best instruction possible to meet the needs of today's students. We have attempted to strengthen the program from its elementary base to its most advanced courses by adopting pedagogical techniques which maximize students' opportunities to make progress in the language. Some of the most important of these opportunities occur outside of the traditional classroom format, such as apprentice teaching or use of the language lab at the advanced level. Although we have set as a goal that our students gain a near-native level of fluency in Spanish before graduation, we fully realize that we are much more than a Berlitz type course in language study. We also want our language students to touch base with some of the traditional components of a liberal education: a strong sense of cultural awareness, and a development of aesthetic sensitivity to the literary text. Only with this balance will our graduates be "more flexible, more successful, and happier in the world of work," and will we as an institution move forward with sure footing in the 1980s.

NOTE

[1] The minimum number of advanced courses in literature (beyond the survey) that we previously required Spanish majors to take was six; we have reduced that number to three. The additional required credits may now be taken in composition/conversation or culture courses.

REFERENCES

"The Dartmouth Intensive Language Model." Typescript from the Department of Romance Languages, Dartmouth College, Hanover, New Hampshire, (n.d.), p. 10.

Gaudiani, Claire. "French Composition Teaching: A Student Generated Text Editing Approach." <u>The French Review</u>, 8, 2 (Dec. 1979), 232-38.

Rivers, Wilga. <u>Speaking in Many Tongues</u>. 2nd. ed. Rowley, Mass.: Newberry House, 1976.

CULTURE X LANGUAGE = SHORT COURSE ABROAD

Fritz H. König
Nile D. Vernon
University of Northern Iowa

Programs abroad and their raison d'être

Since 1979 the University of Northern Iowa has conducted a three-week semester/interim program for undergraduates and graduates. This course serves as a prototype for similar courses to be developed in other languages, and also as basis for the following remarks. This type of course is the latest addition to a group of programs abroad maintained by our institution. Three of them in French/German/Spanish are full-semester or academic year programs; three of them in the same languages are undergraduate eight-week summer programs, a cooperative effort with the other two state universities; three more are eight-week summer graduate programs for our own graduate students and for language teachers nationwide who need professional development or work on their master's degrees.

The reason we in a relatively small Midwestern university maintain such a variety of programs abroad--some of them enroll as many as sixty, others as few as fifteen participants--is twofold:

a) We firmly believe that everyone who studies a language and culture in some depth, and especially those who want to become teachers, should go to a country where the target language is spoken.

b) Our graduate programs abroad are advertised nationally and thus are an excellent recruiting tool, besides serving very practical purposes for teachers. They have helped put our university on the national map.

It is not the intent here to give a full description of our programs. What we would like to do is to concentrate on certain pedagogical aspects which we feel make some of our programs special and particularly successful.

Whenever the creation of a language program abroad is considered, the question has to be asked: why do we want to do this? In most cases the answer will be: to provide the students with a total language and culture immersion experience. Although total immersion programs can also be created on the home campus, they always betray an overpowering artificiality. Simulated "culture," and the fact that American students are speaking the target language poorly to each other while safely ensconsed in predictable and familiar surroundings, mean that this is no acceptable substitute for the experience abroad.

Logically then, the students, once abroad, should not stay in a large dormitory where they will talk English among themselves and with other foreigners there (the major drawback of the summer programs which most European universities offer) nor is much gained by keeping the participants half a day or longer in a formal classroom where they are lectured at; this can be done much better and more peacefully at home. After all, the mind rests easier when you know you have paid only $400 for a whole semester's tuition rather than $1500 or more for a paltry few weeks abroad.

Host families; contact person

It is of top priority then that the students be placed with local families, to insure that they indeed speak the target language at all times when not under our direct supervision. Besides the linguistic benefits, they receive total immersion into the local civilization, the local way of life. In virtually all cases a local contact person finds the families, helps us place the participants, and disburses payments. Initially securing the services of a liaison is no easy task. Contact persons have been found by consulting with officials at city hall, local chambers of commerce or host institutions. Generally, it can be said that the contact person facilitates communication between individual families and the institution and also has the function of impartial troubleshooter should friction and misunderstandings arise.

Obviously, the ideal host families are those who do not accept foreign houseguests simply for economic reasons, but for their own cultural enrichment; then the guests become full-fledged family members. Over the years we have been able to assemble a core of such ideal families in most locations, although each time, depending on enrollment figures, there will invariably be some new families. The new families very often are friends or relatives of a family which has already had an agreeable experience with a foreign houseguest.

Through a succession of newsletters and orientation meetings prior to departure, we prepare the participants for life with the local family. Certain customs and items of etiquette are pointed out and a general exhortation is issued to keep an open mind and to be willing to accommodate to local pecularities, to try various foods, etc.

Ideally, the families--and we encourage this through the liaison-- become allies of the instructors. They give the students certain simple tasks of everyday life to perform, such as making purchases, running errands. To illustrate this we would like to provide a list of tasks compiled by a recent participant of our three-week program in Mexico:

1. I went to the bank and paid a credit card bill, to another bank to deposit money and to yet another to make a loan payment. Each time, Hector signed the check and I wrote out the rest of it.

2. He dropped me off in town with his wallet and a traffic ticket and

I had to find city hall and pay the ticket.

3. When we went to a restaurant, I ordered for everyone.

4. I went to pick up the newspaper every day. One day, Hector told me to pick up two magazines with my newspaper and tell the owner of the stand that I would pay the next day.

5. We went to the market, he told me what we needed and I had to pick out good, ripe tomatoes, turnips, and guava. Then I bought a small chicken and told the lady to cut it up. Each time I had to ask how much it would cost, pay for it, and carefully count my change. Next I had to ask one of the women in the market where I could find the right kind of chili for the turnips and what it was called.

6. Fernando and Teresa, friends of Hector and Consuelo, took me out to eat two or three times, just the three of us, so that I would become accustomed to other people and have to understand them without being able to depend on Hector to translate for me.

7. Whenever we were with friends or family, Hector encouraged everyone to ask me what I had done that day, how I liked Colima, etc. This helped a lot, since I would have to repeat the names of places I had been to that day. The more I repeated them, the better I could remember and pronounce.

8. They sent me out with another friend of theirs, Javier, a 25-year-old lawyer who talks very, very, very fast. Listening to him and understanding was a difficult task but I was forced to do it in order to communicate with Javier.

9. We all watched the news each day together. When I didn't understand, they would explain. We also read the daily paper and listened to the radio at every opportunity.

The educational ramifications, both linguistic and cultural, are obvious. However, we should add that, although we encourage families to create an array of little tasks, not all are willing or able to comply. Normally, strong friendships between host family and guest develop. We know of some cases where correspondence is still being exchanged--in the target language--as long as ten years after the visit. It is also a common occurrence that families or family members get invited by their American guests to visit them in the U.S. We feel that this humanistic aspect, individual friendships, regular communication between people of different nationalities, is the crowning touch of our programs.

<u>Walking classes</u>

We have already mentioned that we do not believe in traditional lecture classes in the foreign location. Instead we concentrate on learning experiences which the students could not readily have at home. In order to facilitate such experiences, we undertake "walking classes." Students, usually in pairs, have to interview representatives of local businesses, agencies, and institutions. We first have them prepare a set of questions. After the interview, there is a class meeting in which the students share the information with their peers. Various benefits accrue from this activity: the students are exposed to a number of different speakers of the target language, they are forced to communicate, they learn to find their way around the city, they gain first-hand knowledge of local institutions, and they become more confident and more independent in using the target language.

In the recent Mexico program, students discovered what it takes to have a phone installed, how much a monthly phone bill might be, and how to make a long distance call. They interviewed the men in a fire station, two policemen, and a cab driver. They went to a funeral home and to a cemetery and asked the cost of casket, funeral, plot, and burial. They asked a priest what his duties involved and what the situation of the Church is in Mexico. They investigated how to put an ad in the local newspaper and inquired as to the educational process for becoming a dentist, a physician, and a lawyer. They talked to an official in the city treasury and asked about the various local taxes a citizen has to pay. Two students spent a day with a teacher in an elementary school, others looked around a hospital for a few hours. This list could be continued ad infinitum. The students can present their findings orally or in writing. The interviews can be improvised or prepared in advance. In the latter case the class frequently holds a brainstorming session to compile a list of places to visit, and the entire group gives suggestions of information to solicit.

While still in the U.S., the students are required to check out prices with realtors, car agencies, and all types of stores for the purpose of comparison on site in the foreign country. In this exercise the prices, although they do give some insight into the cost of living, are immaterial. What counts is the vocabulary, the need to call each object by its proper name.

But not all of the class time is devoted to daily life and "investigative reporting." We do call on local experts to come and give presentations on such topics as "the school system," "the labor union," "local and national politics," which are meant to round out the picture the students have formed, to provide a different and larger frame of reference. Within the same context, visits to museums, factories, farms, and so forth, are made.

Written assignments

To underline the informal, off-campus character of the abroad programs, daily chores are not necessarily conducted in a classroom. One can have a good class in swimsuits, grouped around a pool; in a local bar or restaurant; sitting in the plaza bandstand; on top of a mountain; and for hardy souls, even on a moving bus.

Some instructional strategies involve "capital C" Culture. We give students names of historical personalities: politicians, writers, painters, musicians, etc. The students research biographies in local libraries and report on their findings in writing.

With all their tasks the students have some choices. They deal primarily with the things they are most interested in. This way the motivation is much better and they feel challenged and go to a lot of trouble to complete the assignment.

Many programs abroad require their participants to keep a written diary with daily entries. Our experiences with the diary have been rather bad. Although students are encouraged to react in writing to specific occurrences on any given day, to comment on customs, and so on, most tend to start each entry with: "Today I got up at 7:30; for breakfast I had...." For the time being we have discontinued the assigned diary approach. Instead, the students are encouraged to keep a personal diary, and must compile a comprehensive written report which carefully reflects the impact of the three-week program on their own cultural awareness. Such a report, to be written in the target language, will necessarily demonstrate achieved linguistic growth, and yields several additional benefits:

a) It serves as an informal evaluation tool for the program.

b) It helps develop writing skills.

c) Most importantly, it gives students the opportunity to contrast cultural settings and values, and should enable them to see themselves through the eyes of foreigners. Thus, while being desensitized to their own culture, the students are sensitized to that of another country.

Site selection criteria

It goes without saying that not all locations are equally desirable for such a program. We have exercised great care in placing our abroad programs in medium-sized provincial cities having all the facilities with which we like to be affiliated, including an institution of higher education; but which at the same time do not present the problems of the large city, such as crime, pollution, chaotic traffic, and other stress factors. Above all, we try to find places which have not yet been discovered by the English speaking tourist. This does not mean that we entirely exclude large cities from the program. In Mexico we spend time both in Mexico City and in Guadalajara. But we find that they are not suitable as a permanent site for the program, and that, as a rule, families in large cities are less interested in receiving foreign houseguests.

Student eligibility and staffing

The participants in these programs range from sophomores meeting the minimum prerequisite of one year's college-level study in the target language, to graduate students. Thus, three levels of instruction are necessary: undergraduate intermediate and advanced, and graduate. A minimum of two staff members are needed for this structure, which is designed for up to twenty participants. Graduate students work much of the time on an independent project requiring fewer meetings with an instructor. When enrollment demands, additional staff can be added. Three semester hours of credit are earned for this short course. Two of these credits are gained through the class meetings, the tours and excursions, and through the final paper. The other credit is granted for the time spent living with the local family, where constant use of the language and exposure to the local culture is nearly unavoidable.

Conclusion

It is our belief that the value of this type of program lies in the fact that it gives the student a brief yet organized exposure to the language and culture of another country and people. Most of the students who participate have just completed the second through fourth semester in the target language in which they are contemplating either a major or minor. The semester/interim course affords them the opportunity, early in their academic program, to gain practical experience while earning credits, and above all, to return to the second half of the school year with a higher level of motivation than that of their classmates from the previous semester. And this motivation is truly intrinsic, for they soon discover that they have increased their linguistic abilities and broadened their cultural horizons.

UPGRADING SECOND LANGUAGE SKILLS:
MANPOWER DEVELOPMENT IN A DEVELOPING COUNTRY

Henk Kroes
Rand Afrikaans University

The Setting

For the purpose of this discussion I shall refer in particular to South Africa--the territory where I have been working for so many years and which I know best. This means that my assumption is that South Africa is a developing country. Not everyone may be prepared to accept this without some qualification. After all, many economists refer to South Africa as the industrial giant of the African continent; the infrastructure seems to be there, the intellectual and technical know-how that one usually associates with developed, and not developing societies.

Yet one need only look at the large majority of unskilled or semi-skilled workers, the low level of productivity, the number of adult illiterates, the average income and similar phenomena, to realize that in those areas with which we are concerned today we must treat the South African community as a developing people.

At the same time, however, we have to bear in mind three factors which make this community not quite the same as those elsewhere in Africa. These three factors are:

a) the heterogeneous composition of the South African community;
b) the presence of a very influential and highly developed subgroup consisting mostly of Whites, who have until recently been able to exploit and develop the natural resources of South Africa and at the same time retained responsibility for all areas of endeavor for which academic and technical training were a prerequisite; and
c) the rapidly changing political scene.

In order to place our examination of the communication skills required by such a community into proper perspective, it will be necessary to elaborate briefly on each of these three points.

The South African community is a very heterogeneous community and is divided into a large number of subgroups and cultures along both ethnic and linguistic lines. So we find the approximately five million Whites, consisting of Anglophone as well as Afrikaans-speaking South Africans descended from European stock (since 1652), reinforced by a flow of more recent immigrants. Then we have a substantial Indian population. Some of these speak Indian languages, but the vast majority claim English as their mother tongue (although, be it noted, this English deviates significantly from what could be described as standard South African English). Then we have the large Black majority, most of whom speak one of the Bantu languages of Southern Africa. One could add to this the significantly large group of Colored people who have descended from any combination of these groups and of whom the majority speak a variation of Afrikaans which often has characteristics deviating from standard Afrikaans.

The following table will give a broad indication of the languages and the numbers of speakers who use them as their mother tongue:

<u>Official</u> languages:	Afrikaans		3,421,000
	English		1,423,000
	Both		1,022,000
		Total	5,866,000
<u>Immigrant</u> languages: (mostly German, Portuguese, Greek, Italian and Dutch)			168,000
<u>Indigenous</u> languages:			
Nguni languages:	Zulu		4,026,000
	Xhosa		3,929,000
	Swazi		499,000
	Ndebele		410,000
Sotho Languages:	Tswana		1,719,000
	Northern Sotho		1,604,000
	Southern Sotho		1,453,000
Tsonga			737,000
Venda			358,000
Other			318,000
		Total	15,053,000
<u>Indian</u> languages:	Tamil		154,000
	Hindi		117,000
	Gujerabi		46,000
	Urdu		39,000
	Telegu		31,000
		Total	387,000
<u>Other</u> languages			27,000

<u>TABLE 1</u>: Native languages and no. of native speakers in South Africa. (From Van Wyk 1978: 30-31.)

English and Afrikaans are used for the most part to communicate across language barriers, with a few interesting exceptions:

--Among Blacks in areas such as the Witwatersrand Industrial Zone, Zulu is the most widely used lingua franca.

--On the mines and in industries where a large number of migrant workers are employed from as far afield as Mozambique and Botswana, Fanakalo is often used as a means of communication. It is a pidgin language with a Zulu base containing elements of English and Afrikaans.

Until a few years ago, the more highly skilled professions in the so-called White areas in South Africa were reserved for Whites, and Blacks were regarded as temporary migrant labor (much as the migrant workers in Western Europe). This entrenchment by law of White privileges in the labor field was known as job reservation.

In the rapidly changing political climate in South Africa, and after the Riekert and Wiehahn reports, the legal entrenchment of discriminatory practices in the labor field underwent drastic changes. Two of the most important results were that the "higher" professions were thrown open to all races, and trade unions for Blacks were not only permitted, but encouraged.

Taken in conjunction with the tremendous pace at which the South African economy developed during the same years, the effects of these changes were dramatic. The change from a labor intensive to a capital intensive approach was inevitable, and the urgent need for more highly skilled technicians and artisans on the one hand, and highly trained staff at management and executive level on the other, became apparent. But where were these to come from? Certainly not from the White sector, which already contributed its maximum potential. There was a tremendous need to upgrade and train the hitherto neglected Black workers. When the urgent need for in-service training and other upgrading programs became apparent to the authorities, the private sector was encouraged to undertake such training by generous tax concessions of up to 200% for these programs.

The implications for language and literacy training were far-reaching, particularly when one considers that manpower development had to take place precisely for those who were mother tongue speakers of languages other than the official English and Afrikaans. These implications will be discussed below, after other factors have been presented which have a bearing on both the problems and the suggested solutions.

Second language skills and literacy in South Africa:
an overview of the situation at present.
Literacy: some facts and figures.

It is generally accepted that illiteracy among Whites in South Africa has been reduced to levels that compare very well with the situation in most West European countries. It may safely be assumed that the illiterates listed below are to be found mostly among Blacks and Coloreds. It is for this reason that the population breakdown relevant to this situation is supplied below. Another factor to be considered is that compulsory schooling is gradually taking effect with inevitable consequences for illiteracy among the younger generation. It is for this reason that figures have been supplied for adult illiteracy. One should also bear in mind that a needs analysis for language skills and literacy has to take into account the immediate needs for on-the-job training of adults at present limited to unskilled and semi-skilled work.

1.	Republic of South Africa (Responsibility area of Dept. of Education and Training)	2,930,000
2.	Bophuthatswana	249,000
3.	Ciskei	181,000
4.	Gazankulu	137,000
5.	Ka Ngwane	48,000
6.	Kwazulu	911,000
7.	Lebowa	475,000
8.	Qwaqwa	44,000
9.	Transkei	580,000
10.	Venda	123,000
	Total	5,678,000
Total adult population		15,000,000
Total adult white population		2,200,000

TABLE 2: Adult illiterates in South Africa. (Extract from French 1982)

The dominant role of English and Afrikaans

The need for all members of the community to have adequate command of at least one, and preferably both official languages, may be gauged from the following:

English and Afrikaans are the languages of commerce and industry. It is impossible to be appointed to a senior position if you cannot speak and write at least one of these two languages; it is very difficult to be promoted to a senior position without being bilingual (English and Afrikaans).

On the relative importance of English and Afrikaans to Black workers there has been interesting debate. An investigation undertaken by G. K. Schuring of the Human Sciences Research Council in 1975 among Blacks throughout South Africa revealed, inter alia:

a) English is regarded by Blacks as a prestige language and a language for international communication. It is used at political meetings and at conferences.

b) Afrikaans is the language which, most Black workers claim, is used in the work situation and for transactions with civil servants and shopkeepers.

c) Respondents claim an almost equal oral proficiency in English and Afrikaans, although English has a slight edge over Afrikaans. Respondents claim to be more proficient in written communication in English than in Afrikaans.

d) Letters are often written in English, even to relatives, in preference to the indigenous languages.

e) Blacks read very little Afrikaans, but English newspapers are in demand.

These interesting data should be seen against the background of language attitudes and the 1976 riots in South Africa, said to have been sparked off by the language medium policy of the Department of Bantu Education, as it was then called.

One should bear in mind that, to many Blacks, the Afrikaans language is the language of that section of the White population regarded by them as the oppressors, and, since the Nationalist Party came into power in 1948, responsible for legislation entrenching segregation on ethnic lines. Although the use of the mother tongue as medium of instruction during the first years of primary education is universally regarded as desirable, and this view is (and was) endorsed both by Black educationists and the Departments of Education concerned, the problem centered on what should happen after these first few years at school. It is generally agreed among Black educators that mathematical concepts and scientific terminology cannot at this stage be adequately conveyed in any of the indigenous languages in Southern Africa, necessitating a switch to one of the two official languages at a relatively early stage in formal education.

The problem was that the Department of Bantu Education insisted that both official languages should be used (where possible for an equal number of subjects) as medium of instruction. Black educationists rightly pointed out that the choice of language medium should be left to parents and the community and that "once such a language has been selected, it is completely unnecessary, indeed it may even be gratuitously unjust, to compel the use of yet another foreign language as a medium, and in this way to double the burden of mastery" (ATASA memorandum, 1976).

Unfortunately the Department of Bantu Education did not change official policy (or guard against the interpretation and enforcement of policy by departmental officials) in time to prevent the 1976 riots.
Viewed in retrospect, there is no general agreement that these riots were the result of language policy; in fact, there is good reason to believe that other factors played a significant role.

It is important to realize, however, that public feeling on Afrikaans as medium of instruction since 1976 is such that few schools dare express a preference for Afrikaans as medium of instruction now that parents and schools are completely free to exercise their preference. That English has now, to all intents and purposes, become the official medium of instruction in all Black schools after the first few years of primary education, is generally accepted.

Unfortunately it would be naive to assume that this problem has now been solved. There are large tracts of the country where English is seldom heard except in the classroom, and where every Black child is exposed to spoken Afrikaans from childhood. A study undertaken by the Rand Afrikaans University in 1981 revealed that in many schools so situated, both teacher and pupils would manfully try to wrestle with the complexities of geography or mathematics in English, a language the teacher would barely be able to speak, and pupils did not understand; and at the end of the lesson pupils would put up their hands and ask the teacher to repeat the lesson in Afrikaans!

And so we are faced with the unpleasant situation of very few teachers having the courage to insist on Afrikaans as medium of instruction, even where it is in the best interest of the children entrusted to them to do so. In this way hundreds of thousands of children suffer a severe educational disadvantage and one may only hope that the political climate will eventually allow both parents and teachers to make decisions on educational rather than on political grounds.

At this point it is important to take stock of the teacher situation. The following table reflects projections of needs for teachers in general up to the year 2000 to achieve the teacher/pupil ratio as indicated on the right. In studying these figures, used as a point of departure by the large-scale HSRC Investigation into Education (1982) for teachers as a whole, the following points should be borne in mind:

a) At present, different communities in South Africa are still served by separate Education Departments.

b) This means that statistics enable us to identify and appreciate the backlog for disadvantaged groups.

	Number of teachers		Teacher-pupil ratio	
	1980	2000	From	To
White education	44,722	41,774	1 : 20	1 : 20
Colored education	25,359	32,376	1 : 29	1 : 25
Indian education	8,079	9,994	1 : 27	1 : 23
Black education	95,501	185,523	1 : 48	1 : 39

TABLE 3: Projection of future needs: Teachers required for different communities in South Africa by the year 2000 to achieve or maintain the teacher/pupil ratio as indicated.

The need to train large numbers of teachers for Black education emerges clearly from these figures, and the projection given above only provides for a still very unfavorable ratio of 1 : 39.

Perhaps an even more gloomy picture is conveyed by the following table indicating the educational qualifications of teachers at present employed by the different education departments. The following legend will assist in the interpretation of the data presented:

Std. 6 : Beginning of secondary education (Form 1 in Britain)
Std. 8 : Completion of junior secondary level
Std. 10 : Completion of secondary school (not necessarily
          university entrance level)

	Professional Diploma	Std. 6	Std. 8	Std. 10	Degree
			(Percentages		
White education	+			66	34
Indian education	+		13	80	7
	−		40	60	
Colored education	+	4	57	37	2
	−	31	33	35	1
Black education	+	18	62	19	1
	−	14	70	16	

TABLE 4: Present educational and professional qualifications of all teachers (including language teachers). (HSRC Investigation into Education, 1981.)

There is no reason to assume that the qualifications of language teachers in particular will differ to any marked extent from the qualifications of teachers in general. Again the dire need for upgrading the qualifications of teachers in particularly Black and Colored education is clearly indicated. In the case of Black education (and to a smaller extent in Colored education) the position is aggravated by the fact that, for the teaching of the two official languages, there are few, if any, mother tongue speakers of the target language.

In other words, English and Afrikaans, the two languages which are most important for the needs and aspirations of the Black community, have to be taught by teachers who have themselves learned these languages as a second language. In 80% of the cases these teachers have had formal instruction in the language they teach up to Form 3 (plus a few years, in some cases, at teacher training college); many even less.

Organizations concerned with adult literacy.

A number of privately funded organizations such as the Bureau of Literacy and Literature, Operation Upgrade, and Learn and Teach are actively involved in literacy training for adults. The Human Sciences Research Council is engaged in research to promote literacy. Although these bodies are doing good work, a coordinated effort supported by the state seems to be lacking. That this lack of state support has serious consequences for manpower development will become apparent when efforts aimed at manpower development are discussed below.

The need for new objectives and revised syllabi.

At conferences of language teachers, concern has been expressed at the fact that language learning objectives, particularly in second language learning, have not adjusted to the needs of the consumers. The consumers may here be defined on the one hand as the employers of school leavers, and on the other as the school leavers themselves. Employers in particular claim that schools seem to turn a blind eye to the need for writing skills, and are concerned only with the primacy of speech. Teachers, it is claimed, are ignorant of the communication needs in the second language at the work place.

In the Transkei, one of the new independent Black states in Southern Africa, Afrikaans is being reintroduced as an optional second language at schools simply because work seekers and businessmen need Afrikaans as a bread and butter language in the Republic of South Africa. But note the interesting difference: it is now called "Practical Afrikaans," and is taught at the lower secondary level according to a notional/functional syllabus based, as far as selection and ordering of content are concerned, on a needs analysis of the consumer.

An interesting point here is that the students themselves have not been asked to define their needs or objectives. This would be too unreliable an indicator, it is felt. Applied linguists and other consultants have been asked to conduct an investigation on more scientific lines, and the new syllabus has been designed according to their specifications.

The shift from academic schools to Technikons (Polytechnics), advocated by the HSRC investigation already referred to, may be regarded as another indicator of the gradual shift away from an academic approach to second language learning and toward a practical approach--practical in the sense that the communication requirements (at spoken as well as written level) of commerce and industry must be met. The important trend which emerges from these and other pointers is that the need to upgrade second language skills is being seen not only as a vertical upward movement, but also as a horizontal move towards communication needs in commerce and industry, and away from academic pursuits.

In passing it should be mentioned that employers and managers are beginning to realize that, in South Africa at least, it is necessary to be able to communicate with the Black worker in one of the indigenous languages. This view is supported by the Education Departments. Languages such as Zulu and North and South Sotho are being taught in White primary and secondary schools to mother tongue speakers of one of the official languages and to improve communications across language barriers.

The need for research

It is not generally realized that decisions on second language teaching objectives and methods can no longer be left to chance. It is significant that applied linguistics, the group of interdisciplines most relevant to language teaching and literacy, is beginning to make a major contribution to research in this field. Three years ago there was only one university in South Africa which offered applied linguistics at post-graduate level. Now there are six, and the number of academics capable of doing research calculated to place second language teaching on a sound scientific footing, is growing.

Government policy and new developments

The fact that the South African government launched the large-scale Human Sciences Research Council Investigation into Education in 1981 under the Chairmanship of Prof. J. P. de Lange, is in itself sufficient evidence of government concern with education needs in general. This investigation yielded eighteen important reports, of which one was concerned with languages and language teaching.

State concern with the need to upgrade skills with a view to manpower development is further reflected by the generous tax concessions of up to 200% for in-service training programs undertaken by the private sector. Unfortunately this important incentive is to a large extent neutralized by an important reservation: all in-service training programs directly concerned with upgrading professional skills qualify for tax concessions; but language teaching and literacy programs do not, because they are not regarded as job oriented. Commerce and industry are not encouraged to conduct training programs in second language skills or literacy because of the high cost involved, and because such programs represent only a long-term investment. And the result is that a countrywide drive for manpower development is stranded on a rock of communicative incompetence or illiteracy in a second language.

This has a disastrous effect on in-service training. Many large concerns have discovered to their cost that up to 80% of their Black workers lack the communicative skills in either of the official languages which would enable them to benefit from such programs. Many others are illiterate and cannot benefit for this reason.

By allowing greater individual freedom in the choice of medium for education, the State has defused a political bomb and ushered in, since the riots of 1976, a period of relative peace in Black education. Many educationists fear, however, that many Black pupils are being taught in a language they do not understand, or at best a language in which they do not follow instruction as easily as in the other official language. This state of affairs must be seen as the direct outcome of language attitudes hardened to a large extent by political events before and during 1976. It will be a long time, it is feared, before choice of medium will be based on purely educational considerations.

The need to train large numbers of language teachers, especially for Black and Colored education, has been demonstrated. Bearing in mind the population explosion, it is difficult to foresee how the targets suggested by projections for the year 2000 can be achieved. Even more important is the need to upgrade the language competence and qualifications of language teachers, and again it is the Blacks in South Africa whose need is the greatest.

At present the Department of Education and Training responsible for Black education in the Republic of South Africa has only one small in-service training center which can reach approximately 300 language teachers per year. This is hopelessly inadequate. More research to pinpoint second language needs and to investigate methods of tackling the enormous problems identified by such research is required to tackle the urgent need for manpower development in South Africa.

To enable such research to take place, more applied linguists will have to be trained. The time has passed when policies on second language learning and literacy could be formulated without adequate scientific support for the decision making process. This is particularly true for South Africa, a country with vast potential for prosperity and happiness, but plagued by many problems. Of these, the urgent need to upgrade the skills of millions of Blacks who until now have been denied the opportunity to participate in this prosperity, largely because they lacked the appropriate second language and professional skills, must be regarded as a top priority. The Human Sciences Research Council (HSRC) is playing an increasingly valuable role, not only to coordinate research on language learning and literacy, but also to initiate and undertake valuable research itself. The research data are beginning to provide an invaluable scientific base for decision making and course production.

Lastly, a remark on a problem area which has of late occupied the attention of those who are concerned with literacy programs. I refer to the urgent need for bridge literature--easy reading matter to encourage new literates to continue reading and to develop their newly found skills. Some organizations producing materials on the Paolo Frere model are not getting support from educationists whose main concern is with the welfare of the community rather than to foster the cause of revolution and communism. For the same reason, the South African government or other state agencies can hardly be expected to support such organizations. Unfortunately, other sources of material still have to be found, and this is not easy in a country where so many languages have to be served and the turnover for each language is therefore too small to attract publishers.

In conclusion, I think I am justified in claiming that South Africa presents a most complex spectrum of problems. It is a country which differs in many ways from other developing countries on the continent of Africa, yet shares many of their second language and literacy problems. It is also a country on the move, where constitutional changes and the easing of discriminatory measures hold promise of peaceful change; where economic and industrial potential provide the means for rapid development; where a small but enthusiastic minority of academics, research workers, and teachers are trying to perform miracles. In short, a fascinating country offering a challenge to any academic interested in language learning and literacy.

REFERENCES

French, E. The Promotion of Literacy in South Africa. HSRC, 1982

HSRC Investigation into Education. Reports of the Main Committee on Languages and Language Teaching, (No. 18), 1981.

Van Wyk, E.B. "Language Contact and Bilingualism." In L. W. Lanham and K. P. Prinsloo (eds.), Language and Communication Studies in South Africa, Oxford: Oxford Univ. Press, 1978.

PANEL DISCUSSION

Toward a Definition of Intermediate Applied Language Study

Moderator: **John J. Deveny, Jr.,** Oklahoma State University

Panelists: **James D. Wells,** Oklahoma State University
Thomas G. Deveny, Western Maryland College
James F. Ford, University of Arkansas
Alfred Gage, Oklahoma State Department of Education

Professor Wells, the opening speaker, raises a number of interesting questions which need to be considered in any attempt to define the intermediate level of language study. He emphasizes the need for language teachers to be more goal directed at the intermediate level, and his view is that what constitutes intermediate level is peculiar to each language and each department, but that a solution to this dilemma is indeed possible. The text of his comments follows:

"As a profession we language teachers have been admirably creative in the area of beginning language study. New texts, new methods are being used which seem to be truly innovative and, more importantly, effective. There is, in general, agreement on our goals. We endeavor to acquaint the students with the orthography, phonology, and the grammatical/syntactic patterns of the target language.

"Intermediate language study, on the other hand, seems to be a kind of amorphous pedagogical dumping ground. Most teachers prefer to work with either the beginning or the advanced students. Few actively seek to teach at the intermediate level. We generally have the composition/ conversation classes which contain a heavy dose of grammar review. We vaguely recognize the often serious 'plateau' problems at the intermediate level: it's simply hard work to memorize and use new words, and students don't feel the clear sense of progress that they did in the earlier phases of their language study.

"A wide array of ingredients seem to be put into the intermediate language stew, and the mixture is not always palatable. Among these ingredients are: the desire to expand the students' vocabulary, both active and passive; the desire to expand familiarity with a wider number of syntactic patterns; etc. While these goals are indeed admirable, they are often extremely ill-defined and implemented in a large variety of ways. For example, do we really want to emphasize active vocabulary for the student who plans to be a scientific documents translator? What is, and what should be, the role of literature at the intermediate level? Some texts and programs study the literature as literature. In other texts the literary selections are really little more than a medium to look at the new/old grammar contained therein or exercises in 'comprehension,' whatever that is. Other intermediate texts contain large amounts of cultural materials or even history--again, all these are to one degree or another useful (or maybe only traditional).

"Briefly stated, I think we must be much more strongly goal directed at the intermediate level. When we can define the goals, we can more easily create appropriate materials and design programs for this level of language study. One method of organizing the problem is to identify, however broadly, the use to which the student plans to put his language knowledge when he has completed his work (at whatever level). When exit uses are identified we can prepare for them.

"Some possible exit uses:

1. Terminal, will not use, fulfilling a requirement only.
2. Graduate School--probable teacher, college level.
3. Teacher of the language at high school level.
4. Fair speaking knowledge--travel, etc.
5. Translator of written scientific documents.
6. Reading in a specific field.
7. Enough to use in business (aural/oral).
8. Interpreter.

"These exit categories vary greatly for different languages. Employment for someone capable of translating scientific documents from French to English is not readily available, but someone able to translate Russian, German, Chinese, or Japanese scientific materials has very real prospects for employment. My suggestions raise many problems since no program can satisfy all the varied needs that we can identify. For example, look at ancient Greek: not even a spoken language, it should be simple, yet precisely at the intermediate level the students must go in five totally different directions:

1. Biblical or Koine Greek
2. 4th and 5th Century Prose, Plato et al., Attic Greek
3. Herodutus, Ionic Greek
4. Domma Poetry--like Attic but different
5. Poetry: Homer (dialect problem).

I don't want only to raise problems and provide no answers; but the answers really prove to be peculiar to each language and the flexibility of any given department. One possible method might be to collapse all intermediate sections into a one hour hardcore grammar/grammar-review session and then divide the other two hours into highly individualized subsections. Perhaps these grammar sessions would be an ideal place to use computer-assisted instruction.

"Once we realistically identify the uses to which our students will put their language skills beyond the 'intermediate' level, it becomes easier to identify their needs. Then those needs can and should be met creatively."

Professor Thomas Deveny, the second speaker, sees the intermediate level as the bridge between elementary and advanced language study and thus necessarily defined by what precedes it and what follows it. He focuses on intermediate language study as a process of development of both active and passive skills which incorporates a cultural dimension. His remarks follow:

"In language study, the term 'intermediate' implies a bridge between elementary and advanced levels of study. As such, an examination of intermediate language must inevitably take into account what precedes and what follows.

"At Western Maryland College, a small, private liberal arts institution, we have a language proficiency requirement of competency equal to one year of college study. Consequently, not all students are required to study language at the intermediate level, and those who do so are frequently fulfilling an option within a Liberal Arts distribution requirement. Therefore, there is a very high attrition rate between elementary and intermediate: only about 25% of our first-year students continue to the second year. Needless to say, these are usually the best students from elementary, and they are joined by incoming freshmen with a very good language preparation from high school. (We use the listening and reading comprehension achievement tests from the Educational Testing Service in Princeton, N. J., to determine placement; we place students in first semester intermediate who obtain a score in the range of 510-550). The proportion of students who continue their language studies beyond intermediate is even smaller, 10% to 15%. Consequently, our total enrollment resembles a pyramid: a broad base with little at the top.

"One of the main reasons, I believe, for the high attrition rate is that students feel they have not achieved an adequate level of competency for them to continue. A strong intermediate program, then, can only follow a strong elementary program. One major criterion of such a program is that all major grammatical points in the target language be introduced. All too often, one hears remarks such as: 'We didn't have time to cover the past subjunctive in elementary.'

"No matter how strong the first-year course, the jump to second-year language study is often a major hurdle. At the elementary level, we are mainly concerned with language manipulation, but in intermediate we suddenly emphasize the linguistic level of expression of personal meaning (Rivers 1976: 14). One way of providing a bridge between these two activities and therefore offering a smoother transition from elementary to intermediate is to adopt an intensive language model in which the third semester continues student participation in drill sessions. These drill sessions, run by apprentice teachers (undergraduate or graduate teaching assistants) help break the traditional (and very limiting) format of only three hours of contact time with the target language at the intermediate level. They are the ideal setting for additional work at the level of language manipulation, and thus serve to reinforce vocabulary and grammatical structures that can then be used with more facility in personal expression in the meetings with the professor. This manipulation will perhaps be of greatest value at institutions where two years of language study are required, and the disparity in preparation among the students is much greater than at a school such as my own.

"The need for increased contact time, then, is essential for development of oral/aural skills at the intermediate level. Another way to meet this need is to increase use of the language laboratory. Unfortunately, this valuable pedagogical tool is often abandoned after elementary study, but there is an increasingly large pool of authentic language materials that can make the lab a viable component of second-year study. In Spanish, for example, Radio Nacional de España now has a tape transcription service available in the United States which consists of cassette recordings that summarize the month's news and speak about a monographic theme; a basic level program is tentatively planned for next year. Music, both folk and contemporary songs, can provide valuable cultural insights while it helps develop listening comprehension skills. In addition, there are video cassette programs which can also be used as supplementary language lab exercises.

"What typically follows intermediate level is composition/conversation courses or surveys of literature. In order to better prepare students for these advanced level courses, we intend to transform our second semester intermediate into an advanced grammar course. By providing a more in-depth grammar study at this level, we hope to eliminate basic errors which often plague students who continue their language study, so that at the advanced levels we will be able to concentrate on writing instead of grammar.

"The readings and class discussions at the intermediate level can come from a wide variety of sources, but I feel it necessary that they introduce students to the culture of the countries where the language is spoken. Cultural myopism has reached epidemic proportions among college students in our country, and intermediate classes offer an ideal format to begin its cure, both among the majority of students who will have little contact with the language and culture after finishing their second-year language studies, and among those who will continue.

"These approaches to teaching intermediate language seek to accelerate the development of competency levels in both active and passive skills while stimulating students' cultural interests. In this way, we hope to make the intermediate course truly a 'bridge' experience and therefore change the shape of our pyramid enrollment configuration."

Professor Ford sees the intermediate level as a place for the development of skills in such a way as to emphasize receptive skills over production skills, and he chooses reading as the most important area to be developed at the intermediate level. These are his views:

"The intermediate level is the most critical phase of language study. At this point attrition will have claimed some 80% of the students who began elementary language and it will claim 50% more of the intermediate group. Therefore, what is done at this level is of the utmost importance, both for those who will exit after the intermediate course as well as for those who may choose to continue their language study. It may seem on the surface that we have two distinct groups of intermediate students which should perhaps be dealt with separately and differently; however, from the point of view of 'skills maintenance' these two seemingly disparate groups are quite similar in that the skill that needs the most attention and development is reading.

"As far as the 'terminal' group is concerned, reading is the skill that atrophies least when one leaves the classroom and does not spend long periods of time in the language milieu. The student who chooses to continue beyond the intermediate level is confronted with courses which are primarily reading-based (e.g., surveys of literature, culture and civilization) and when reading has not been stressed at the intermediate level, these students become anxious and frustrated because of their inability to read and understand the textbooks of such courses. It is for these reasons that we should go about the teaching of reading at the intermediate level very seriously and very thoroughly, leaving nothing to chance or osmosis. Simply using a reader or readers which students decode with a bilingual dictionary is not teaching reading; neither is assigning voluminous amounts of material. Reading, like the other language skills, must be taught systematically. A large portion of time must be devoted to teaching and practicing recognition skills and the texts and materials used must be carefully chosen to reinforce this type of instruction.

"Too many existing intermediate textbooks are simply extensions of elementary texts, and their authors seem to assume that in learning a language through formal classroom instruction, one progresses in the four skills simultaneously. Too often we teachers rather unthinkingly accept this assumption and teach accordingly. The result is that at the end of the intermediate sequence, our students speak, understand, and write very poorly, but worst of all, they haven't learned to read.

"The second priority I would assign to listening comprehension. Throughout the entire language learning experience, this is certainly the most neglected skill. When one finds oneself in the language milieu, the most difficult communication process is not making oneself understood, but understanding the variety of voices, registers, and dialects inevitably encountered.

"Taped material is generally used at the elementary level to provide native models for the segmental and suprasegmental features of the language and to drill high frequency grammatical patterns. Unfortunately, in too many programs there is no further use of out-of-class taped material. Thousands of unmaintained and broken down language labs notwithstanding, the technology exists (both hardware and software); we have only to integrate it into our programs. A great deal can be done with the simple audio cassette and an inexpensive player, which almost everyone owns these days.

"In conclusion, let me state that my reordering of skills priorities at the intermediate level would be as follows:

1) reading,
2) listening comprehension,
3) speaking,
4) writing.

Obviously, in this order the receptive skills are emphasized over the productive skills. It is not to suggest that the productive skills be ignored, but that the receptive skills take precedence. I wish to end by stating emphatically that this is not an arbitrary ordering based on personal preference. While space does not permit references, there is a great deal of literature on language acquisition which supports this re-ordering of skills not only at the intermediate level, but at the elementary as well."

Dr. Gage defines different levels of language study in terms of specific proficiencies that can be expected of students. His remarks refer particularly to a secondary education setting and can easily be adapted to a university situation. The following text, from the Foreign Language Post (Oklahoma State Department of Education 1982) forms the basis for his remarks.

"The following are some suggested proficiencies adapted from work done by Dr. Gail Guntermann of Arizona State University. They include the basic areas of listening comprehension, speaking, reading, and writing skills starting with one level of modern foreign language study. Although they are not meant to be slavishly adhered to, they do, nevertheless, represent a point of departure from which you can write your own list of expected minimal proficiencies.

Level I - Survival Proficiency

Speaking. The student should be able to:
1. obtain food, shelter, and transportation for survival;
2. acquire through oral and written language information essential to their basic social and travel needs;
3. establish and maintain at least superficial friendships through greetings, farewells, and exchanges of personal information;
4. open or maintain conversations by inquiring or giving the most basic information about health, weather, the time, or the date;

5. carry out common classroom functions, such as requesting and giving information, asking permission, borrowing items, and solving simple problems;
6. express wishes (I want _____.);
7. express ability and inability to do things;
8. recount past events and activities that are common to their daily lives, at least through the use of the simplest indicators of past time, such as the simple past tense forms and adverbial expressions;
9. describe places, people, and things well enough for them to be identified by a listener who is familiar with them;
10. make simple requests of others.

Most students would be able to express these meanings in such a way that they could be understood most of the time.

Listening. Students are able to comprehend what is said and identify the purposes of native speakers within the bounds of the material they have studied. They can understand recombinations of this same material and are able to grasp meanings somewhat beyond the level of their speaking ability when listening to clear speech directed to them at normal speed, or when the speaker's gestures, the context, or other clues are available. They are unperturbed when exposed to the natural speech of native speakers in person or through the media; they are capable of discerning some words and phrases from the flow of speech.

Reading. Students command sound/symbol relationships and read recombinations of the material studied during the course; they are also able to gather some very basic information from newspapers and magazines, read with comprehension signs and other written material (including maps and schedules) encountered in the performance of the basic survival functions.

Writing. In addition to writing exercises for learning the grammar and vocabulary, students are able to spell the words and sentences that they can read and use orally, write notes and messages, and fill out basic travel forms.

Level II - Expansion Level

Speaking. The student should be able to:
1. maintain relationships at a deeper level: introduce and meet people; share experiences, opinions, common problems, express personal feelings; issue invitations and accept or decline; make social plans;
2. influence others' actions: request help, get others to do things, give and respond to instructions (expressed through indicative or

       other simple forms), give advice;
3. agree, disagree;
4. make excuses;
5. request and report information on matters of common interest related to their daily lives;
6. identify and describe people, places, objects; compare and contrast;
7. paraphrase and summarize, with the limitations of the topics and materials studied;
8. request information by telephone.

Listening. During the second year of study, listening practice should be expanded to include many exercises at the macro level (i.e., language as it is spoken naturally). Learners should be able to comprehend more than they can say. When listening to native speakers, they can identify the topic and attitudes of the speakers when the material is familiar, concrete, and nontechnical and when the speech is clear. Even when much of what they hear is new to them they are able to decipher parts of the message as they recognize words and phrases.

Reading. At this level, students read short, carefully edited stories and articles and peruse newspapers and magazines for specific information. They comprehend nontechnical instructions; simple invitations, notes, and letters written by native speakers; advertisements; and jokes and cartoons containing material within their proficiency limitations.

Writing. Students write simple telephone messages, friendly letters, paragraphs, and very short compositions; and they can fill out forms related to travel, school, and so forth.

Career Exploration. Learners are apprised of careers requiring languages, the proficiency levels necessary in careers that interest them, and their own interests and preferences. Those who have identified a possible career are helped and encouraged to seek out appropriate vocabulary and apply it in their language development exercises.

Level III - Basic communicative proficiency.

Speaking. The student should be able to:
1. express approval, disapproval, and blame;
2. report on current school events and major world events;
3. explain facts and relationships such as cause and effect;
4. make suggestions and recommendations;
5. give directions and instructions;
6. influence others: command, request, beg, insist, permit, prohibit, threaten, etc.;
7. express (and hide) emotions and respond to others' feelings;
8. joke, share leisure activities, apologize, argue;
9. make guesses and predictions.

Listening. Learners can now comprehend enough of any clear, standard message dealing with an everyday topic to surmise the message most of the time. They are able to identify others' purposes and intentions within the bounds of their own experience with the target language and culture. They can converse at some length on topics of everyday interest, although native speakers must often restate their messages in more than one way for comprehension to be complete.

Reading. While students continue to read carefully edited messages, they also read simple stories and articles and illustrated material on their own for enjoyment as well as for specific information. With the aid of a dictionary, they can read with general comprehension unedited words in standard, nontechnical language.

Writing. Students are now capable of writing outlines, instructions, short skits, longer letters, and compositions.

Career Awareness. Learners continue to seek information on careers, and those who identify a possible career seek further information about it and its linguistic requirements. They can practice some skills related to their own areas of professional interest.

At this level, the areas of study interact considerably as students are able to use the target language to gain information about careers, the culture, and related topics from the satellite areas. The curriculum is much more integrated.

Level IV - Expanded Proficiency

Speaking. The student should be able to:
1. state his or her opinions and defend them;
2. give logical explanations;
3. report on world events;
4. discuss literature;
5. interpret nontechnical conversation for speakers who do not know English.

Listening. In face-to-face encounters students can now comprehend native speakers who are dealing with everyday topics. Students should be able to surmise the message of television news programs.

Reading. Students can now read newspapers, magazines, selected short stories, short plays and, with the aid of a dictionary, some short novels.

Writing. Students are now capable of writing short, nontechnical reports or research papers. With the use of a dictionary they can translate into or out of the target language nontechnical materials of moderate length" (pp. 71-77).

From the preceding discussions, we can see that the intermediate level of language study is probably the most difficult to define and work with. It is the level where students of extremely varied backgrounds collect, thus presenting a great challenge to the teacher. It is the level where adequate educational process is known with least certainty. It is, in short, the area of greatest challenge.

REFERENCE

Rivers, Wilga. Speaking in Many Tongues. 2nd ed. Rowley, Mass.: Newberry House, 1976.

FROM THEORY TO PRACTICE AND BACK:
HOW RECENT FUNCTIONAL METHODS GIVE FORM TO NEW
OBJECTIVES IN SECOND LANGUAGE TRAINING

by Pierre Trescases
University of New Brunswick

Structuralists are out, functionalists are in. Such would seem (particularly from a European point of view) to be the 1980s perspective for one in search of a new methodology. As a result many second language (SL) teachers are looking forward, although somewhat apprehensively, to this new (communicative) panacea. Times are a'changing and, with the help of efficient marketing techniques, we might indeed be soon flooded with no-nonsense functional/communicative (FC) methods. It is therefore important that we take a good look at what we are buying.

In a recent article, C. Germain and R. LeBlanc (1982: 665) wonder about the rationality of stating characteristics of pedagogical materials "not yet to be really found on the market." This statement applies to students in the public school system and in universities (the type of learners with which we will be concerned here) and not to students with specific needs and purposes (the primary target of the functional approach). But the above statement could also mean that there is to date no genuine FC method on the market. This is precisely the question, which is threefold: Is the FC approach applicable to learners in the school system? To what extent are the new methods "functional"? To what extent are they contributing to a renewal of SL teaching?

To attempt to answer these questions, however partially, we will examine recent beginning French methods,[1] more or less avowedly derived from the FC approach, and will study how some key concepts in this approach have been applied in La Méthode Orange (1980), Cartes sur table (1981), Sans Frontières (1982), Archipel (1982). To this end, we will again deal summarily with three questions: Which needs? Which contents? Which methodology?

A. Which needs?

The analysis of all four methods, while revealing a common preoccupation with the learner's needs, brings out--as could be expected--the lack of a clear definition of the concept more than it helps delimit it. In that regard, it is significant that R. Richterich is not very explicit in CT. This could be considered as an attestation not only that his 1972 model for an analysis of language needs has not been improved but that it is simply not workable. Richterich somewhat reluctantly states that "elaborated out of necessity in the most general manner, the method could be used in the most varied circumstances" (Guide: 4). He elaborates on the adaptability of the materials to local conditions and to the factual experience of the individual learners; this amounts to saying that the more general the method, the more adaptable it is to the learners' specific needs. Such a statement, if not necessarily contradictory, is assuredly not very challenging for the profession. Elsewhere the author speaks of "a common project: the learning of French" (Guide: 5) as if unconsciously referring to a link that would in the end unite all existing disparities in a common objective. This is echoed by the introductory sentence to the textbook, which states, "the student will find all the elements that he needs in order to learn French" (my underline). This again could be interpreted as a shift of emphasis from the fulfillment of behavioral objectives to the learning process itself. In actual fact both coexist characteristically in Richterich and the FC approach. Well, more than ten years after his model for defining adults' language needs, there has been no significant progress. "Objectives needs" are passed over in silence, while giving shape to the notional/functional contents; and "subjective needs" continue to elude all definition while gaining in importance. In the same first page of introduction the learner's "interest, desire, need for learning" appear as key pedagogical elements while the confusion between needs and motivation remains. The other methods reveal the same lack of a clear definition of the concept of needs and the unapplicability of it. (For O1 see Carnet: 8; for AR see Livre: 11-12).

In short, what these four methods show is that the concept of needs as defined, or rather ill-defined, by the FC approach, is not applied and consequently hardly applicable as such to the general student in our schools and colleges. It is significant that either "interest, desire, need to learn" are packed together (CT), or else the authors switch to the notions of "internal" motivation (O1) or "expectations" once they have arbitrarily selected the notions and functions to be learned. Practice-oriented research should in our opinion steer away from the concept of needs, and for that matter, of integrative vs. instrumental motives, to focus on two directions:

1. How better to fulfill learners' "expectations" within the framework of the course.

    This covers two interrelated aspects:
    a.) Success breeds success. As S. Savignon (1972: 65) puts it, "Interest in learning the language appears to be rather a function of past success."
    b.) As advocated by some functionalists, the notion of fulfilling a pledge between the teacher and the individual lecturer as to some tasks to be performed can be a source of "internal" motivation allowing some limited amount of individualized instruction (O1). Clearly, the focus should be on what motivates students once they are within the four walls of the classroom and how to go about achieving it.[2] Therefore the question should be:

2. How to have students communicate no matter what.

To this end, group dynamics should be directed toward

a.) breaking down usual learning habits;
b.) facilitating and developing interaction in the classroom.
In short, what should be aimed at is increasing the amount of communication and student input; and finding out which type of exchanges are most motivating, which speech acts are most conducive to interaction within the class and the classroom--all as a function of their active, creative, affective, or cultural input.[3]

B. Which (language) contents?

From what precedes it appears that one of the basic equations of the FC approach, the translation of needs into "motivating" objectives, is distorted from the start in these recent methods. How then is the basic concept of communicative competence dealt with in the new methods? Is it furthered by the use of a language for communication and of a notional/functional content to be taught?

In the FC approach the accent is placed on the social communicative function of language. The fundamental presupposition is that of the acquisition of communicative know-how ("savoir-faire") enabling the learner to "perform" speech acts in "authentic" sociolinguistically marked language situations. To study whether and how this can be achieved, a few equally basic questions need to be answered: Which language is taught? Is the learner exposed to and/or taught several registers? The basic assumption here is that communicative competence implies knowledge and use of social registers.

As far as the lexicon is concerned, in OI and SF there is no evidence in the instructions or in the textbook itself of a desire to expose and still less to have the students practice more than one speech register. The reference of OI to the Français Fondamental is significant. Lexical items belonging to familiar spoken French are scarcely used (copain, fac, etc.; but sympathique unabbreviated, etc.) in SF. In OI (Carnet: 25) equivalents given for formidable are "standard" words--étonnant, extraordinaire, inouï, etc.--and never the equally "current" (to use their definition of communication) terms used in conversational French, especially among this group of speakers/learners (teenagers). On the contrary, CT (69) proposes an activity where students have to give more familiar equivalents such as "C'était chouette!" for "Extraordinaire". However, the 700 word lexicon (close to the Français Fondamental) contains very few such "familiar" phrases. AR proves the most radical by systematically introducing students to this register and even more marked ones, and also to the significance of switching registers (see Introduction, p. 16, and Situation 5 in Livre du professeur, p. 55). "Familiar French" is thus introduced in Unit 1 in several situations. (One of them involves a child uttering an ungrammatical sentence.) More slangy terms, also put in quotation marks in the dialogues, are introduced from Unit 2 in socially marked situations (portraying a crane driver, a migrant worker and hoodlums). Note here how they are all packed together, and linked by their speech to the burglars in Unit 3, whereas the computer programmer and the photographer use more "correct" forms. One has yet the impression that, after this shock exposure, phrases in quotation marks become less frequent and amount to the same few recurring terms (widespread slang terms, abbreviations, interjections) and structures of spoken French.

Notwithstanding the avowed "communicative" objectives, the four methods are rather cautious in their use of speech registers at that level. One could therefore conclude that: 1) two methods do not essentially depart from the structuralist conception of a "neutralized" language and do not take into consideration the notion of language situations; 2) in the other two methods the students are sensitized to the existence of several registers but they are not asked to practice forms clearly marked as very familiar. CT systematically proceeds to expose students to different situations and registers, though very slowly (phonological differences between spoken and written French are explicitly dealt with in the last unit, varieties of accents in French in the unit before). AR lays more stress on exposing students to sociolinguistic rules of discourse, but does not propose any new techniques to achieve this aim.

Were learners not able to operate transfers from their native language, their communicative competence in SL would be most limited indeed, and this for two further reasons: 1) non-verbal means of communication are not taken into account, nor is "expressive intonation" (except in AR); 2) sociocultural connotations are ignored. The Canadian adaptation of Ol remains in that respect, and for good reason, superficial. "Authentic" documents have been mainly used to trigger linguistic and "communicative" activities as well as to represent authentic spoken language. They have not been exploited to introduce the learner to the other culture; nor have speech acts. This is no departure from previous approaches, and the notion of a culturally "neutralized" content at the beginner's level is still widely accepted (Galisson 1980: 126). Now, this is the contradiction with an approach that sets communicative competence as the learner's goal. Which leads to the closely related questions: Is communicative competence attainable without sociocultural competence? And how can the latter be taught and learned? Here again going from theory to practice can bring us back to the sobering reality of the classroom (how to teach communicative competence and how to define it first of all). This may also help us to rethink the theory.

Considering, in particular, the concept of interlanguage (and language does include knowledge and use of social rules) one should further study and redefine the applicability of the broadly defined concept of communicative competence to SL teaching. One should also be careful not to replace linguistic competence by another kind of competence as unrealistic to achieve for learner and teacher as was linguistic competence. This being said, one should nevertheless recognize that no departure from previous approaches and no stress on communicative competence is possible without taking into consideration the sociolinguistic component from the start. What one should aim at, however, if one considers the components of communication beyond the purely linguistic to be an essential part of communication, and as such a motivating force (see Besse 1982: 65-87) is a restricted developing communicative competence. At the beginner's level, this could be achieved mainly by sensitizing learners to the various elements in the communicative situations they are exposed to and confronted with (social registers, cultural connotations, gestures, etc.). This constitutes a prerequisite (fulfilled, and very partially at that, in only two of the four methods under review) to any practice in communication, however limited it may and must remain at first.

C. Which methodology?

Has the FC approach, by its focus on the learner, his autonomy and individual learning strategies, contributed to a renewal in course planning and classroom activities?

1. Are these learner-centered methods?

Interestingly enough, 01, conceived for high school students, is rather discrete in its reference to these concepts. In the final stage of each unit, that of role playing, students are expected to demonstrate a limited know-how and "a certain autonomy" (Guide: 9).

In AR, J. Courtillon dissociates herself from behaviorism to fully embrace the new creed whose concepts appear in the introduction, and are "very concretely explained" in the "pedagogical card" for each unit. However, despite the rhetoric, nothing "concrete" is really offered within the frame of the audio-visual methodology except for the use of "directions" in role playing ("une méthodologie du ré-emploi par le moyen de canevas de jeux de rôle"). Now, while this is rightly putting the emphasis on the "production phase" and the acquisition of a communicative comptence, this is not sufficient to guarantee that the focus will be on the learner (Livre: 13). Courtillon, for that matter, admits on the same page that we know little about learning and learning strategies. She nevertheless shifts the problem to the learner and the teacher. In the case of needs, the learners have not been entitled to any choice; in that of learning strategies they are made fully responsible.

In CT, Richterich does more than advocate the autonomy of the learner. Having realized the importance of breaking learners of some of their habits, he makes the "learning of learning" a full-fledged domain, leading, like grammar and communication, to three types of activities ("sensibilisation/découverte/pratique").

2. Towards a communicative methodology?

Germain and Leblanc (1982) write that how to teach is not a matter of the FC approach but of a pedagogy of communication. The distinction is not relevant. The problem remains: How to teach or acquire a communicative competence besides the linguistic one? The study of these four recent methods has not revealed any new "communicative methodology." In fact two of them, 01 and AR, make use of the audio-visual method (while stressing cognitivism to the detriment of behaviorism) with a renewed and increased emphasis on expression. The lack of any rigid methodology is of course inherent in the approach itself, and in its applicability to learners in the school/college system. It is worsened by the absence of a model of a cognitive speaker and a grammar of communication, and by the difficulty of defining and applying key concepts.

These methods nevertheless reveal elements that could help constitute a FC methodology (somewhat along the lines of the outline proposed by G. Dalgalian 1981):

a.) The first phase of the lesson aims at "creating the need to express oneself and to communicate," and therefore sets the tone ("ambiance" in AR) and the objectives to be achieved through the ensuing activities. This is what Richterich calls "learning triggers" ("déclencheurs d'apprentissage"). They partake of an active pedagogy calling for the learners' creativity (see 01, Guide: 8).
b.) Authentic or pseudo-authentic documents are used to foster learners' creativity and autonomy, to develop their communicative and cultural competence, and to set up authentic communicative situations leading to the practice of specific speech acts. Only AR makes full use of these documents but again without always giving precise directions as to their exploitation in the classroom.
c.) The importance given to simulation and role playing. This latter activity, to be constructed with the help of a "framework," lies at the core of the methodology in AR. This might, however, favor a return to traditional dialogue playing, when in fact more interactive activities should be developed.
d.) The variety of activities involving all skills and integrating the learning of grammar in the overall learning process. This is well exemplified by Richterich in CT within the frame of shorter learning sequences (as advocated by Dalgalian). However, role plays and interactive tasks are not, in our opinion, given the importance they could have had in an otherwise thought-provoking textbook.

This cursory review of four methods for beginning French students has brought out some of the difficulties in applying the functional/communicative approach, while revealing its potential. The challenge for the profession lies now in realizing these potentialities. This can only benefit second language teaching, be it functional or not.

NOTES

[1] The four methods have been thus designated in the text:

a) O1: La Méthode Orange 1 by A. Reboullet et al. Montréal: C.E.C., 1980 (Canadian version by M. Duplantie); Carnet: Carnet du Professeur (Teacher's Handbook).

b) CT: Cartes sur table by R. Richterich and B. Suter. Paris: Hachette, 1981; Guide: Guide d'utilisation (Teacher's Guide).

c) AR: Archipel (Units 1-7) by J. Courtillon and S. Raillard. Paris: Didier, 1982: Livre: Livre du professeur (Teacher's Handbook).

d) SF: Sans Frontières by M. Verdehlan et al. Paris: CLE, 1982; (no Teacher's Handbook was available to us).

[2] As J. Yalden (1981: 16) puts it: "It may not be so much attitudes towards the language and the culture it represents, but the act of communicating itself, that will provide the necessary drive."

[3] As R. Galisson (1980: 107) writes: "Or quand l'authenticité ne sera plus conditionellement liée aux décors, aux materiaux employés, aux personnages en présence, mais à la qualité et/ou l'intensité du vécu exprimé, la classe pourra devenir, comme le monde extérieur, un lieu où naitront et se développeront d'authentiques situations de communication."

REFERENCES

Besse, H. "Pour une didactique des différences communicatives." Revue de Phonétique Appliquée, 61-62-63 (1982), 65-87.

Dalgalian, G., S. Lieutaud, and F. Weiss. Pour un nouvel enseignement des langues. Paris: CLE, 1981.

Germain, C., and R. LeBlanc. "Quelques caractéristiques d'une méthode communicative d'enseignement des langues." The Canadian Modern Language Review, 38 (1982), 4, 665-679.

Galisson, R. D'hier à aujourd'hui. La didactique générale des langues étrangères. Paris: CLE, 1980.

Richterich, R. Langues vivantes: modèle pour la definition des besoins langagiers des adultes. Strasbourg: Conseil de l'Europe, 1972.

---, and J. L. Chancerel. L'identification des besoins des adultes apprenant une langue. Strasbourg: Conseil de l'Europe, 1977.

Savignon, S. *Communicative Competence: An Experiment in Foreign-Language Teaching.* Philadelphia: Center for Curriculum Development, 1972.

Yalden, J. *Communicative Language Teaching: Principles and Practice.* Toronto: OISE, 1981.

TRANSLATION/INTERPRETATION IN SPECIAL PURPOSE SECOND LANGUAGE INSTRUCTION: AN EXPERIMENT

Fritz Hensey
University of Texas at Austin

Translation has traditionally been a major component of second language instruction. Except for medieval Europe and late twentieth century America, the history of language teaching in the West has involved some type of translation activity. In his historical overview, Kelly states that "the history of language teaching is dominated by translation" (1969: 25). Attitudes towards translation have varied over time, with corresponding ups and downs in its status vis-à-vis second language instruction (Eppert 1977; Thomas 1976).

While the audiolingual, four skills approach is usually opposed to the incorporation of translation or interpretation (hereafter T/I) in the FL class, there are a number of scholarly voices suggesting reconsideration. Simultaneously and perhaps not coincidentally, there has been an impressive increase in the amount of professional T/I training available in this country.

This paper describes an experimental application of T/I activities to the teaching of an intermediate course of Spanish for prospective students of medicine and related health/social services. Since this is the writer's first attempt to use T/I as a major motif in such a course, the results are still inconclusive. Nevertheless, the experience so far has been positive enough to warrant continuation of the experiment.

Proponents of behaviorist/audiolingual approaches to FL instruction are not enthusiastic about T/I. Some feel that the skills required render T/I appropriate only for advanced and possibly special-purpose courses. Others are diffident or openly hostile to T/I in this context, considering such activities a source of interference, compound bilingualism, and dependence on the surface structures of the native language. Occasionally, a writer will suggest a few translation exercises to illustrate the structural differences involved; Mills (1977) proposes the use of translation in contrastive analysis, while Brown (1980) makes a similar proposal regarding error analysis. Rivers et al. describe translation exercises (1976: 136-9) but also criticize the so-called grammar/translation method as unrealistic (107-10). For Grittner, translation activities are ". . . a step away from the development of direct communicative skill" (1977: 238-9). On the whole, the literature on applied linguistics and methodology tends to make short shrift of T/I in the second language classroom.

Meanwhile, in Europe and somewhat less in America, various trends are making themselves felt: special purpose FL instruction, syllabuses based on other than structural criteria, instruction in intercultural communication, and the often poorly defined communicative and cognitive approaches. In the area of special purpose instruction, one of the major target populations for FL (specifically, Spanish) teaching materials is the medical profession and related social services. One may cite such recent publications as Jarvis and Lebredo (1980), Teed and Raley (1982), Sylvester et al. (1982), Savariego (1982), Escandon (1982), and Savariego (1983). The Escondon text makes use of the interpretation motif in the form of "bilingual projects," while the Savariego (1983) video materials typically show Anglo health workers learning to interpret for Hispanic patients or hospital visitors. The need for making doctors, nurses, and other helping professionals minimally competent in Spanish is clear and present: a growing population of Hispanics of limited English speaking ability who need medical and other social services.

The training of translators and interpreters has burgeoned in the United States to the extent that almost yearly surveys are required to chart the increase of institutions offering T/I training. One may see this in the surveys taken by the American Translators Association in 1975, with some 30 institutions cited, and by the same association in 1981, with nearly triple that number (ATA, 1981). It is likely that the forthcoming directory of the Translating and Interpreting Education Society will show further increases (TIES, 1983).

In defense of a reconsideration of T/I in FL instruction, several scholars have discussed the audiolingualists' objections and presented their own arguments. Juliane House, for instance, claims that many objections are based on limited conceptions of T/I and on a failure to consider effective uses which might be made of such activities in the FL class. She claims that such uses include:

a. the establishment of pragmatic equivalents as a tool for communicative competence;
b. improvement of both reception and production in the target language;
c. explicit comparison of the two cultures;
d. practice in the production and evaluation of texts in both native and target languages (House 1977: ch. 7).

House is concerned less with T/I in language teaching than with the classification and evaluation of translations. She observes that students of a second language need to learn to perform motivated communicative acts and to make creative use of the target language. The main point of T/I is not, in her view, the particular teaching methods used; rather, it is the application of a given T/I model to second language instruction (ch. 8, passim).

Widdowson devotes a sizable portion of his book on applied linguistics to communicative (including T/I) activities, relating them to discourse analysis and suggesting a range of possible exercises which far exceeds that of most intermediate texts. He proposes three levels of translation: structural translation, which relates to the form of the target utterance ("The postman opened the door" = "Le facteur ouvrit la porte"); semantic translation, focusing on the message or deep structure common to the two languages (= "Le facteur a ouvert la porte"); and pragmatic translation, which considers the likely effects of the utterance, e.g., in terms of topicalization (= "C'est le facteur qui a ouvert la porte") (1979: 101-3). Widdowson recommends a combination of communicative and T/I exercises, considering the pragmatic and semantic types of translation to be the most useful to the FL learner interested in achieving communicative competence. He expresses the cognitive viewpoint in stating that "...the process of learning a foreign language should be presented not as the acquisition of new knowledge and experience, but as an extension or alternative representation of what the learner already knows" (111).

Peter Newmark's introduction to translation strongly defends the use of T/I in FL instruction. He believes translation should be one of the main aims of the language learner, arguing that the so-called grammar/translation method was rejected because it was bad grammar, bad translation, and too much of both. Newmark attacks the four skills approach as "selfish and self-centered" and urges students of FL to acquire something socially useful, such as learning to communicate between cultures (1981: ch. 5).

Newmark echoes Widdowson's pragmatic and semantic classifications with his own communicative and semantic ones. A communicative translation is meant "to produce on its readers an effect as close as possible to that obtained on the readers of the original," while a semantic one should "render, as closely as the...structures of the second language allow, the exact contextual meaning of the original" (39).

Other scholars have urged reconsideration of the role of T/I in second-language teaching. Bradley (1977a and b) proposes for the teaching of Spanish the use of simultaneous and consecutive interpretation techniques; the course described below is, in fact, based far more on pragmatic interpretation then on (written) translation. The literature on interpretation, and particularly its teaching, is rather scanty in comparison with that on translation. Gerver and Sinaiko (1977) covers a wide range of interpretive activities, while parts of Brislin (1976) address problems of both simultaneous and consecutive. For consecutive and conference interpretation, Seleskovitch (1978) and Bowen & Bowen (1980) are valuable as teaching texts.

Friesen laments the decline of translation in FL teaching and criticizes current approaches as leading to an ability to "communicate on the level of foreign language competence equivalent to that of a three-year-old native speaker" (1975: 113). Wandruszka defends translation and the linguistic analysis that goes with it as "...il solo metodo veramente efficace per acquisitare una competenza plurilingue, una coscienza interlinguistica" (1973: 53).

The Spanish for Medical Personnel course in question is being given at the University of Texas at Austin during the spring semester of 1983. At this stage, four T/I activities have formed the course motif and have taken up the bulk of class time. Two of them, "Conversaciones y Consultas" and "Charlas Profesionales," involve role playing in simulations of relatively authentic situations. The translation tasks make use of official documents published bilingually. The laboratory activity, which is the weakest of the four, comprises an adaptation of rather dated materials; hopefully, with the appearance of new texts for this market, better lab tools will become available. There should be greater use of movies and videotape. A systematic approach to evaluating interpretation will be implemented, based possibly on the criteria of Barik (1971) or Bradley (1977b).

Impressions so far, which cannot be properly tested until near the end of the course, suggest that this use of T/I activities in an intermediate, special purpose Spanish class produces positive results in the following areas:

a. response to assessed needs of students (over half have worked in hospitals, doctors' offices, or social services);
b. use of authentic, available, and easily adaptable materials;
c. implementation of a communicative, situational syllabus which permits a systematic if superficial review of basic grammar;
d. daily practice in simulated cross-cultural communication;
e. achievement of a high degree of motivation as reflected in attendance, performance, and morale;
f. stimulus to self-actualization by making the student partly responsible for evaluating his own work;
g. increased professionalization of a level of FL instruction whose status and function are not always well defined.

REFERENCES

American Translators Association. Survey of U.S. Colleges and Universities Offering Training for Translators. Ossining, NY: ATA, 1975.
_____. 1981 Survey of Schools Offering Translator and Interpreter Training. Ossining, NY: ATA, 1982.

Barik, H. "A Description of Various Types of Omissions, Additions, and Errors of Translation Encountered in Simultaneous Interpreting." META, 16 (1971), 199-210.

Bowen, D., & M. Bowen. Steps to Consecutive Interpretation. Washington, D.C.: Pen & Booth, 1980.

Bradley, D. (1977a). "La traducción simultanea como materia en una carrera de lenguas." Yelmo 32 (1977), 25-7.

_____. (1977b). "La interpretación consecutiva y la enseñanza avanzada de lenguas." Yelmo 33 (1977), 21-4.

Brislin, R. Translation: Applications and Research. New York: Gardner Press, 1976.

Brown, H. D. Principles of Language Learning and Teaching. Englewood Cliffs, N.J.: Prentice Hall, 1980.

Carbajo, A. Spanish for Doctors, Dentists, Oculists, Optometrists, and Nurses. Miami, Fl.: Language Research Press, 1963.

Eppert, F. "Translation and Second Language Teaching." Canadian Modern Language Review 34, 1 (1977), 50-61.

Escandon, R. Bilingual Vocabulary for the Medical Profession. Cincinnati: South-Western Publishing Co., 1982.

Friesen, A. "Why Teach Translation and How?" In M. Batts (ed.), Translation and Interpretation: The Multicultural Context. Vancouver, B.C.: Canadian Association of Teachers of German, 1975.

Gerver, D., and H. Sinaiko, Language Interpretation and Communication. New York: Plenum Press, 1977.

Grittner, F. Teaching Foreign Languages. 2nd ed. New York: Harper & Row, 1977.

House, J. A Model for Translation Quality Assessment. Tubingen: TBL Verlag Gunter Narr, 1977.

Jarvis, A., and R. Lebredo. Medical Personnel Workbook. Lexington, Mass.: D. C. Heath, 1980.

Kelly, L. 25 Centuries of Language Teaching. Rowley, Mass.: Newbury House, 1969.

Mills, G. "Contrastive Analysis and Translation in Second-language Teaching." Canadian Modern Language Review 33, 5 (1977), 732-45.

Newmark, P. Approaches to Translation. New York: Pergamon Press, 1981.

Orleb, E. & R. Cadice. El Cuerpo humano. New York: Milliken Publishing Co., 1971.

Rivers, W., et al. A Practical Guide to the Teaching of Spanish. New York: Oxford Univ. Press, 1976.

Savariego, B. Talk to the Patient in Spanish/ Hablele al paciente en español. Cincinnati: South-Western Publishing Co., 1982.

_____. Spanish for Health Professionals. (Videotape and texts). Dallas: University of Texas Health Science Center, 1983.

Seleskovitch, D. Interpreting for International Conferences. Washington, D.C.: Pen & Booth, 1978.

Sylvester, N., et al. Medical Readings in Spanish. Lavallette, N.J.: Holt, Rinehart & Winston, 1982.

Teed, C., and H. Raley Conversational Spanish for the Health Professions. Lavallette, N.J.: Holt, Rinehart & Winston, 1982.

Thomas, J. "Translation, Teaching, and the Bilingual Assumption." TESOL Quarterly 10, 4 (1976), 403-10.

TIES. Directory of Programs in Translation and/or Interpretation. (Personal communication from E. Arjona). 1982.

Wandruszka, M. "Traduzione, interlinguistica, ed insegnamento delle lingue." in G. Petronio (ed.), La traduzione: saggi e studi, Trieste: LINT, 1973.

Werner, D. Donde no hay doctor. Palo Alto, Ca.: La Fundación Hesperian, 1981.

Widdowson, H. Explorations in Applied Linguistics. Oxford: Oxford Univ. Press, 1979.

STRATEGIES FOR THE USE OF AUTHENTIC MATERIALS

Nancy Anne McClure Zeller and Bernice Melvin
Austin College

Foreign language teachers always supplement inadequate textbooks with realia. Such realia are, however, rarely integrated into the study of the language. Instead they are usually presented as "show and tell" objects, an enjoyable break between dull grammar sessions and uninteresting dialogues or readings. At Austin College our concept of authentic materials encompasses realia, but it includes as well materials normally excluded from classes at all levels due to their perceived linguistic and conceptual complexity. We prefer to integrate these materials into the course of study, to use them to teach language and culture. In order to do this, new strategies beyond "show and tell" must be developed.

What are authentic materials? "Authentic" refers to those language artifacts that exist independently of the teaching establishment. Authentic materials are created by native speakers for native speakers, and they exist to inform, entertain, or persuade. "Materials" that are authentic include some familiar old standbys such as short stories, fables, fairy tales, and other short forms of literature, but other materials qualify as authentic as well. Less commonly used authentic materials include newspaper and magazine articles, television and radio broadcasts, advertisements, pop songs, record jackets, labels, statistics, correspondence, flyers, brochures, interviews, etc. Authentic materials are not those created by foreign language teachers to demonstrate a particular grammar point or encompass a minimum vocabulary. We all have our favorite example of such non-authentic material. French teachers cite the Harris and Lévêque dialogue in which every sentence has verbs in the various conjugations of the subjunctive. Read aloud, such materials remind one more of an Ionesco play than reality in a foreign country. In fact, Ionesco has co-authored a textbook that capitalizes on the absurdity of most beginning language texts (Benamou and Ionesco, 1969). Some notions about the use of authentic language materials clearly should be challenged.

The first of these notions is that authentic materials can only be used after students have been given some introduction to grammar. This notion has fathered countless textbooks with inane reading passages and dialogues that have no reason for existence except that they illustrate particular grammar concepts. However, we at Austin College believe with Neuner et al. (1981: 50) that authentic materials can practically replace current texts IF comprehension strategies are taught from the very beginning of a course of study. Successful classroom experience has proven to us that authentic language materials can be used at all levels of language instruction, even with first semester beginners, IF appropriate tasks guide the student to understanding.

There must be some selection criteria, of course, and we consider length and content the most important (Schulz 1981: 43-53; Langer 1981: 452). For example, a lengthy, abstractly poetic essay is of no use in beginning classrooms, but then few teachers would be tempted to select such materials. Level of linguistic difficulty concerns us less. Because we do not demand that our students understand every word, but rather proceed from global comprehension, and because we teach strategies for building comprehension, we consider interest a more important factor. If the teacher finds the material interesting, he or she is more likely to impart that interest to the students. If students find the material interesting and/or see that their teacher is enthusiastic, it is our experience that they can accept a high level of ambiguity without frustration. The attitude that guesses and mistakes and self-correction are an acceptable way (or even the optimum way) to comprehend, fosters a climate of excited exploration in the classroom and leads to an emphasis of inferencing, one of the higher cognitive skills involved in reading (Van Parreren and Schouten-Van Parreren 1981: 236). While some consideration must be given to text selection, we consider it secondary to the designing of appropriate tasks to accompany the materials.

To make materials accessible even to beginning students, different strategies are required. We begin with the assumption that our students do not check their knowledge and experience of the real world at the door to our language classes and that they can, and should, use this knowledge as a context for understanding foreign language materials. Our scheme of task design is consistent with a view of comprehension as a complex cognitive process in which meaning is constructed. The three-part scheme we have developed represents our practical application of recent research in psycholinguistics and second language reading and our systematization of what has proven successful in actual classroom use (Swaffar 1981: 176-194; Van Parreren & Schouten-Van Parreren 1981; Phillips 1975; Hosenfeld et al. 1981: 419; Kolers 1972: 84-91; Goodman 1982; Neuner et al. 1981).

We have successfully used the following three-part scheme for designing tasks based on the belief that comprehension is a process that requires the student to work with the material more than once, and to test initial assumptions through successive, goal-oriented activities. We divide the tasks into: 1) orientation tasks, 2) tasks which emphasize words and structures, and 3) tasks which foster production, each task building on the understanding gained from the previous one (Cates 1982). This three-part scheme is appropriate to all levels of language instruction, but the specific tasks involved differ in complexity depending on whether the students are beginning, intermediate, or advanced. The basic guiding principle we work from in designing exercises is that global understanding should precede specific. There are, of course, other factors to consider when writing exercises. One should take into account level of instruction, age of students, course syllabus, time available in class, time available for preparation, and accessibility of equipment. In other words, exercises should fit the situation.

Additionally, exercises should not assume total comprehension of everything in the material. Most teachers are trained to pinpoint failure rather than reinforce the successes of their students, and this expectation or assumption of total understanding must be overcome before good exercises can be devised. Exercises should build on what students already know, the first tasks utilizing extralinguistic clues, cognates, loan words, knowledge of genre, Western culture, etc. Subsequent exercises should lead students from global understanding of the material toward detailed, specific comprehension following the sequence of comprehension before production. Earlier exercises should require a restructuring of the information through list making, categorization, chronologies, etc., rather than pinpointing discreet information through the use of wh-questions (who, what, when, where, why). Final production exercises should ask the students to be creative and convey information in the context of the material, to produce original utterances or writings based on their understanding of the material. Such production exercises are preferable to mere dialogue memorization or model sentence repetition, which are essentially uncreative uses of the language.

The French, German, and Spanish examples that follow the body of this paper illustrate these general guidelines for writing exercises and our three-part exercise scheme. It is assumed that the reader will make frequent reference to these examples.

Orientation exercises draw attention to the material as a whole. Students may be asked to identify the genre, the structure, the characters or the major divisions of the material. Such preview or orientation exercises are a necessary first step because they demarcate the conceptual and linguistic boundaries within which the student will work (Swaffar 1981: 182). Students can tell much about a text without looking up a single unknown word if the exercises encourage them to capitalize on extra-linguistic clues such as accompanying pictures, graphics, headlines, layout, structure, or genre. This foreknowledge serves to disambiguate the material, often more effectively than glosses or footnotes. Students work in a context which they have been able to discover themselves, and this can make a big difference in the range of vocabulary, expectations of syntactic complexity, and possible interpretation.

Exercises that deal with words and structures should require students to recognize and then reorganize the information in the material according to categories designed to further comprehension, i.e., cognitive categories. The student may be asked to list words or phrases related to selected themes, locate significant information, note redundancies, order material chronologically, locate and list examples of selected grammar points, recognize cognates and loan words, locate topic sentences or main ideas, note nonlinguistic structures such as key changes in music or visual aspects of film. These tasks involve first a recognition of the ideas in the material; and reorganization exercises are actually an initial, highly controlled form of interpretation. With more advanced students, more numerous and demanding word and structure exercises can be assigned.

Production exercises represent the goal of the other tasks because they best allow the students to express or communicate ideas gained from the materials in the target language. Production tasks can be as simple as pantomiming content, completing simple sentences, or improvising a sketch or interview based on the material; or they can be as complex as a composition, a debate, or a new version of the material. These exercises should be designed so that production grows naturally and logically from the previous exercises that focused on comprehension (Cates 1982). The level of complexity of production exercises can be tailored to the needs and abilities of the students.

There are many advantages to this approach with authentic materials. Not only are such materials diverse and readily available, but they are inherently more interesting than textbooks. The interest factor--meaning both student and teacher interest--is the greatest single recommendation for using authentic materials. But there are additional benefits. Students respond positively to using authentic materials. They recognize them for what they are: authentic artifacts of the culture whose language they are learning. They also appreciate the fact that they are being taught strategies which they can later use in dealing with similar materials in nonclassroom situations. Because they have been taught ways to construct meaning, they will not be overwhelmed by the wide variety of information that will confront them if they ever travel to the foreign locale (and most of our students take a language hoping and expecting to do so). The strategies we teach will allow them to extract information, guess at content, reorganize concepts, learn vocabulary, and in general deal with ambiguities in all their contact with the culture. They quickly learn that this is far more valuable or manageable than memorizing word lists or grammar rules, filling in blanks or answering questions which exist solely to use specific structures or vocabulary items.

Because authentic materials are versatile, they can be used as the basis for an entire course or can supplement commercial texts, thus returning a great deal of control to the teacher. The German section at Austin College has built its entire curriculum around authentic materials, while the Spanish and French sections relate individual pieces of material to units in existing textbooks. They are, however, used by all three languages from the first semester on.

With so many advantages it is appropriate to ask why authentic materials are not universally employed in our high schools and colleges. Our contact with sixty high school language teachers last summer at our NEH Institute on authentic materials provided us with some answers. Constraints of time, energy, and money, together with the requirements of school boards, have prevented teachers from straying too far from adopted texts. Some teachers we worked with were not even allowed to use their school's photocopier. The short-term solution to such practical problems lies in networking, the systematic sharing of successful materials within school districts or regions. The long-term solution will be a process of re-education of administrators and teachers, and increasing the availability of suitable materials and exercises in textbook form.

Another reason authentic materials are not universally used is that most teachers have no training or experience in handling such materials. Typically, teachers inundate their students with a flood of wh-questions which focus on individual words or structures and can usually be answered without any understanding of the material. Such techniques focus on what students may not know instead of building comprehension from what they already know. Our strategies thus imply a radical change in the way languages are taught, learned, and tested. And frankly, the thought of such a revolution is unsettling to many. We at Austin College have developed strategies that work for us, and we believe others can use them just as effectively.

REFERENCES

Benamou, Michel, and Eugène Ionesco. Mise en train. London, Toronto: The Macmillan Company, 1969.

Cates, G. Truett. "Three Steps to Fluent Reading." Session 459: Developing Second Language Reading Skills, MLA Convention, Los Angeles, 29 Dec. 1982.

_____, and Janet K. Swaffar. Reading a Second Language. Washington, D.C.: Center for Applied Linguistics, 1979.

Gollasch, Frederick V. (ed.). Language and Literacy: The Selected Writings of Kenneth S. Goodman. Boston: Routledge and Kegan Paul, 1982.

Hosenfeld, Carol, et al. "Second Language Reading: A Curricular Sequence for Teaching Reading Strategies." Foreign Language Annals, 14, 5 (Dec. 1981), 415-422.

Hudelson, Sarah, ed. Learning to Read in Different Languages. Washington, D.C.: Center for Applied Linguistics, 1981.

Kolers, P. A. "Experiments in Reading." Scientific American, 227 (1972), 84-91.

Langer, Judith A. "From Theory to Practice: A Prereading Plan." Journal of Reading, 25, (Nov. 1981), 152-156.

Mackay, Ronald, Bruce Barkman, and R. R. Jordan (eds.). Reading in a Second Language: Hypotheses, Organization and Practice. Rowley, Mass.: Newbury House, 1979.

Neuner, G., et al. Übungstypologie zum kommunikativen Deutschunterricht. Munich: Langenscheidt, 1981.

Phillips, June. "Second Language Reading: Teaching Decoding Skills." Foreign Language Annals, 8, 3 (Oct. 1975), 227-32.

"References and Select Bibliography on Reading." System, 9, 3 (Fall 1981), 275-85.

Schulz, Renate A. "From Word to Meaning: Foreign Language Reading Instruction after the Elementary Course." Session 459: Developing Second Language Reading Skills, MLA Convention, Los Angeles, 29 Dec. 1982.

_____. "Literature and Readability: Bridging the Gap in Foreign Language Reading." Modern Language Journal 65, 1 (Spring 1981), 43-53.

Swaffar, Janet King. "Reading in the Foreign Language Classroom: Focus on Process." Die Unterrichtspraxis, 14, 2 (Fall 1981), 176-194.

Van Parreren, C. F., and M. C. Schouten-Van Parreren. "Contextual Guessing: A Trainable Reader Strategy." System, 9, 3 (Fall 1981), 236 & 238.

Wanat, Stanley F. (ed.). Language and Reading Comprehension. Washington, D.C.: Center for Applied Linguistics, 1977.

WER SAGT DASS MÄDCHEN DÜMMER SIND

Wer sagt, daß Mädchen dümmer sind,
wer sagt, daß Mädchen albern sind,
wer sagt, daß Mädchen schüchtern sind –
der spinnt, der spinnt, der spinnt!

Wer sagt, die Mädchen traun' sich nicht,
wer sagt, sie seien immer weinerlich
und meckerig und zappelig –
der hat'n Stich, 'n Stich, 'n Stich!

Mädchen sind genau – so schlau – wie Jungen,
Mädchen sind genau – so frech – und schnell,
Mädchen haben auch so viel Mut wie Jungen,
Mädchen haben auch ein dickes Fell.

Wer sagt, daß Mädchen schwächer sind,
wer sagt, daß Mädchen immer zickig sind,
wer sagt, daß Mädchen affig sind –
der spinnt, der spinnt, der spinnt!

Wer sagt, die Mädchen fürchten sich
und petzen und sind zimperlich,
sind also blöd und hinderlich –
der hat'n Stich, 'n Stich, 'n Stich!

Mädchen sind genau – so schlau – wie Jungen,
Mädchen sind genau – so frech – und schnell,
Mädchen haben auch so viel Mut wie Jungen,
Mädchen haben auch ein dickes Fell.

aus: „Wer sagt, daß Mädchen dümmer sind",
DAS GRIPS-LIEDERBUCH
von Volker Ludwig/Birger Heymann,
Verlag Heinrich Ellermann, 1978

I Orientierung

Hören Sie sich das Lied zweimal an! Beantworten Sie folgende
Fragen:
1. Dieser Text ist
   a) ein Gedicht   b) ein Artikel   c) eine Reklame
   d) ein Lied   e) ein Märchen

2. In diesem Text geht es um
   a) Argumente und Ideen   b) Personen und Handlungen

3. Die Sänger von diesem Lied sind
   a) ein Mannerchor   b) zwei Alte Damen
   c) Kinder   d) Elvis Presley

4. Charakterisieren Sie diese Musik!
   z.B. Sie ist "modern" oder "punk" oder "für meine Eltern,"
   u.s.w.

II. Worter und Strukturen

1. Machen Sie zwei Listen von Attributen oder Charakteristiken,
   positive und negative!

2. Sehen oder hören Sie Wiederholungen in diesem Lied? Wenn ja,
   identifizieren Sie die Worte oder Wortgruppen, die mehr als
   einmal vorkommen!

3. Die Form von Strophe I kann man auf folgende Formel reduzieren:
   "Wer sagt, X , der spinnt."
   Finden Sie andere Strophen mit dieser Form!

4. Sind "der spinnt" und "der hat 'n Stich" positive oder
   negative Eigenschaften (Charakteristiken) ?

5. Finden Sie Zeilen, die etwas uber die Meinung der Sänger
   aussagen, d.h. wo sieht man, was die Sänger über den Satz
   denken, "Mädchen sind dümmer als Jungen?"

III. Produktion
1. Schreiben Sie einen Dialog zwischen zwei Personen! Person A
glaubt, daß Mädchen dümmer sind. Person B glaubt das nicht.
Nehmen Sie Sätze oder Satzteile aus dem Text des Liedes!
2. Erfinden Sie ein Interview mit den Komponisten dieses Liedes.
Mogliche Fragen für die Interviewten sind:
Für wen ist dieses Lied gemeint? Wo wollen Sie dieses Lied
spielen? Wo kann ich dieses Lied hören? Was für eine Funktion
soll dieses Lied erfüllen?

Changez votre vie

et donnez lui un sens.
Quittez vore solitude,
étendez
le choix de vos relations,
faites le premier pas,
découvrez l'amitié,
partagez la tendresse,
souriez au bonheur
et à l'amour, trouvez
votre vraie raison
de vivre

Uni-Centre

MARIAGES - RENCONTRES

Résidence St-Nicolas
1er étage
98, rue St-Nicolas
NANCY

Tél. 336.42.82

Mariages - Rencontres

- **Secrétaire médicale**, 21 ans, châtain, yeux noisette, douce, féminine, sérieuse, sportive, **désire épouser garçon** loyal, sportif, gentil, sincère, 22 à 26 ans. Ecrire ou téléphoner à UNI-CENTRE. N° 585.

- **Elle adore la nature**, lecture, sport, pleine de vie, enjouée, dynamique, âgée de 25 ans, employée de banque, blonde aux yeux bleus, **recherche un futur mari** qui sache apprécier ses qualités. Ecrire ou téléphoner à UNI-CENTRE. N° 586.

- **Divorcé, 58 ans**, sans charge, retraité de l'armée (5 500 F/mensuels), sympathique, agréable, courtois, bricoleur, espere rencontrer dame, physique agréable, bonne éducation, affectueuse, pour avenir partagé. Ecrire ou téléphoner à UNI-CENTRE. N° 587.

- **Vendeuse**, 37 ans, physique agréable, moderne, très gaie, douce, sensible, attachée à la vie de famille, **désire mariage avec Monsieur** sincère, bonne presentation, éducation, ayant qualités morales, acceptant sa fille de onze ans. Ecrire ou téléphoner à UNI-CENTRE. N° 588.

- **Célibataire, 27 ans**, directeur technico-commercial, grand brun, distingué, sympathique, ambitieux, aimant beaucoup la campagne, épouserait **jeune fille** jolie, gaie, sincère, niveau secondaire. Ecrire ou téléphoner à UNI-CENTRE. N° 589.

- **22 ans, profession libérale**, beau brun aux yeux bleus, 1,80 m, soigné, élégant, adore sport, musique, désire mariage avec jeune fille mignonne, douce, gaie, bon milieu. Ecrire ou téléphoner à UNI-CENTRE. N° 590.

- **Gentille jeune femme** de 31 ans, maman d'une fillette de 8 ans, douce, agréable, excellente maîtresse d'intérieur, épouserait Monsieur sincère, sérieux, travailleur, âge en rapport. Ecrire ou téléphoner à UNI-CENTRE. N° 580.

- **Jeune maman** de 23 ans, agent hospitalier, célibataire, agréable, plutôt jolie, ambitieuse, gaie, aimant vie familiale, **souhaite mariage avec gentil garçon**, doux, affectueux, sincère, bonne éducation, acceptant sa fillette. Ecrire ou téléphoner à UNI-CENTRE. N° 591.

- **Vendeuse, la cinquantaine**, jolie femme, blonde, élégante, dynamique, souffrant beaucoup de la solitude, **souhaite ardemment rencontrer un homme** sincère, pour union durable et harmonieuse, mariage si affinités. Ecrire ou téléphoner à UNI-CENTRE. N° 582.

- **Chef d'équipe**, divorcé, age de 44 ans, bel homme, soigné, bonne présentation, gai, esprit ouvert, désire refaire sa vie avec dame coquette, gentille, compréhensive, même ayant enfant. Ecrire ou téléphoner à UNI-CENTRE. N° 583.

- **Très beau garçon** ayant beaucoup d'allure, 30 ans, comptable, 1,81 m, brun, études superieures, forte personnalité, sportif, aimant nature, musique, **souhaite mariage avec jeune fille**, douce, gaie, ambitieuse, physique agréable, ayant éducation, instruction. Ecrire ou téléphoner à UNI-CENTRE. N° 584.

Si vous désirez des renseignements sur ces personnes retournez dès aujourd'hui le bon ci-dessous sous pli fermé à UNI-CENTRE

Célibataire	Veuf (e)	Divorce (e)	Date de naissance
NOM .... Prenom		Profession	
Adresse		Ville	Tel
Je ne travaille pas le lundi	le samedi	et les autres jours	
Je suis libre à partir de	le soir	le matin	heures

Je desire sans engagement recevoir une documentation et des renseignements complementaires sur n°

Mariages-Rencontres

I.
1) Ce texte se compose de: a) chansons   b) petites annonces
                             c) recettes   d) offres d'emploi

2) Ces annonces sont: a) des demandes d'emploi
                       b) des offres d'appartements
                       c) des ventes d'autos
                       d) des recherches de mariage

II.
1) Lisez les annonces et faites une liste d'adjectifs pour décrire les femmes.

2) Relisez les annonces. Faites une liste d'adjectifs qui décrivent les hommes.

3) Trouvez quatre professions.

4) Relisez les annonces et trouvez un garçon pour N° 585.

5) Dans les annonces trouvez deux amies pour N° 583.

III.
1) Faites des phrases completes pour décrire les personnes dans les annonces suivantes.
   Ex. N° 585. Voilà une secrétaire médicale qui désire épouser un garçon loyal et sportif.
   Ex. N° 591. Voilà une jeune maman ambitieuse qui souhaite épouser un garçon doux et sincère.
   a) N° 589
   b) N° 584
   c) N° 580

2) Ecrivez une petite annonce pour une des personnes suivantes: Lois Lane, Napoléon, Marie-Antoinette, Astérix

3) Ecrivez votre propre petite annonce.

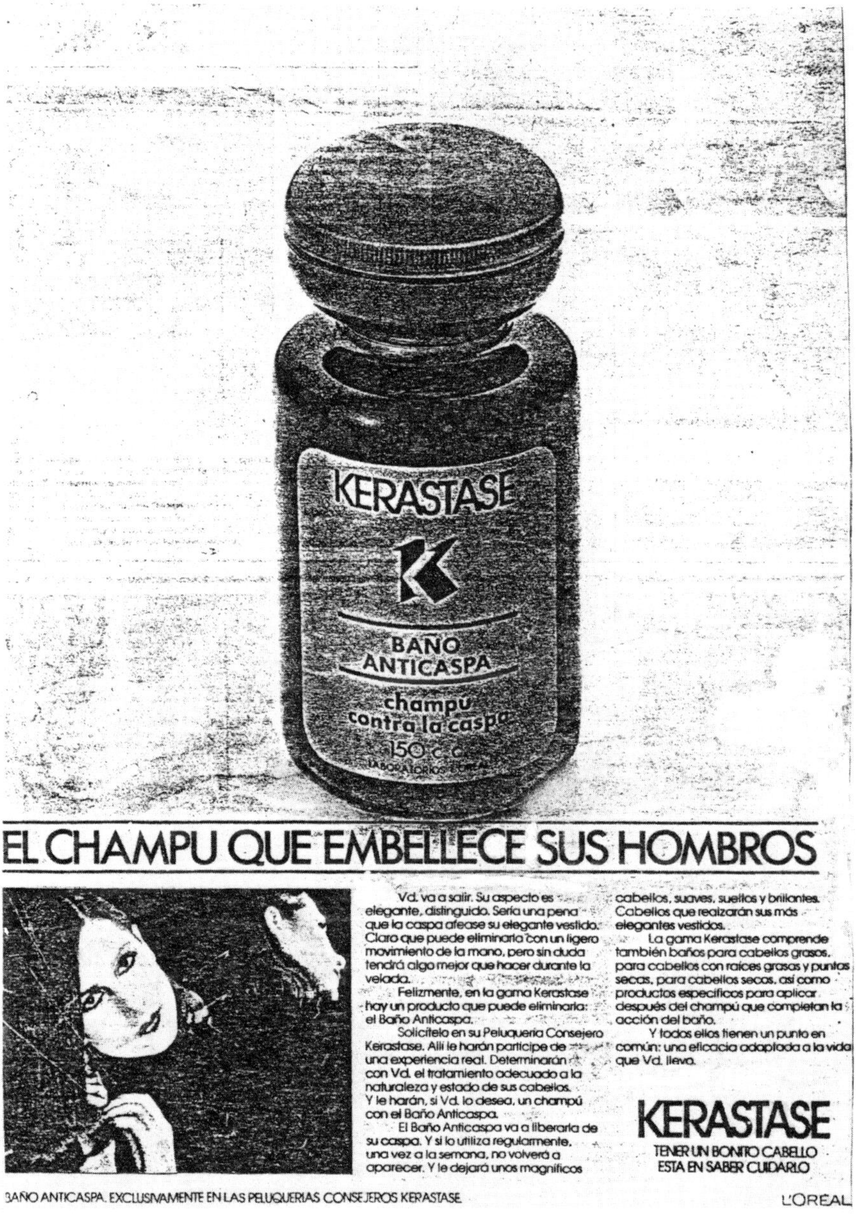

EL CHAMPU QUE EMBELLECE SUS HOMBROS

Vd. va a salir. Su aspecto es elegante, distinguido. Sería una pena que la caspa afease su elegante vestido. Claro que puede eliminarla con un ligero movimiento de la mano, pero sin duda tendrá algo mejor que hacer durante la velada.

Felizmente, en la gama Kerastase hay un producto que puede eliminarla: el Baño Anticaspa.

Solicítelo en su Peluquería Consejero Kerastase. Allí le harán participe de una experiencia real. Determinarán con Vd. el tratamiento adecuado a la naturaleza y estado de sus cabellos. Y le harán, si Vd. lo desea, un champú con el Baño Anticaspa.

El Baño Anticaspa va a liberarla de su caspa. Y si lo utiliza regularmente, una vez a la semana, no volverá a aparecer. Y le dejará unos magníficos cabellos, suaves, sueltos y brillantes. Cabellos que realzarán sus más elegantes vestidos.

La gama Kerastase comprende también baños para cabellos grasos, para cabellos con raíces grasas y puntas secas, para cabellos secos, así como productos específicos para aplicar después del champú que completan la acción del baño.

Y todos ellos tienen un punto en común: una eficacia adaptada a la vida que Vd. lleva.

KERASTASE
TENER UN BONITO CABELLO
ESTÁ EN SABER CUIDARLO

BAÑO ANTICASPA. EXCLUSIVAMENTE EN LAS PELUQUERIAS CONSEJEROS KERASTASE.   L'OREAL

Kerastase "Baño Anticaspa"

I.
1. Este texto está basado en ____ unos personajes, acontecimientos
   ____ unas ideas, razonamientos
2. Este texto es: ____ un cuento, ____ un artículo de prensa,
   ____ un anuncio, ____ una guía
3. Identifique el producto que se venden
4. Fíjese en la distribución del texto gráfico en la página, y señale las principales divisiones del textoñ

II.
1. Encuentre la siguiente información el texto:
   a) dónde se vende el producto.
   b) dónde se habla de los diferentes tipos de cabello.
   c) dónde se habla de los efectos de la caspa.
2. Haga una lista de cuatro adjetivos o frases que describan un bonito cabello.
3. Ordene cronológicamente los siguientes acontecimientos:
   ____ Ud. se quita la caspa con la mano.
   ____ La caspa afea su vestido.
   ____ Ud. sale de su casa.
   ____ Udñ se pone un vestido elegante.
4. Encuentre 5 verbos en el futuro.
5. Escriba de nuevo las frases donde se encuentran esos verbos usando la construcción de futuro inmediato "VOY A + Infinitive"

III.
1. El profesor piensa que este texto está basado en
   a) el efecto de la caspa en los vestidos
   b) las ventatas del champú "Baño Anticaspa"
2. Usando la lengua del texto escriba 2 frases que contrasten un champú normal.

3. Usando la lengua del texto, escriba una frase que hable de la caspa y la vida social.

4. ¿Es el autor de este anuncio imparcial y objetivo con respecto al "Baño Anticaspa"? Justifique su opinión citando frases del texto.

DEVELOPING MOTIVATION AND SPONTANEITY IN CONVERSATION: IDEAS ON THE DESIGN OF CLASSROOM DIALOGUE AND GAMES

Anthony D. Northey
Acadia University

For teachers of modern foreign languages the ability to speak the target languages has been one of the most sought after goals. In recent times great attention seems to have been paid to the development of conversational skills. But by and large recent texts (in the field of German, at least) have failed to provide adequate guidance for putting into practice the language structures they teach. True, very few books have not made the components of their drills sound more like the normal spoken word; they include some type of model dialogue in each chapter and, of course, sections labelled "conversation" or "guided conversation" intended to get the student to speak. Yet how "guided" are these conversations? Looking at fairly recent North American textbooks for German one finds instructions that read like this: "Ask your neighbor to describe his or her living quarters. Ask whether there is a bath or shower or wash basin. Ask for the location in terms of what is near. Inquire with whom he or she shares quarters, what means of transportation is available to go to the university, and what the monthly rent is" (Helbling et al. 1979: 79). One cannot quarrel with the choice of topic of the conversation, only with the way the student is left to cope with the mechanics of putting all these instructions into operation. Invitations such as "Begin a conversation with two or three persons sitting near you" or "Tell a classmate, a group or the class as a whole..." (Helbling et al. 1979: 39; Jespersen & Peters 1980: 55), such invitations, accompanied sometimes by sample questions, commands, or sentences, are not enough.

The newer approaches try to take the student out of the somewhat sterile atmosphere of filling in blanks or altering sentences in order to drive home one grammatical point, and instead confront him with a realistic situation in communication he must deal with in the classroom. The necessary grammatical and lexical material is then brought in to accomplish the task, which has meant that traditional priorities in the presentation of grammar have been subject to a reconsideration, long overdue.[1] Yet for all its attractiveness the new way of learning has its dangers. Following only the dictates of the conversational situation could mean exposing the student to too many grammatical topics at one time. A certain conversation (in German) might require the use of several cases, a variety of prepositions, tenses, and the like, not to mention vocabulary. Should everything be individually learned only as it applies in one conversational circumstance and all systemized treatment of grammar be eschewed? How much variety can the learner, especially the beginner, handle? A welter of forms and vocabulary, with no distinct pattern he can pick out and hold onto, might discourage him and rob him of his motivation just as much as the most rigorous pattern drill composed of unconnected sentences could. One or two grammar difficulties and a modest amount of vocabulary are all one can hope to introduce in one dialogue.

The beginner may face several problems: inhibitions, for instance, some superficial, some more deeply rooted, like the fear of exposing oneself in front of the instructor and fellow students; or motivational problems, deriving from the fact that students cannot see how the language they are learning can become functional for them. Then there is a specific difficulty relating to dialogue. As everyone knows from daily communication, conversation shows varying degrees of randomness; that is, although there is a certain amount of predictability to typical conversations, one cannot account for the specific twists and turns they may take. On the one hand a model dialogue for the classroom can be highly structured. In this case it must be memorized like the parts in an amateur play. Indeed, many instructors like to use various dramatic forms to practice speaking. Yet since conversation often progresses quite haphazardly, learning a dialogue by heart has not prepared the student to cope with the vagaries in conversation. No room is left for the art of adaptation, however slight, which the beginner needs to practice. On the other hand, merely to require a superficial learning of the script and then demand that the student "ad lib" is too much to ask. Probably only the very experienced actor has developed the ability to "cover up," that is, to sense, without receiving the all-important cue line, that it is time for him to speak. And leaving the students to set the pattern of the conversation themselves after having given them a few "starter sentences" also puts too big a burden on them. "Where do I begin?" they will probably ask, feeling dismayed and tongue-tied.

These problems should be borne in mind when addressing the question of creating practice dialogues for the classroom. The solution lies not only in carefully planned dialogue but also in making the student as well as the instructor aware of the strategies available in speaking. Normally one would choose everyday conversational situations as a basis and give the classroom dialogue the most rudimentary beginning (some type of greeting, probably), a middle section, and perhaps as an end some kind of goodbye or sign-off, although the end can be more vaguely defined. The central principle of construction, however, is that there be, insofar as possible, no rigidly fixed sequence of sentences, that is, no forced interdependence between statements other than a question needing some form of answer. The conversation should be short, three or four exchanges, at least in its initial stages. The following example of a dialogue, a typical get-to-know-one-another situation standard to almost all texts, would appear in the earliest phase of language practice:

A: (Guten Tag). Ich heisse A.   Hello. My name is A.
Wie heissen Sie?   What's your name?

B: (Guten Tag.) Ich heisse B.   (Hello.) My name is B.
Studieren Sie hier in W.?   Are you studying here in W.?

A: Ja. (Ich studiere) Mathematik und Deutsch. Und Sie? (Was studieren Sie?)	Yes. (I'm studying) mathematics and German. And you? (What are you studying?)
B. Biologie.	Biology.
A: Ach so. Wohnen Sie hier in W.?	Oh. Are you living here in W.?
B: Ja. Wo wohnen Sie?	Yes. Where do you live?
A: (Ich wohne) in K.	I'm living in K.
B: Ach ja. Schön. Na ja... Auf Wiedersehen.	I see. That's nice. Well... Goodbye.
A: Auf Wiedersehen.	Goodbye.

This very rudimentary but not wholly unnatural dialogue can be handled in German with a minimum of vocabulary and grammatical forms. No one sentence depends on another. They can all stand alone and be presented in almost any order; a pair of conversation partners could ask each other where they live before asking what they are studying. They could even ask each other's name after having spoken for a while. It is not just this variation that is important. A change in the pattern is, in fact, manageable for beginners, and they should be encouraged to switch sentences and questions around when the dialogue is repeated. They are conditioned to the fact that conversation will not necessarily follow the path they have imagined. The dialogue design should try to achieve this "controlled randomness," a compromise between extemporaneous and memorized dialogue. The student knows all the things that can occur, but not the order in which they will.

Dialogues are probably best carried out by dividing the class into groups of four or by having it form one large group, each student speaking with as many others as possible in the ten or fifteen minutes allotted for practice. In any case, whether in small groups or one large "free-for-all" situation, the students must be encouraged to stand up from their seats and move about without books or notebooks. The higher noise level generates excitement while providing a screen, as it were, behind which the inhibited will feel more free to speak. The instructor should not merely stand by as an advisor, as one book recommends, but take full part, going from group to group or individual to individual (Jespersen & Peters 1980: x). This should not prevent the instructor from interrupting his or her participation to clear up a specific problem someone may be having.

One might wish to practice a dialogue like the one outlined above first in groups, then move on to the more open classroom "free-for-all," pretending that it is a party at which one gets to know as many people as possible. A straight repetition of the three questions and answers will be too tedious over a period of ten or fifteen minutes. Therefore the instructor might want to interrupt practice to add a sentence or phrase. This points to another desirable feature of practice dialogue: it should be easily expandable. One segment of the previous conversation can be enlarged by a question with the verb <u>finden</u> ("to find" in the sense of "to like"):

A: Wohnen Sie hier in W.?   Do you live here in W.?

B: Ja. (Ich wohne hier.)   Yes. (I live here.)

A: Und wie finden Sie W.?   And how do you like W.?

If the sentence one adds can be used more than one time, so much the better.

A: Was studieren Sie?   What are you studying?

B: Mathematik und Deutsch.   Mathematics and German.

A: So...Wie finden Sie   Oh...How do you find
   Mathematik?   mathematics?

B: Ach (ganz) interessant. (gut,   Oh, (fairly) interesting
   so-so, schwer)   (good, so-so, difficult)

A: Arbeiten Sie viel in Mathe?   Do you work a lot in math?

B: Ach, so-so.   Oh, so-so.

Of course this one addition is not fundamental to the exchange of words. It may be added by the speaker; no misfortune, however, if it is left out. There will be no gap that cannot be bridged. This exemplifies a corollary of "controlled randomness": if the parts of a dialogue are linked loosely enough then one part can be dropped without danger of bringing the conversation to a standstill. Again, the students must be made aware of this fact; for it, like the knowledge that the sequence of word exchanges is not crucial, will give them more self-confidence and induce them to speak freely within the bounds that have been set. At the same time it should be pointed out that a one-word response like "interessant" can be spoken several ways. At a relatively early stage therefore the language learner becomes aware of communicative elements in tone of voice and accompanying facial expressions. Similarly he will learn to appreciate the use of time fillers like <u>ja</u>, <u>na ja</u>, <u>ach</u>, and, later on, whole phrases: <u>ich glaube ...</u> ("I believe ..."), <u>ich weiss nicht</u> ("I don't know"), <u>ich bin nicht sicher</u> ("I'm not sure"), and so on. These are legitimate delaying tactics found in many languages and employed by native speakers to gain time to formulate a reply.

It has been seen that a simple three or four sentence dialogue can be significantly expanded with a minimum of extra vocabulary and grammar. Another factor to be considered in designing manageable dialogues is the reusability of dialogues or dialogue segments in conversations that occur in later practice sessions. The following dialogue, for instance, might appear several weeks into a German course after the introduction of the dative case. Each student is asked to think of names of several fictitious friends (male, female, couples). The general rule of this exercise is that the student must pretend to know at least 80% of the people he is asked about. The person he meets and speaks to is an old friend.

A: Grüss dich. Wie geht's dir? — Greetings. How are you?

B: Tag. Ach, ganz gut und dir? — Hi. Oh, quite good and you?

A: Auch gut. Du kennst doch Bruno Weber, nicht (wahr)? — Fine too. You know Bruno Weber, don't you?

B: Ja, natürlich. — Yes, of course.

A: Wie geht es ihm? — How is he?

B: Prima! — Great!

A: Das freut mich. — I'm pleased (about that).

B: Wie geht's deiner Freundin? — How's your girlfriend?

A: (Der) Irene? Na ja, so-so. — Irene? Well, so-so.

B: Nur so-so? Das tut mir leid. — Only so-so. Sorry to hear that.

etc.

The dialogue holds true to the principles of construction discussed earlier. A controlled randomness exists; parts could be left out. Yet even before the whole class gets up to practice this conversation it can be pointed out that portions from a previous dialogue can be brought in to augment this one.

A: Du kennst doch Bruno Weber? — You know B.W., don't you?

B: Ja, natürlich. — Yes, of course.

A: Wie geht's ihm? — How is he?

B: Oh ... ganz gut. — Oh ... o.k.

(A: Was macht er jetzt?) — (What is he doing now?)

B: Ja ... (Du weisst,) er studiert nicht mehr in München. Er wohnt jetzt in Frankfurt. (Ich glaube,) Er arbeitet bei IBM. (Bei IBM oder Control Data, ich bin nicht sicher.) Er findet den Job interessant, aber (ich glaube,) er findet Frankfurt nur so-so.	Well ... (You know) he isn't studying in Munich anymore. He's living in F. now. (I believe) He's working at IBM. (At IBM or Control Data, I'm not sure.) He finds the job interesting, but (I think) he only likes Frankfurt so-so.

(For this example I have chosen mainly words from previous examples. It can be assumed, however, that the student will have more material at his disposal by this time.)

Dialogues recreate--approximately at least--everyday situations. The closeness to the actual experience adds flavor. When games are used in the classroom the excitement of playing the game adds incentive to speak and can make the learner forget his inhibitions. Games may mimic true-to-life conversation or adapt it slightly. Again, a relatively limited number of sentences, one or two new grammatical elements, and a minimum of vocabulary are put to use by the players until one or, better still, several or all are successful in achieving the objective of the game. In the following example each class member writes down the days of the week on a note-size piece of paper and each one, in secret, chooses a day on which he or she is going to give a party and at the same time two days on which he or she is somehow occupied, making a brief note of the reason (work, visit Aunt Doris, etc.). The object of the game is to speak to as many persons in the class as one can and to try to get as many as possible to attend one's party. If invited on a certain day that is free one must accept, however; having agreed to attend, one cannot accept any other invitations for that day. If an invitation must be refused, an explanation must be given. The dialogue accompanying the game might look like this:

A: Ich will (möchte) Mittwoch eine Party machen. Kannst du kommen?	I want (I'd like) to give a party Wednesday. Can you come?
B: Ich möchte kommen, aber ich soll (muss) eigentlich arbeiten.	I would like to come, but I should (must) really work.
A: Schade.	Too bad.
B: Aber ich möchte Samstag eine Party machen. Willst du kommen?	But I would like to give a party on Saturday. Do you want to come?
A: Samstag? Ja. Samstag kann ich. (Ich muss nichts machen.) Wann soll ich dort sein?	Saturday? Yes. Saturday I can come. (I don't have to do anything.) When should I be there?

B: Ach, sagen wir 7 Uhr.   Oh, let's say 7 o'clock.

A: O.K. Samstag um 7 Uhr.   O.K. Saturday at 7 o'clock.

This game involving the use of modal auxiliaries to formulate invitations has a companion piece: two lists of about seven items each, one listing drinks, the other snacks, are displayed. Half the class receives slips of paper of one color, the other half slips of another. Each member of one group secretly writes down two beverages and two snacks he will accept (perhaps one beverage and one snack can even be accepted twice, the other two only once.) Everything outside the few items a player can accept must be declined (with a reason, if possible). The members of the other group each (secretly) choose two items from each list; they must offer one drink and one snack three times, the other only once. The object of the game is to see whether one can get rid of all the items one has to offer or whether one is offered the things one wishes.

Both examples just cited allow variation in the accompanying dialogue. The other necessary element is the invitation or offer and its acceptance or rejection; reasons for the latter may be omitted if the student cannot think of one quickly. The two games also show a desirable feature for all games, namely that all players interact with others at the same time, leaving no one class member exposed while others look on. The instructor, who takes part as usual, calls a halt to the game after about eight to ten minutes. The games do not have to produce a winner; it is in fact better if several players can be successful.

Playing against the clock can add a competitive note, as in the following game: the instructor distributes among the members of the class items belonging to four or five categories (some books, magazines, notebooks, pencils, and newspapers, for example), enough objects so that each player has one or two. A timer is set to ring after four or five minutes and the students ask each other to take things, hand objects over, give them away, lay them down, let them drop, pick them up, and so on. A player can only acquire or get rid of an object by request, his own or someone else's. The object of the game: whoever has two objects in hand when the bell rings is in the winning group. In the dialogue that goes with it the students practice commands or perhaps polite requests, using subjunctives and conditionals:

A. Würden (Könnten) Sie mir bitte   Would (Could) you please
    die Zeitschrift geben?   give me the magazine?

B: Dürfte (könnte) ich bitte den   Would I be allowed (Could)
   Bleistift haben (nehmen)?   I have (take) the pencil?

By supplying half the class with blue slips of paper, the other half with yellow slips (both pinned to clothing), the distinction between formal and informal form of address can be injected into the exchange. Those with slips of like color address each other with the informal form, those with slips of paper with different colors use the formal form of address. Like other dialogues those used specifically in games can possibly be expanded, in the case above, to include practice of adjective endings or relative clauses:

A: Würden Sie mir das Buch geben?	Would you give me the book?
B: Welches Buch?	Which book?
A: Das schwarze (Buch) da.	The black one (book) there.
or	
Das Buch, das Sie da haben.	The book, that you have there.

The request is not carried out until the object has been defined by an adjective or relative clause (or both).

There is a further step in dialogue practice which should be mentioned briefly, the "planned role play" (German <u>Planspiel</u>), which brings together material from a number of dialogues and games. Each member of the class is given a role and, possibly but not necessarily, a new identity. He or she receives a card which lists information and several tasks to be performed. Taking the party situation used before, the following example shows two sample cards:

You are the <u>host</u>. Name: T.W. Info: Student (Biology), hobbies: soccer, tennis. Tasks: 1. Greet your guests, ask how they are, talk with them. 2. Offer them food and drink. (Additional food and drink or anything not set out is in the fridge in the kitchen.) 3. If serving becomes too much for you, ask some of your guests to help. 3. Extra cassettes are next to tape recorder.	You are a <u>guest</u>. Name: B. R. Info: Student (History), hobbies: tennis, stamps. Tasks: 1. Meet as many people as you can and speak with them. Some (with like color name tags) you know; some (with different color tags) you don't. 2. You drink only mineral water. (If there is none, ask host.) 3. Find out where Miss Braun works. 4. Get your host to change the the rock music you don't like.

etc.

Both general and specific instructions bring the students to interact with others. Since the sentence material they are to use is not spelled out, they must rely on previous experience to find an appropriate way to cope with the problems they have been given. It is not essential that all points on the card be satisfied, nor even be dealt with in the order given. The instructor calls an end to the play after about fifteen to twenty minutes, then may wish to check to see whether the students have actually performed the various tasks assigned to them, whether student A did find out where Miss

Braun works or whether he got his mineral water in the end. At the same time it becomes evident to the class that the instructor can police the level of their activity. This threat, however, should hardly be necessary, since role-play, like games and correctly designed dialogue, should by itself offer enough stimulus to speak.

NOTE

[1] Jespersen & Peters (1980: ix) speaks of a "thematic" approach. A German text with a strong functional approach is Neuner et al. (1979).

REFERENCES

Helbling, Robert E., Wolf Gewehr, Dieter Jedan, and Wolff A. von Schmidt. First-Year German. 2nd ed. New York: Holt, Rinehart & Winston, 1979.

Jespersen, Robert C., and George F. Peters. Using German. New York: Harper & Row, 1980.

Neuner, Gerd, Wolf-Dieter Ortmann, Reiner Schmidt, and Heinz Wilms. Deutsch aktiv. Berlin: Langenscheidt, 1979.

THE METALEX PROJECT

Jonathan J. Webster
National University of Singapore

1.0 Significance of overall problem

Metalanguage is defined herein to mean those "expressions and phrases used for talking about language" (Longman Dictionary of Contemporary English). Students encounter metalanguage in the classroom to the extent that their textbook and teacher talk about or explain the workings of the English language. The curriculum designer has certain expectations for what students should learn; the teacher has certain expectations for what students can learn. To what extent are students expected to have a conceptual awareness for how language works? To what extent are they capable of understanding and talking about how language works? What we wish to study and describe is that metalanguage by which students recognize and refer to patterns of correct usage. How does the student's metalanguage compare with the curriculum designer's? What is the relationship between the teacher's expectations for what students have learned/can learn and the students' actual metalinguistic competence? Of methodological significance will be our design of a research instrument capable of assessing the students' metalinguistic competence. Of pedagogical significance will be our comparison of students' acquired repertoire and command of metalinguistic expressions with the intentions of the curriculum designer and the expectations of the teacher.

2.0 Research objectives

Initially, we hope to ascertain what the curriculum designer regards as an acceptable form of metalanguage to be used in textbooks and by the teacher for the purpose of introducing targeted grammatical items. The method of investigation here will be an analysis of texts and syllabi. In order to describe the actual use of metalanguage in the classroom, however, it will be necessary to observe and even record the teacher's metalanguage as he or she goes about the task of teaching those grammatical items targeted for instruction by the curriculum designer. The teacher's metalanguage is most likely influenced by such factors as (1) experience with and appreciation for a given orientation/approach to language as a field of study, (2) interpretation of the curriculum designer's aims and intentions, and (3) expectations regarding the students' capabilities and performance limitations.

Finally, as regards the students, we intend to assess the manner and extent of their metalinguistic development, and to ascertain the association between such development and the learners' background. The data source will be the students' responses to a specially designed test, the Learning English Grammar Survey (LEGS).

3.0 Methodology of the project
3.1 Text-based elicitation

In the ENGLISH Syllabus for the New Education System, there are 134 language items constituting the language core. As pointed out in the same text, "These (items) are listed IN GRAMMATICAL TERMS such as verbs (tenses), nouns (countable and uncountable), pronouns, adjectives, adverbs, prepositions, articles, conjunctions, concord, etc." We therefore have a ready list of targeted grammatical (language) items, and clearly the curriculum syllabus designer expects the teacher to employ this same metalanguage of the text and syllabus in the classroom.

3.2 Field-based observation

Recordings of actual class sessions will enable us to observe the teachers' metalanguage in use as they go about their task of communicating those materials provided by the curriculum/syllabus designer. Specifically our attention will be focused on the teachers' practice of naming grammatical items and explaining their role in the language.

3.3 Response-based information

Sociolinguistic research techniques and methods of data analysis have been coordinated in this study of the metalanguage associated with the instruction and learning of the English Language at various levels of education in Singapore.

3.3.1 Learning English Grammar Survey (LEGS)

Learning English Grammar Survey (LEGS) is the title of a multiple-task research design implemented for the purpose of discovering the correlation between a student's socioeducational background and the development of his metalinguistic competence. There were two primary objectives, then, to be considered in the formulation of the research design; first, to determine the manner and extent of metalinguistic development; and second, to ascertain the association between such development and the socioeducational background of the learners.

3.3.1.1 LEGS task one: Grammatical Term Association

Participants are requested to fill in fifteen slots down the middle of a page with any words or phrases which they might consider appropriate in the blank portion of the following statement to appear on the same page:

" '_____' is an example of a word or phrase which one might use in a description or explanation of English grammar."

The term 'sentence' is provided in the first slot to serve as a prompt for this term-association task.

This task is deliberately placed at the head of the LEGS task flow due to the relative ease with which most participants approach such an exercise. Moreover, as will be most obvious from the discussion of succeeding tasks, such an arrangement necessarily avoids the imposition of any bias in the selection of terms.

In the course of analyzing the data, our attention will be primarily directed toward the identification of those terms selected by more than one individual. Any observable tendency toward selection of a given term by participants is of significance and requires notice. When it becomes evident that such a tendency is characteristic of the total survey population, then it may be concluded that such terms belong to the class of terms hereafter referred to as common core metaterminology. Those terms lacking unanimity may reveal emphases characteristic of a given group or cluster of groups. It should be pointed out, however, that the failure of participants to select a term does not preclude the possibility of its use; rather it suggests the presence of other terms which are relatively more salient and therefore more likely to be cited.

3.3.1.2 LEGS task two: Odd Item Out

Participants are provided with a series of four items and asked to perform the following tasks: (1) identify the odd item; (2) describe in grammatical terms what distinguishes this item from the rest of the set; (3) state in grammatical terms how one could class the remaining members of the set; and finally (4) give a replacement item for this set. Note the example provided below:

Example: a. books
b. cup
c. pencil
d. wallet

The odd item is _____ .

How in GRAMMATICAL TERMS can you distinguish this item from the rest of the set? _____

How in GRAMMATICAL TERMS can you class the remaining members of the set? _____

Give a replacement item for this set? _____

Each O.I.O. set is designed in such a way as to test the participant's ability to recognize, name, and exemplify those grammatical items targeted for instruction by the curriculum/syllabus designer.

3.3.1.3 <u>LEGS task three: Eliciting metalinguistic expressions for grammatical processes</u>

Participants are requested to provide short-answer replies for a series of correction cum description items such as the following:

How would you describe what is grammatically incorrect about the following sentences?

1. I is happy to see you again.
2. The boys has worked hard.
3. We works from dawn to dusk.

Participants may also be asked to give a brief account describing what grammatical process is at work affecting certain grammatical changes between a given pair of sentences. For example,

What grammatical changes (excluding punctuation) are necessary to change the following sentences from _____ speech to _____ speech:

1. a. He said, "I am very tired."
   b. He said that he was very tired.
2. a. Mary said, "The customs officer is checking everything very thoroughly."
   b. Mary said that the customs officer was checking everything very thoroughly.
3. a. They said, "We will go when we have finished the exercise."
   b. They said that they would go when they had finished the exercise.

Here we are hoping to observe the students' metalanguage in use as they go about describing grammatical processes at work in the English language.

3.3.1.4 LEGS Background Questionnaire

The information obtained therefrom includes all necessary demographic data, e.g., sex, age, schools attended, information about the participant's language background and experience.

4.0 Implementing LEGS

LEGS in its initial format has already been administered to first and second year students at National University of Singapore enrolled in EL102 and EL202 (English Language) respectively; the results are presently under review.

Preliminary analysis of the responses of second year students to LEGS task one (Grammatical Term Association) and the first ten sets of task two (Odd Item Out) are presented here with discussion of the implications for future implementation of LEGS.

4.1 Tabulated Results for Grammatical Term Association:

As the frequency list below indicates, few terms evidenced as wide appeal as those which refer to parts of speech, e.g. noun, verb, adverb, adjective, etc.

TERM	FREQ	PCT
noun/noun phrase	123	63.7
verb/verb phrase	120	62.2
adjective/adjectival phrase	113	60.0
adverb/adverbial phrase/adverbials	107	57.5
clause	103	53.4
phrase	76	39.4
preposition/prepositional phrase	75	38.9
tense	73	37.8
conjunctions/conjunct	59	30.6
article	46	23.8
word	44	22.8
morpheme	39	20.2
pronoun	38	19.7
subject	37	19.2
syntax	32	16.6
adjunct	26	13.5
aspect	24	12.4
object	23	11.0
punctuation	23	11.9
phoneme	22	11.4

Also, the choice of prompt for this task, <u>sentence</u>, may have influenced respondents to select such terms as "clause," "phrase," and "word." The overall tendency among participants seems to have been to cite terms which refer to syntactically definable entities, rather than properties or processes.

4.2 Tabulated Results for Odd-Item-Out

4.2.1. a. I
b. he
c. me
d. she

```
OM01
     CODE
          I
     0.   *** (     6)
          I
          I
     1.   ******* (    23)
          I
          I
     3.   ***************************************** (       161)
          I
          I
     4.   ** (     3)
          I
          I
          I.......I.......I.......I.......I.......I
          O      40      80      120     160      200
          FREQUENCY

VALID CASES    193       MISSING CASES      0
```

As the frequency listing indicates for OM01 ("The odd item is ____"), 161 out of 187 participants (86.1%) participants identified the odd item as (c) me; of these, only 61 (37.9%) cited the fact that 'me' is an object pronoun as the distinguishing factor which sets this item apart from the rest of the set. In their own words, 'me' is a "pronoun object," "object," "objective pronoun," "object pronoun," "pronoun used at end of a sentence," "objective," "pronoun in predicate case"; also that 'me' is "objective," or in "objective case." As many as 40 (24.8%) gave no reason, with the remaining 60 offering such explanations as "reflective pronoun," "possessive pronoun," "personal pronoun," "relative pronoun," "reflexive pronoun," "first person pronoun" (note that item a is the first person subject pronoun 'I').

As for participants' ability to class the remaining members of the set, out of 161 correct responses to OM01, a total of 114 (70.8%) correctly identified the set as consisting of "pronouns," "personal pronouns," or, more significantly as being "pronoun subject," "nominative pronoun," "subjective pronoun," "subject pronoun," "subject," "subjective," "subjective case," "nominative case," "nominative," "pronoun used at beginning of a sentence."

As many as 148 respondents (91.9%) correctly substituted a subject pronoun when asked to give a replacement for the odd item. Of the 187 participants responding at all to this first set, only 12 failed to provide a replacement item.

Ranked in order of difficulty, then, as shown in OMOSCAL1, SUBSTI(tute)1 ("Give a replacement item for this set.") had the lowest percentage of error, only 12%, while OMO1 ("The odd item is ___") had slightly higher at 14%. However, both response categories in which respondents were expected to express themselves in GRAMMATICAL TERMS obtained a much higher percentage of errors than either OMO1 or SUBSTI1. We should note, however, that a nil response for either ITEMID1 ("How in GRAMMATICAL TERMS can you distinguish this item from the rest of the set?"), CLASS1 ("How in GRAMMATICAL TERMS can you class the remaining members of the set?"), or SUBSTI1 was calculated into the percentage of error. Only if one failed to identify the odd item would the case be excluded from processing. Of the 124 incorrect responses for ITEMID1, 45 were actually missing, while of the 67 incorrect responses for CLASS1, 24 were missing. In each instance, the fact that the respondent started the set but left subsequent parts blank, would seem to suggest a lack of knowledge, or at best some degree of uncertainty on the part of the respondent as to how to reply.

```
ITEM..    ITEMID1      CLASS1       OMO1         SUBSTI1
RESP..   0    1 I   0    1 I    0    1 I    0    1 I    TOTAL
      - - I -ERR- - - - -I -ERR- - - - -I -ERR- - - - -I -ERR- - - - -I
  O     I             I             I             I             I
  M  4  I   0   53I   0   53I    0   53I    0   53I       53
  O     I - - - - -ERRI             I             I             I
  S     I             I             I             I             I
  C  3  I  54    9I   4   59I    2   61I    3   60I       63
  A     I             I - - - - -ERRI             I             I
  L     I             I             I             I             I
  1  2  I  45    1I   3    8I    4   42I    5   41I       46
        I             I             I - - - - -ERRI             I
        I             I             I             I             I
     1  I  16    0I  16    0I   11    5I    5   11I       16
        I             I             I             I - - - - -ERRI
        I             I             I             I             I
     0  I   9    0I   9    0I    9    0I    9    0I        9
        I - - - - - - - -I - - - - - - - - - -I - - - - - - - - - -I - - - - - - - - -I
SUMS      124   63    67   120   26   161   22   165        187
PCTS       66   34    36    64   14    86   12    88
ERRORS      0   10     4     8    6     5   13     0         46
```

193 CASES WERE PROCESSED
6 (3.1%) WERE MISSING

STATISTICS:
COEFFICIENT OF REPRODUCIBILITY = 0.9385
MINIMUM MARGINAL REPRODUCIBILITY = 0.7620
PERCENT IMPROVEMENT = 0.1765
COEFFICIENT OF SCALABILITY = 0.7416

4.2.2   a. run
        b. sing
        c. teach
        d. life

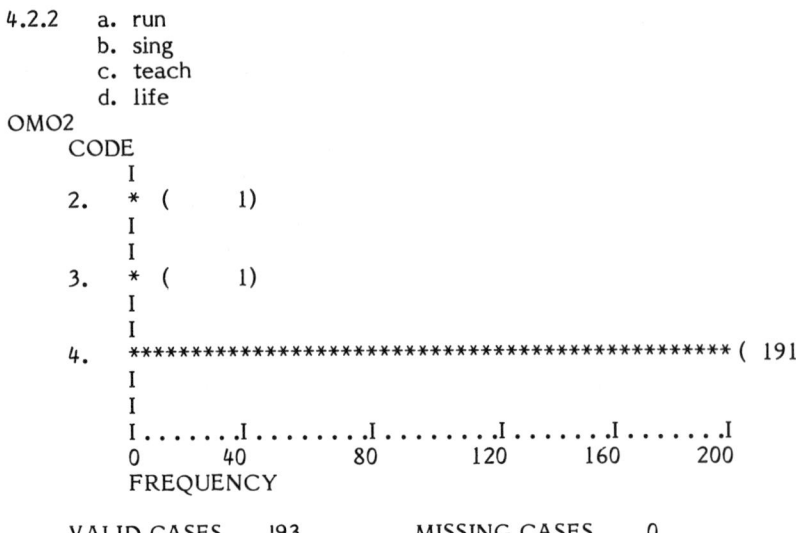

VALID CASES   193   MISSING CASES   0

Only 2 out of 193 respondents did not select (d) <u>life</u> as the odd item in the second set. Of the remaining 99%, 181 correctly took note of the fact that 'life' is a noun, 185 described the remaining members of the set as verbs, and 187 replaced the odd item with a verb. Altogether, 173 participants responded without error for each response category of the second set.

```
      ITEM..   ITEMID2    CLASS2    SUBSTI2    OMO2
      RESP..   0    1 I   0    1 I  0    1 I   0    1 I   TOTAL
             - -I-ERR- - - - -I-ERR- - - - -I-ERR- - - - -I-ERR- - - - -I
      O     I         I          I         I         I
  M   4 I   0   173I   0   173I   0   173I   0   173I   173
  O        I- - - - - -ERRI         I         I         I
  S        I         I          I         I         I
  C   3 I   8     9I   4    13I   4    13I   1    16I    17
  A        I         I- - - - - -ERRI      I         I
  L        I         I          I         I         I
  2   2 I   2     0I   2     0I   0     2I   0     2I     2
           I         I          I- - - - - -ERRI      I
           I         I          I         I         I
      1 I   0     0I   0     0I   0     0I   0     0I     0
           I         I          I         I- - - - - -ERRI
           I         I          I         I         I
      0 I   1     0I   1     0I   1     0I   1     0I     1
           I- - - - - - - - -I- - - - - - - - -I- - - - - - - - -I- - - - - - - - -I
      SUMS    11   182    7   186    5   188    2   191   193
      PCTS     6    94    4    96    3    97    1    99
      ERRORS   0     9    4     0    4     0    1     0    18
```

193 CASES WERE PROCESSED
0 (0.0%) WERE MISSING

STATISTICS:
COEFFICIENT OF REPRODUCIBILITY = 0.9767
MINIMUM MARGINAL REPRODUCIBILITY = 0.9676
PERCENT IMPROVEMENT = 0.0091
COEFFICIENT OF SCALABILITY = 0.2800

4.2.3. a. tall
        b. and
        c. heavy
        d. strong

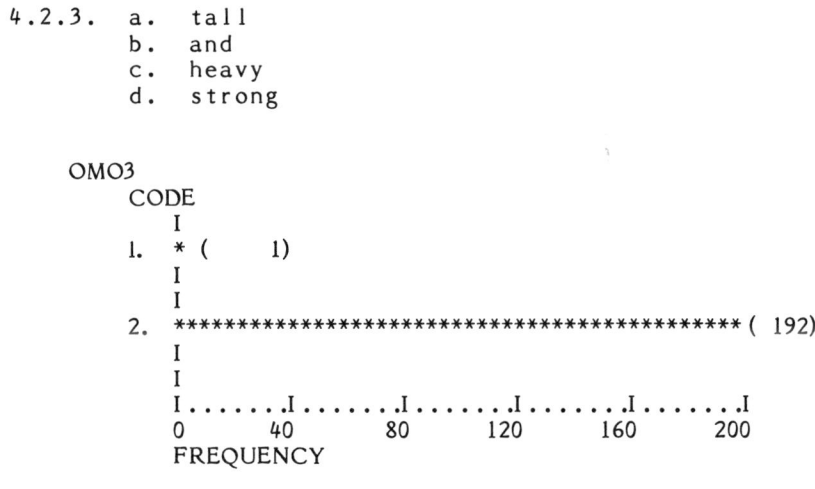

```
OM03
    CODE
        I
     1. * (     1)
        I
        I
     2. *********************************************** ( 192)
        I
        I
        I......I......I......I......I......I
        0     40    80    120   160   200
        FREQUENCY
```

VALID CASES   193   MISSING CASES   0

Similarly with OMO3, only one out of 193 respondents failed to identify (b) <u>and</u> as the odd item. Altogether 170 responded without error to each response category. They identified 'and' as being either a "conjunction," "connective," "coordinator," or "conjoining word"; they stated that the remaining members of the set were "describing words," "noun modifiers," "adjectival words," "descriptive," or simply "adjectives"; and they replaced the odd item with an adjective.

```
ITEM..   ITEMID3      SUBSTI3      CLASS3       OMO3
RESP..  0    1 I    0    1 I    0    1 I    0    1 I   TOTAL
     I-ERR-----I-ERR-----I-ERR-----I-ERR-----I
 0   I           I           I           I           I
 M 4 I    0  170I    0  170I    0  170I    0  170I    170
 O   I       ERRI           I           I           I
 S   I           I           I           I           I
 C 3 I    8   13I    8   13I    5   16I    0   21I     21
 A   I           I------ERRI           I           I
 L   I           I           I           I           I
 3 2 I    1    0I    0    1I    1    0I         1I      1
     I           I           I------ERRI           I
     I           I           I           I           I
   1 I    0    0I    0    0I    0    0I    0    0I      0
     I           I           I           I------ERRI
     I           I           I           I           I
   0 I    1    0I    1    0I    1    0I    1    0I      1
     I----------I----------I----------I----------I
SUMS     10  183      9  184      7  186      1  192    193
PCTS      5   95      5   95      4   96      1   99
ERRORS    0   13      8    1      6    0      0    0     28
```

193 CASES WERE PROCESSED
0 (0.0%) WERE MISSING

STATISTICS:
COEFFICIENT OF REPRODUCIBILITY = 0.9637
MINIMUM MARGINAL REPRODUCILIBITY = 0.9650
PERCENT IMPROVEMENT = -0.0013
COEFFICIENT OF SCALABILITY = -0.0370

4.2.4 a. my
    b. him
    c. it
    d. her

Excluding missing cases, we note that only 76.6% identified (a) my as the odd item. Of that number, 27 did not reply to ITEMID4, 34 did not reply to CASE4, and as few as 9 did not render a SUBSTI(tute). Nonetheless, there was a higher percentage of error for SUBSTI4 than any of the other response categories. As may be noticed, however, upon closer examination of the above set, the first item, my, is odd for two reasons, one being that it is a possessive adjective, the other being that it is in the first person (while the rest are all third person object pronouns). No one mentioned them as a replacement item, but then the other items were all singular in reference. 60 respondents substituted a first person object pronoun. Those indicating third person singular other-than-object pronouns were treated as having given an 'incorrect' response.

```
     OMO4
        CODE
            I
       0.  *** (     9)
            I
            I
       1.  *************************************************    (  141)
            I
            I
       2.  *** (     9)
            I
            I
       3.  ******** (    33)
            I
            I
       4.  * (     1)
            I
            I
            I
            I......I.......I........I........I.......I
            0       40      80       120      160     200
                         FREQUENCY

       VALID CASES   193        MISSING CASES   0
```

ITEM..	SUBSTI4		CLASS4		ITEMID4		OMO4		
RESP..	0	1 I	0	1 I	0	1 I	0	1 I	TOTAL
	I -ERR-	- - - - I	-ERR-	- - - - I	-ERR-	- - - - I	-ERR-	- - - I	
0 I	I		I		I			I	
M 4 I	0	30I	0	30I	0	30I	0	30I	30
O I	I - - - - - - -ERRI		I		I			I	
S I	I		I		I			I	
C 3 I	24	21I	14	31I	6	39I	1	44I	45
A I	I		I - - - - - -ERRI		I			I	
L I	I		I		I			I	
4 2 I	37	10I	35	12I	19	28I	3	44I	47
I	I		I		I - - - - - -ERRI			I	
I	I		I		I			I	
1 I	30	0I	26	4I	27	3I	7	23I	30
I	I		I		I		I - - - - - -ERRI	
I	I		I		I			I	
0 I	32	0I	32	0I	32	0I	32	0I	32
I	I- - - - - - - - - I - - - - - - - - - I - - - - - - - - - I - - - - - - - - - I
SUMS	123	61	107	77	84	100	43	141	184
PCTS	67	33	58	42	46	54	23	77	
ERRORS	0	31	14	16	25	3	11	0	100

193 CASES WERE PROCESSED
9 (4.7%) WERE MISSING

STATISTICS:
COEFFICIENT OF REPRODUCIBILITY = 0.8641
MINIMUM MARGINAL REPRODUCIBILITY = 0.6399
PERCENT IMPROVEMENT = 0.2242
COEFFICIENT OF SCALABILITY = 0.6226

In fact, however, such an analysis unjustifiably ruled against those for whom the third person versus first person distinction was more salient. Moreover, the fact that the third item (c) *it* may act as either subject or object would seem to further argue against treating *any* third person pronoun as incorrect. Thus, we revised our analysis accordingly with the outcome given below.

```
ITEM..   CLASS4        ITEMID4       OMO4          SUBSTI4
RESP..  0     1  I    0     1  I    0     1  I    0     1  I   TOTAL
      --I-ERR-----I-ERR-----I-ERR-----I-ERR-----I
0       I         I         I         I         I
M   4 I   0   51 I    0   51 I    0   51 I    0   51 I   51
0       I-----ERR I         I         I         I
S       I         I         I         I         I
C   3 I  30   18 I   11   37 I    4   44 I    3   45 I   48
A       I         I-----ERR I         I         I
L       I         I         I         I         I
4   2 I  34    7 I   29   12 I    6   35 I   13   28 I   41
        I         I         I-----ERR I         I
        I         I         I         I         I
    1 I  28    1 I   29    0 I   18   11 I   12   17 I   29
        I         I         I         I-----ERR I
        I         I         I         I         I
    0 I  15    0 I   15    0 I   15    0 I   15    0 I   15
      --I---------I---------I---------I---------I
SUMS    107   77    84   100    43   141    43   141   184
PCTS     58   42    46    54    23    77    23    77
ERRORS    0   26    11    12    10    11    28     0    98
```

193 CASES WERE PROCESSED
9 (4.7%) WERE MISSING

STATISTICS:
COEFFICIENT OF REPRODUCIBILITY = 0.8668
MINIMUM MARGINAL REPRODUCIBILITY = 0.6644
PERCENT IMPROVEMENT = 0.2024
COEFFICIENT OF SCALABILITY = 0.6032

4.2.5 a. books
       b. cup
       c. pencil
       d. wallet

OMO5
     CODE
          I
       0. ***(7)
          I
          I
       1. *** (172)
          I
          I
       2. *** (10)
          I
          I
       3. ** (2)
          I
          I
       4. ** (2)
          I
          I
          I......I......I......I......I......I
          0   40   80   120   160   200
          FREQUENCY

     VALID CASES   193   MISSING CASES   0

92% of all those responding to OMO5 correctly identified the odd item as (a) books; this odd item, moreover, was described as being plural: "plural noun," "plural form," "plural item," "plural object," "plural common noun;" while the remaining members of the set were labeled as being "singular in number." What is striking, however, is the higher percentage of errors for SUBSTI5 than for either ITEMID5 or CLASS5. Some respondents substituted other plural nouns in place of books.

```
          ITEM..  SUBST15      OMO5        ITEMID5      CLASS5
          RESP..   0    1 I   0    1 I   0    1 I   0    1 I  TOTAL
               -----I-ERR-----I-ERR-----I-ERR-----I-ERR-----I
          O    I         I         I         I         I
          M  4 I    0  154I    0  154I    0  154I    0  154I   154
          O    I------ERRI         I         I         I
          S    I         I         I         I         I
          C  3 I   14    4I    1   17I    1   17I    2   16I    18
          A    I         I------ERRI         I         I
          L    I         I         I         I         I
          5  2 I    0    1I    0    1I    1    0I    1    0I     1
               I         I         I------ERRI         I
               I         I         I         I         I
             1 I    3    7I   10    0I    9    1I    8    2I    10
               I         I         I         I------ERRI
               I         I         I         I         I
             0 I    3    0I    3    0I    3    0I    3    0I     3
               I---------I---------I---------I---------I---------I
          SUMS     20  166    14  172    14  172    14  172      186
          PCTS     11   89     8   92     8   92     8   92
          ERRORS    0   12     1    1     2    1    11    0       28
```

                193 CASES WERE PROCESSED
                  7 (3.6%) WERE MISSING

        STATISTICS..
        COEFFICIENT OF REPRODUCIBILITY = 0.9624
        MINIMUM MARGINAL REPRODUCIBILITY = 0.9167
        PERCENT IMPROVEMENT = 0.0457
        COEFFICIENT OF SCALABILITY = 0.5484

4.2.6   a. to
          b. in
          c. under
          d. a

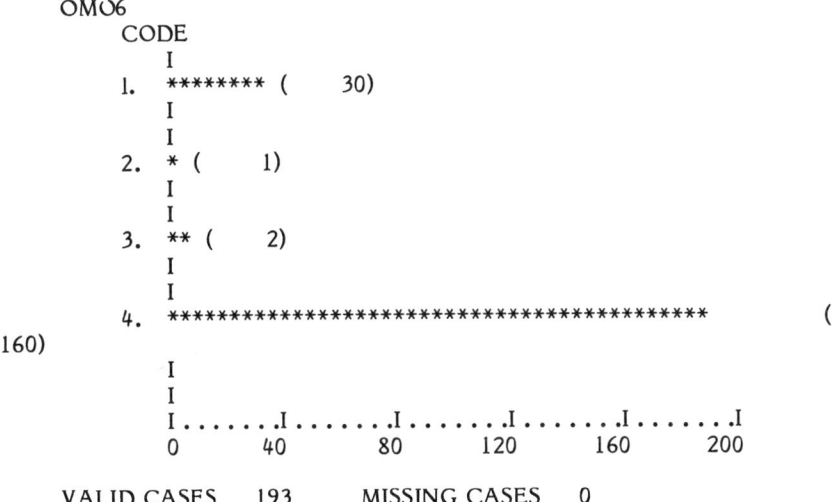

```
OMO6
        CODE
            I
       1.   ******** (     30)
            I
            I
       2.   * (       1)
            I
            I
       3.   ** (      2)
            I
            I
       4.   ******************************************         (
160)
            I
            I
            I......I......I......I......I......I
            0      40     80     120    160    200
       VALID CASES   193      MISSING CASES    0
```

A total of 160 respondents (83%) identified the odd item as (d) a. OMOSCAL6 would seem to indicate, however, a higher percentage of errors in the OMO6 category than in any other. The reason appears to have more to do with the design of the questionaire and subsequent tabulation of results than with the actual question itself. Note, for example, the curious tendency for respondents to select (a) to as the odd item, while at the same time obtaining correct answers for ITEMID6 ("article"), CLASS6 ("prepositions") and even SUBSTI6. What most likely happened is that some respondents while in the process of completing OMO6 actually placed the item itself, the article 'a', in the blank portion (of the statement, "The odd item is _____."), so that during tabulation what had in fact been a reference to the article 'a' was treated as the item label (a) for the preposition 'to'.

		ITEM..	OMO6		ITEMID6		CLASS6		SUBSTI6		TOTAL
		RESP..	0	1 I	0	1 I	0	1 I	0	1 I	
		-----I	-ERR-----I		-ERR-----I		-ERR-----I		-ERR-----I		
0		I		I		I		I		I	
M	4	I	0	137 I	0	137 I	0	137 I	0	137 I	137
O		I	------ERR I		I		I		I		
S		I		I		I		I		I	
C	3	I	26	16 I	7	35 I	6	36 I	3	39 I	42
A		I		I ------ERR I		I		I		
L		I		I		I		I		I	
6	2	I	6	6 I	8	4 I	7	5 I	3	9 I	12
		I		I		I ------ERR I		I		
		I		I		I		I		I	
	1	I	1	1 I	1	1 I	2	0 I	2	0 I	2
		I		I		I		I ------ERR I		
		I		I		I		I		I	
	0	I	0	0 I	0	0 I	0	0 I	0	0 I	0
		I----------I----------I----------I----------I							
SUMS			33	160	16	177	15	178	8	185	193
PCTS			17	83	8	92	8	92	4	96	
ERRORS			0	23	7	5	13	0	8	0	56

193 CASES WERE PROCESSED
0 (0.0%) WERE MISSING

STATISTICS:
COEFFICIENT OF REPRODUCIBILITY = 0.9275
MINIMUM MARGINAL REPRODUCIBILITY = 0.9067
PERCENT IMPROVEMENT = 0.0207
COEFFICIENT OF SCALABILITY = 0.2222

We have attempted to remedy the situation though, by reassigning a positive value to the first item. Note the revised listing for OMOSCAL6 given as follows:

```
          ITEM..   ITEMID6      CLASS6      SUBSTI6       CMO6
          RESP..  0    1 I    0    1 I    0    1 I    0    1 I  TOTAL
                 -I-ERR-----I-ERR-----I-ERR-----I-ERR-----I
       O          I         I         I         I         I
       M    4 I   0   162I   0   162I   0   162I   0   162I   162
       O          I------ERRI         I         I         I
       S          I         I         I         I         I
       C    3 I  10    12I   7    15I   4    18I   1    21I    22
       A          I------ERRI         I         I         I
       L          I         I         I         I         I
       6    2 I   5     2I   6     1I   2     5I   1     6I     7
                 I         I         I-------ERRI         I
                 I         I         I         I         I
            1 I   1     1I   2     0I   2     0I   1     1I     2
                 I         I         I         I------ERRI
                 I         I         I         I         I
            0 I   0     0I   0     0I   0     0I   0     0I     0
                 I---------I---------I---------I---------I
       SUMS      16   177    15   178    8   185     3   190    193
       PCTS       8    92     8    92    4    96     2    98
       ERRORS     0    15     7     1    6     0     3     0     32
```

193 CASES WERE PROCESSED
0 (0.0%) WERE MISSING

STATISTICS:
COEFFICIENT OF REPRODUCIBILITY = 0.9585
MINIMUM MARGINAL REPRODUCIBILITY = 0.9456
PERCENT IMPROVEMENT = 0.0130
COEFFICIENT OF SCALABILITY = 0.2381

4.2.7   a. must
           b. be
           c. may
           d. will

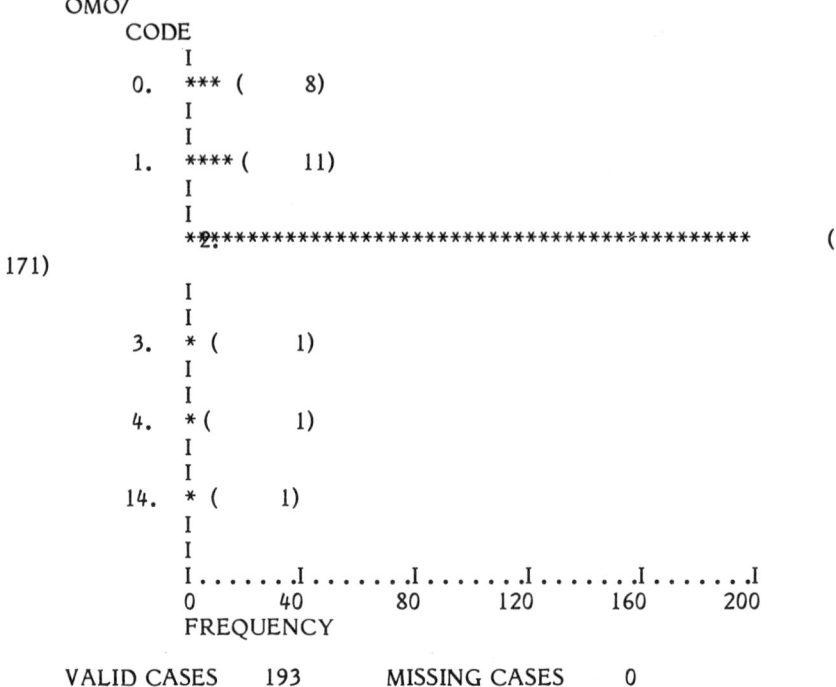

OMO7 was designed to test participants' ability to distinguish between the verb 'to be' and the modals. Nearly 20% of those correctly citing item (b) as the odd item, had difficulty with response categories ITEMID7 and CLASS7, while only 6.5% substituted an item other than a modal verb. As many as 24 respondents (over half those responding 'in error' to CLASS7) failed to give any answer at all for CLASS7.

ITEM RESP	CLASS7 0	CLASS7 1	ITEMID7 0	ITEMID7 1	SUBSTI7 0	SUBSTI7 1	OMO7 0	OMO7 1	TOTAL
	-ERR-		-ERR-		-ERR-		-ERR-		
M O S C A L 7 4	0	109	0	109	0	109	0	109	109
	------ERR								
3	17	26	17	26	6	37	3	40	43
			------ERR						
2	19	4	19	4	5	18	3	20	23
					------ERR				
1	7	0	6	1	3	4	5	2	7
							------ERR		
0	3	0	3	0	3	0	3	0	3
SUMS	46	139	45	140	17	168	14	171	185
PCTS	25	75	24	76	9	91	8	92	
ERRORS	0	30	17	5	11	4	11	0	78

193 CASES WERE PROCESSED
8 (4.1%) WERE MISSING

STATISTICS:
COEFFICIENT OF REPRODUCIBILITY = 0.8946
MINIMUM MARGINAL REPRODUCIBILITY = 0.8351
PERCENT IMPROVEMENT = 0.0595
COEFFICIENT OF SCALABILITY = 0.3607

4.2.8   a. tall
        b. thin
        c. shorter
        d. kind

```
OMO8
    CODE
        I
     0. * (      1)
        I
        I
     1. * (      1)
        I
        I
     2. * (      1)
        I
        I
     3. ********************************************** (   184)
        I
        I
     4. *** (    6)
        I
        I
        I......I......I......I......I......I......I
        0      40     80    120    160    200

VALID CASES   193         MISSING CASES   0
```

Just over 95% of the respondents selected item (c) <u>shorter</u> as the odd item. 19 of that number failed to describe the odd item as being the "comparative form"; instead, they either left the item blank (2.6%) or made some reply, e.g. "superlative," "adverb," etc. As many as 12 respondents did not even reply to CLASS8; 126 described the remaining members of the set as "adjectives," 24 referred to them as "positive adjectives," while others mentioned "noncomparative adjective," "adjective of the first order," etc. Four respondents who picked (c) still entered a comparative adjective for SUBSTI8; whereas 174 substituted a "noncomparative" adjective in the SUBSTI8 slot.

```
ITEM..      ITEMID8      CLASS8       SUBSTI8       OMO8
RESP..    0     1 I    0     1 I    0     1 I    0     1 I    TOTAL
       -----I-ERR-----I-ERR-----I-ERR-----I-ERR-----I
  O    I          I          I          I          I
M 4 I      0   144I    0   144I    0   144I    0   144I     144
  O    I------ERRI          I          I          I
  S    I          I          I          I          I
  C 3 I    11    22I   12    22I    9    24I    1    32I      33
  A    I          I------ERRI          I          I
  L    I          I          I          I          I
  8 2 I     8     0I    7     1I    0     8I    1     7I       8
       I          I          I------ERRI          I
       I          I          I          I          I
    1 I     6     1I    6     1I    3     4I    6     1I       7
       I          I          I          I------ERRI
       I          I          I          I          I
    0 I     0     0I    0     0I    0     0I    0     0I       0
       I----------I----------I----------I----------I
SUMS        25   167      25   167     12   180      8   184     192
PCTS        13    87      13    87      6    94      4    96
ERRORS       0    23      12     2      9     4      8     0      58
```

193 CASES WERE PROCESSED
1 (0.5%) WERE MISSING

STATISTICS:
COEFFICIENT OF REPRODUCIBILITY = 0.9245
MINIMUM MARGINAL REPRODUCIBILITY = 0.9089
PERCENT IMPROVEMENT = 0.0156
COEFFICIENT OF SCALABILITY = 0.1714

4.2.9   a. John has moved to Canada
        b. I had planned to go, but . . .
        c. I have taught here for three years.
        d. Sam has good intentions, but . . .

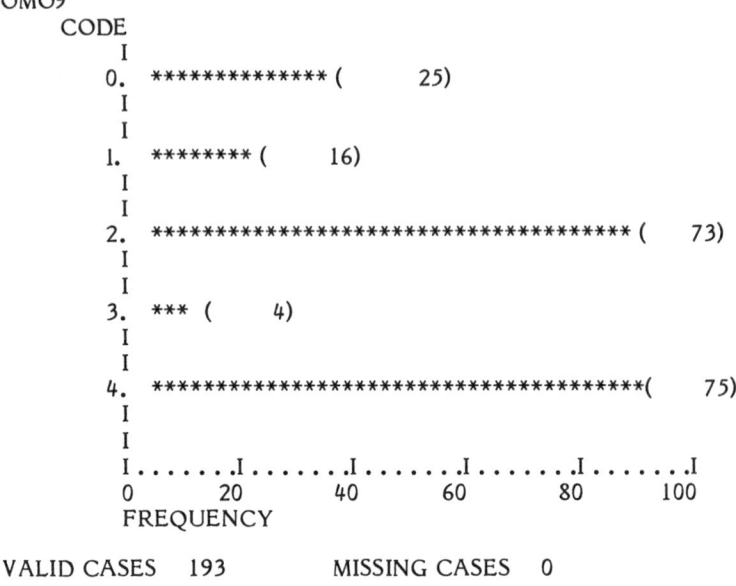

Respondents split quite evenly between items (b) and (d). Those who identified (b) <u>I had planned to go, but</u> . . . as the odd item did so for the following reasons: "past tense" (18 respondents), "past perfect" (17), "past perfect tense" (20), etc. They described the remaining members of the set as being "present" (21), or "present perfect" (33)--evidently not noticing that (d) is not present perfect. When it came to substituting a replacement for the odd item, as many as 60 (out of the 73 that cited (b) as the odd item), or 82.2% wrote in a sentence in present perfect. While one cannot classify all members of the set as being present perfect, this is considered an acceptable substitute because it is present, not past tense.

		CLASS9		ITEMID9		OMO9		SUBSTI9		TOTAL
ITEM.. RESP..		0	1	0	1	0	1	0	1	
		-ERR		-ERR		-ERR		-ERR		
M O S C A L 9	4	0	21	0	21	0	21	0	21	21
		-ERR								
	3	35	4	1	38	1	38	2	37	39
		-ERR								
	2	15	2	12	5	6	11	1	16	17
						-ERR				
	1	59	0	58	1	56	3	4	55	59
								-ERR		
	0	32	0	32	0	32	0	32	0	32
SUMS		141	27	103	65	95	73	39	129	168
PCTS		84	16	61	39	57	43	23	77	
ERRORS		0	6	1	6	7	3	7	0	30

193 CASES WERE PROCESSED
25 (13.0%) WERE MISSING

STATISTICS:
COEFFICIENT OF REPRODUCIBILITY = 0.9554
MINIMUM MARGINAL REPRODUCIBILITY = 0.6964
PERCENT IMPROVEMENT = 0.2589
COEFFICIENT OF SCALABILITY = 0.8529

On the other hand, those who chose (d) as the odd item, cited the following reason: "present tense" (31), "lexical verb" (1), "is not followed by a verb" (1), "one place structure verb" (3), "main verb" (1), "not in perfective aspect" (1), etc. The remaining members of the set were described as being "past" (10)--neglecting to note the present perfect in (a)--"perfect tense" (16), "2 place verb structure" (4), "perfective" (2), "perfective aspect" (2), etc. Altogether 48 respondents substituted a replacement in present perfect. Four put theirs in simple past; seven employed past perfect.

```
ITEM..   CLASS9        ITEMID9       OMO9          SUBSTI9
RESP..   0     1  I    0     1  I   0     1  I    0     1  I    TOTAL
-----I-ERR-----I-ERR-----I-ERR-----I-ERR-----I
   O     I           I           I           I           I
M  4 I   0    29 I   0    29 I   0    29 I   0    29 I    29
   O     I------ERR I          I           I           I
   S     I           I           I           I           I
   C  3 I  11    10 I   7    14 I   1    20 I   2    19 I    21
   A     I           I------ERR I          I           I
   L     I           I           I           I           I
   9  2 I  14     4 I  12     6 I   4    14 I   6    12 I    18
         I           I           I------ERR I          I
         I           I           I           I           I
      1 I  74     0 I  73     1 I  62    12 I  13    61 I    74
         I           I           I           I------ERR I
         I           I           I           I           I
      0 I  26     0 I  26     0 I  26     0 I  26     0 I    26
         I----------I----------I----------I----------I
SUMS    125   43    118   50    93   75    47  121           168
PCTS     74   26     70   30    55   45    28   72
ERRORS    0   14      7    7     5   12    21    0            66
```

193 CASES WERE PROCESSED
25 (13.0%) WERE MISSING

STATISTICS:
COEFFICIENT OF REPRODUCIBILITY = 0.9018
MINIMUM MARGINAL REPRODUCIBILITY = 0.6801
PERCENT IMPROVEMENT = 0.2217
COEFFICIENT OF SCALABILITY = 0.6930

4.2.10 a. Bob is a tall man
        b. Paul is a nice man.
        c. John is a Canadian.
        d. She was born in Canada.

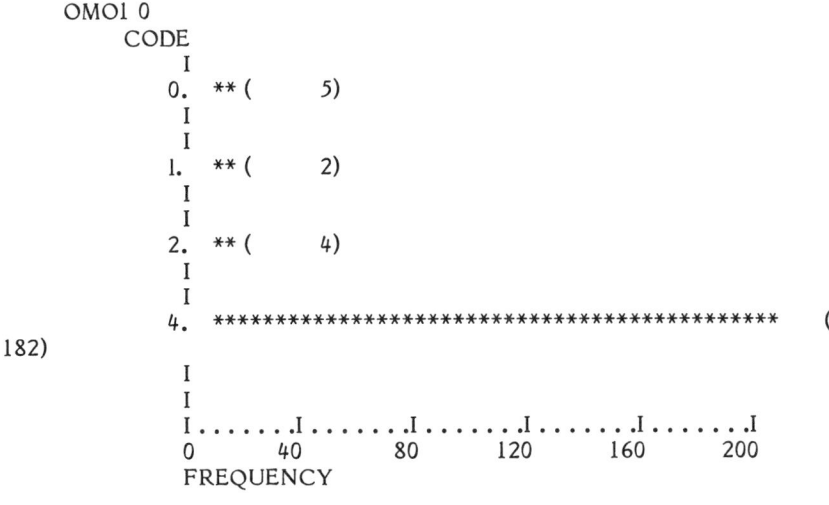

VALID CASES   193   MISSING CASES   0

182 respondents (94.3%) correctly identified (d) <u>She was born in Canada</u> as the odd item. Responding to ITEMID10, they offered the following explanations: "past tense" (88 respondents), "passive" (12), "past perfect" (2), "past tense plus perfective aspect" (1), "prepositional phrase" (1). Altogether 91 participants described the other items in the set as being "present," while 144 substituted a replacement in simple present for SUBSTI10. Five respondents, however, substituted a replacement in simple past.

```
ITEM..   ITEMID10    CLASS10     SUBSTI10    OMO10
RESP..   0    1  I   0    1  I   0    1  I   0    1  I   TOTAL
-----I-ERR-----I-ERR-----I-ERR-----I-ERR-----I
O        I           I           I           I           I
M   4 I  0    107I   0    107I   0    107I   0    107I   107
O        I------ERRI           I           I           I
S        I           I           I           I           I
C   3 I  24    19I   8     35I   10    33I   1     42I   43
A        I           I------ERRI           I           I
L        I           I           I           I           I
1   2 I  26     0I   20     6I   5     21I   1     25I   26
         I           I           I------ERRI           I
         I           I           I           I           I
    1 I  10     0I   9      1I   9      1I   2      8I   10
         I           I           I           I------ERRI
         I           I           I           I           I
    0 I  2      0I   2      0I   2      0I   2      0I
         I----------I----------I----------I----------I
SUMS     62   126    39   149    26   162    6    182    188
```

PCTS	33	67	21	79	14	86	3	97	
ERRORS	0	19	8	7	15	1	4	0	54

193 CASES WERE PROCESSED
5 (2.6%) WERE MISSING

STATISTICS:
COEFFICIENT OF REPRODUCIBILITY = 0.9282
MINIMUM MARGINAL REPRODUCIBILITY = 0.8231
PERCENT IMPROVEMENT = 0.1051
COEFFICIENT OF SCALABILITY = 0.5940

4.3 Interpretation of Data

As the above data analysis has shown, respondents evidenced less difficulty with those sets where the focus of recognition was on parts of speech, e.g., noun, verb, conjunction, adjective, article, prepositions, rather than on syntactic properties or processes. Moreover, although respondents may have been unable to describe the odd item or other members of the set in metalinguistic terms, some were still able to recognize the odd item and provide a suitable replacement.

Our analysis also revealed certain sets, e.g. OMO9, characterized by more than one dimension of contrast. Where recognized, steps need to be taken to enhance the singularity of focus in each set.

5.0 Benefits to be derived from this project

If we agree that the primary objective of language instruction should be to inculcate the skills necessary to enable the student to operate effectively in society; if we agree on the importance of teaching students to recognize grammatical items and produce patterns of correct usage in order to achieve the primary objective, then we must agree on the need to attach significance to the means whereby the curriculum/syllabus designer, teacher, and student all choose to refer to these same grammatical items and processes.

In order to achieve our objectives, steps must be taken to facilitate the continuity and elevate the quality of feedback along the chain of instruction from the learner to the teacher to the curriculum/syllabus designer. For this reason, we wish to observe, as objectively as possible, pupils' ability to recognize, name and produce targeted grammatical items. Having done so, we may then compare teachers' expectations for their students' capabilities with their actual performance. In her study of the relationship between teachers' expectations and students' knowledge of mathematical terminology for the elementary grades, Elwanda B. Murphey concluded "that teachers are not adequately diagnosing students' knowledge of mathematical terms." How accurate are teachers' expectations regarding their students' abilities to recognize, name, and produce targeted grammatical items?

Next, we wish to compare students' use of metalanguage with that of their teachers and the curriculum/syllabus designer. To what extent are they shared systems? To what extent do pupils acquire their own private metalanguage? To what extent is their metalanguage indicative of faulty or incomplete learning? Failure to diagnose pupils' misuse of text and classroom metalanguage, in effect, perpetuates a "confusion of tongues" which may defeat the educator's purpose for introducing such items and terms in the first place.

Forthcoming from the METALEX project, then, should be valuable insight into the nature of metalanguage in use with important implications for future syllabus design and classroom instruction. Moreover, with this increased awareness among educators of the form and function of metalanguage in the classroom, there should be some movement toward a standardization of metalinguistic terms of reference.

REFERENCE

Murphy, Elwanda Bray. The Relationship between Teacher's Expectations and Students' Knowledge of Mathematical Terminology for the Elementary Grades. Ed.D. dissertation, Northwestern State University of Louisiana, 1980.

PRACTICAL APPLICATIONS OF CURRENT LINGUISTIC AND
PSYCHOLOGICAL THEORIES ON SECOND LANGUAGE
ACQUISITION

Kurt Kraetschmer
University of Nebraska at Omaha

In spite of ongoing research in psychology and linguistics, it is still impossible to explain how a child learns to comprehend, speak, read, and write his or her mother tongue. The way in which a person acquires a second, third, fourth, or even more languages is an even greater puzzle. Although psychologists and linguists are making intensive efforts to explore mental and cerebral processes connected with language production and perception, it is still virtually impossible to explain in scientific (i.e., neurophysiological) terms what happens if a person "acquires" one or several languages. Certainly, numerous theories and hypotheses have already been proposed to elucidate this or that aspect of first and second language acquisition; yet, hitherto proposed explanations are highly hypothetical and cannot be validated on the basis of scientific data.

Given our ignorance concerning both first and second language acquisition, it is not surprising to see an incessant appearance and disappearance of methods designed for language learning. Again and again, one hears the claim that a method has been developed that provides the most efficient way of learning a language and enables the learner to reach optimal competence with a minimum amount of time and effort. Some of the most notorious methods utilized in past language instruction have been labeled as "Direct Method," "Grammar Translation Method," and "Audiolingual Method." More recently, "Community Language Learning" has been advocated, and claims have been made that such methods as "The Silent Way," "Suggestopedia," and "Total Physical Response" greatly exceed the efficacy of traditional methods. For example, the so-called "Thomas method," offered at private language centers in Beverly Hills, Washington, D.C., and New York City, boasts that it can teach anyone how to speak, read, and write German, French, or Spanish in just ten days.[1] Proponents of "Superlearning" make equally tenacious claims:

> At Iowa State University, students learned a whole semester of Spanish in two weeks--seven times faster than usual, and they had fun learning. In Washington, D.C., students learned Latin in a fraction of the usual time. In California, students learned a Slavic language three times faster. The U.S. Navy Atlantic Fleet Training Center in Virginia reported good results with an accelerated learning project. (Ostrander & Schroeder 1979: 45)

In view of such claims, it is imperative to determine whether there really exists a discrepancy in the efficacy of various methods used in second language instruction, or whether unexpected results can be achieved with any method, given optimal learning environment and motivation of the student. At the moment it is impossible to answer this question because presently available data are insufficient to permit a comparison of the results obtained with various methods. What is possible, however, is to identify those factors that seem to be mainly responsible for the alleged superiority of certain innovative approaches to second language learning and teaching. This paper attempts to accomplish this task by analyzing critically the main principles of those methods which make the strongest claims and by furnishing an explanation for the usefulness of certain teaching and learning techniques. In doing so, the paper focuses first on psychological parameters of the problem and then on neurolinguistic parameters.

1. Psychological Parameters

In a general fashion, one might state that the idea of student-centered (as opposed to teacher-centered) learning could be the cause for the unprecedented results obtained in some of the innovative approaches. The heightened awareness of students' individual needs and abilities may be the result of recent movements in psychology and linguistics. In psychology, we have seen the trend away from Skinner's behaviorism towards "cognitive psychology." In linguistics, Chomsky's generative/transformational grammar has superseded ideas of structural linguists such as Bloomfield, Sapir, and others. Probably even more influential for the pedagogical practice in language teaching are the ideas of such authors as Carl Rogers (1951) who advocate "client-centered" therapy. Rogers's ideas, which emphasize the "fully functioning person," lead one to believe that many traditional methods--not only in language instruction, but also in other pedagogical areas--placed too much emphasis on one specific style of learning which favored one type of student and neglected other types.

What has been brought to the fore in recent approaches to second language learning is the total involvement of the learners, i.e., the development of their intellectual capacities as well as the fulfillment of their affective and emotional needs. Thus, motivating the student not only on the intellectual level but also on the emotional and affective levels has become a central task in language instruction. The way in which this total involvement or "holistic learning" is accomplished differs from method to method; yet certain techniques have been developed that are widely used and seem to have gained worldwide recognition.

1.1. Biofeedback

The idea that a relaxed state enables the learner to achieve better results in his intellectual pursuits is possibly as old as some of the most ancient meditation techniques. To date, several techniques have been proposed for reaching a relaxed state, and they can be classified in the following fashion: 1. pharmaceutical agents; 2. progressive relaxation; 3. transcendental meditation; 4. electromyographic feedback.

Among the teaching methods which attach primary importance to relaxation, suggestopedy deserves special mention. According to Lozanov (1978: 258), "joy, absence of tension and concentrative psycho-relaxation" is the most fundamental principle of suggestopedic learning. The importance of the relaxed state of the learner, underscored by Lozanov and proponents of "superlearning," has recently been brought into focus by research in speech and language rehabilitation. DiSimoni (1981: 345), for example, in his discussion of alternative and augmentative intervention strategies, states: "Biofeedback is a promising alternative nonlinguistic approach to the rehabilitation of language which is yet in its germinal state." The research by Guiora, Brannon, and Dull (1972) seems to point in the same direction. Guiora's psychoanalytically oriented research on empathy, language-ego, and inhibition apparently vindicates increased utilization of relaxation techniques in second language instruction.

1.2. Role-playing.

A second strategy that seems capable of increasing the effectiveness of second language instruction is the involvement of the learner through role-playing. Recently, some of the psychosocial benefits of role-playing have been pointed out by Stern (1980) who argues that role-playing contributes to heightened self-esteem and self-confidence, increased capacity for empathy, and lowered sensitivity to rejection.

What is particularly interesting are the parallels that exist among role-playing, psychodrama, and therapeutic techniques in psychoanalysis. Sigmund Freud's exploration of the subconscious and the "Unbewusste" has been accomplished through techniques very similar to some of those used in role-playing. One of the recent movements in psychoanalysis, Lacan's "école de la cause," continued Freud's efforts by integrating linguistics into psychoanalysis, and presents as one of its key principles the idea that "le sujet se constitue par le langage."[2]

Role-playing is definitely not an invention of contemporary pedagogy in second language instruction, but has been utilized for a considerable time in traditional methods. Yet its value has been reaffirmed by so-called "communicative" approaches which consider the student's ability to communicate more important than his mastery of grammar rules. As obvious, role-playing can be an excellent means to motivate a student's creative potential. The emphasis on developing the student's creative abilities is actually another element that seems to enhance the efficacy of instruction.

1.3. Multimodality and multisensory activities.

The utilization of the student's creative abilities in several areas has become an important factor in recent approaches to second language learning. Multimodality and multisensory activities, such as dancing, singing, skits, cooking demonstrations, etc., can enhance considerably a student's motivation by allowing him to integrate his personal interests into the learning process. It goes without saying that all these activities lend themselves to valuable practice of grammar, vocabulary, pronunciation, semantics, and phonology.

Besides the above mentioned parameters of second language instruction characteristic of recent approaches, which can be most adequately examined from the perspective of psychology, there are other parameters which can be investigated from the viewpoint of linguistics, especially psycholinguistics and neurolinguistics.

2. Linguistic Parameters

Since the appearance of Albert and Obler's (1978) study of the bilingual brain, it has become obvious that psycholinguistic and neurolinguistic considerations can be highly relevant to second language learning and teaching. What has become particularly clear during recent years is the importance of neurophysiological processes to both language acquisition and language use. Unfortunately, our present knowledge is insufficient to explain all the neural processes that occur when a person acquires, uses, or loses--due to brain injury--one or more languages. In spite of Lenneberg's (1967) pioneering work on the biological foundations of language and ever increasing research on aphasia, apraxia, agnosia, and other speech and language impairments, we are still ignorant concerning the ways in which the human brain accomplishes the many stages of language processing. The answers that have been proposed so far are to a large extent speculations, and one must exercise caution in subscribing to assumptions that are frequently made nowadays without sufficient scientific validation. What is particularly difficult to answer is the question of brain functions and second language acquisition. Given our fragmentary and sometimes contradictory information about language organization in the monolingual brain, investigation of bilingual brain functions is a challenging enterprise indeed.

Despite a considerable lack of scientific evidence, authors have not refrained from proposing solutions to various questions concerning brain functions and language processing. Some time ago, Walsh and Diller (1978) attempted to provide a neurolinguistic foundation to methods of teaching a second language. These authors examined how various methods, e.g., Direct Method, Multiple Approach of de Sauze, and Winitz and Reeds' method ("Rapid Acquisition of a Foreign Language by the Avoidance of Speaking"), activate different areas of the cerebral cortex. In their conclusion, Walsh and Diller (1978: 13) emphasize the current lack of knowledge and present only a hypothetical finding: "...very different neural pathways and mechanisms are employed by students using different methods of language teaching." In a more recent study, Walsh and Diller (1981) proposed neurolinguistic considerations on the optimum age for second language learning. In this study too, they reach only a speculative conclusion stating that there might be certain neurolinguistic advantages of early bilingualism, although superior language learning capabilities can be found in adults, too.

Like most authors, Walsh and Diller focus on the left cerebral hemisphere and do not pay sufficient attention to the potential capacities of the right hemisphere. Yet, in the aftermath of Albert and Obler's (1978) study, one has reason to believe that increased recruitment of the right hemisphere might lead to heightened efficacy of second language learning. Although it is still difficult to prove in neurophysiological terms the potential value of so-called "right hemisphere strategies" (e.g., music, kinesthetic and visuospatial activities, rhymes, rhythmic exercises), past and present pedagogical practice gives strong support to the claim that utilization of such strategies can enhance the effectiveness of second language learning.

Several authors have already recognized the usefulness of learning techniques which, from a neurolinguistic perspective, might be labeled as "right hemisphere strategies." Thus, authors like Schulz, Burkey, Vogel, and Morris (1982) have proposed textbooks that integrate a variety of diverse elements (pictures, songs, drawings, and communicative language forms) and constitute excellent learning aids. From a neurolinguistic viewpoint, it is obvious that extensive use of these elements can make the learning process more efficient by involving not only the left hemisphere, which contains the main language centers in most individuals, but also the right hemisphere, whose linguistic capacities are still not fully explored despite intensive research by such authors as Krashen (1976) and Searleman (1977).

The strongest and most convincing support for the potential usefulness of right hemisphere strategies for language learning comes from speech and language rehabilitation. According to proponents of the so-called "Melodic Intonation Therapy," developed by Sparks, Helm, and Albert (1974), it is the recruitment of the right hemisphere that warrants success in the treatment of speech and language impaired patients. Thus, Sparks (1981: 265) states: "Research strongly suggests that the right hemisphere is involved in processing the prosody of propositional language as well as nonpropositional utterances."

It must be left to future research to explore the full potential of each of the two hemispheres and their interactions during first and second language acquisition processes. For this exploration, intensive cooperation among psychologists, speech pathologists, and language teachers seems highly desirable. Although psychologists have the equipment to design sophisticated experiments suitable for examining various cognitive processes, their data have only limited validity unless they can be corroborated by data obtained in real life situations; and it is the language teacher who is in a position to provide such data. By the same token, speech and language pathologists are capable of furnishing information on language processing in the abnormal brain, and can thus shed light on various aspects of language acquisition or reacquisition which go unnoticed in observations of the normal brain.

3. Conclusion

As the foregoing discussion has shown, second language learning is an extremely complex process, and many areas of research are needed to advance present-day knowledge concerning cognitive and neurophysiological processes relevant to this process. Improving the efficacy of second language instruction necessitates the joint effort of psychologists, linguists, and language teachers. The last especially are in a position to make valuable contributions to ongoing research, because they can validate on the practical level what others propose as theoretical assumptions.

NOTES

[1] For an interesting comment on this method, see the Magazine of United Airlines, October 1982, p. 10.

[2] The reader interested in Lacan's work is encouraged to consult the original French texts.

REFERENCES

Albert, Martin, and Loraine Obler. The Bilingual Brain. New York: Academic Press, 1978.

DiSimoni, Frank. "Therapies Which Utilize Alternative or Augmentative Communication Systems." In Language Intervention Strategies in Adult Aphasia. Ed. Roberta Chapey. Baltimore: Williams & Wilkins, 1981, pp. 329-346.

Guiora, Alexander, Robert Brannon, and Cecilia Dull. "Empathy and Second Language Learning." Language Learning, 22 (1972), 111-130.

Krashen, S. D. "Cerebral Asymmetry." In Studies in Neurolinguistics. Ed. H. Whitaker and H. A. Whitaker. Vol. 2. New York: Academic Press, 1976, pp. 157-191.

Lacan, Jacques. Ecrits. Paris: Editions du Seuil, 1966.

Lenneberg, Eric H. The Biological Foundations of Language. New York: John Wiley & Sons, 1967.

Lozanov, Georgi. Suggestology and Outlines of Suggestopedy. New York: Gordon and Breach, 1978.

Ostrander, Sheila and Lynn Schroeder. Superlearning. New York: Dell Publishing Co., 1979.

Rogers, Carl. Client Centered Therapy. Boston: Houghton Mifflin Company, 1951.

Schulz, R., R. Burkey, U. Vogel, and M. Morris. Lesen, Lachen, Lernen. New York: Holt, Rinehart and Winston, 1982.

Searleman, Alan. "A Review of Right Hemisphere Linguistic Capabilities." Psychological Bulletin, 84 (1977), 503-528.

Sparks, Robert. "Melodic Intonation Therapy." In Language Intervention Strategies in Adult Aphasia. Ed. Roberta Chapey. Baltimore: Williams & Wilkins, 1981, pp. 265-282.

_____, N. Helm, and M. Albert. "Aphasia Rehabilitation Resulting from Melodic Intonation Therapy." Cortex, 10 (1974), 303-316.

Stern, Susan. "Drama in Second Language Learning from a Psycholinguistic Perspective." Language Learning, 30 (1980), 77-100.

Walsh, Terrence, and Karl Diller. "Neurolinguistic Foundations to Methods of Teaching a Second Language." IRAL, 16 (1978), 1-14.

_____. "Neurolinguistic Considerations on the Optimum Age for Second Language Learning." In Individual Differences & Universals in Language Learning Aptitude. Ed. Karl Diller. Rowley, Ma.: Newbury House, 1981, pp. 3-21.

INTENSIVE LANGUAGE PROGRAMS: PAST, PRESENT, AND FUTURE

John J. Deveny, Jr.
Oklahoma State University

Although the term "intensive language instruction" remains largely undefined (Benseler & Schulz 1979: 9), the intensive language experience has become an important force in contemporary education. References to such programs in the professional literature date back nearly sixty-five years, and approximately forty years ago national defense requirements gave intensive programs the impetus they needed to become established as an efficient, effective, and very usable form of foreign language instruction. Under the aegis of such pragmatic considerations, the intensive experience took a form which, even after several decades of evolution, is still discernible today in many such programs (Benseler & Schulz 1979: 1-2).[1]

A review of current literature on intensive programs reveals that, by and large, they tend to be given in French, German, and Spanish. There are notable exceptions, however: in Canada, for instance, where French immersion programs abound, there are also to be found intensive programs in Hebrew. At Concordia College, in Minnesota, we find summer intensive language camps which offer intensive instruction not only in the "big three" languages, but also in Norwegian, Russian, and Swedish. In Ireland, there are intensive Irish language programs. And at Oklahoma State University, we have a summer intensive program offered in Chinese.

The instructional efficiency and immediate effectiveness of such programs are well known and are undoubtedly main factors in the continued flourishing of intensive programs. An intensive language program, although extremely rewarding to most students, is also extremely taxing. The amount of time and energy which students typically devote to an intensive language course far exceeds the time and energy that they would devote to their regular studies. The fatigue factor thus generated, which must be considered by instructional personnel in order to avoid pushing students too hard at critical junctures in the course, puts some real limits on what can be achieved in an intensive program.

In addition to this problem, there is the question of how much of the material is retained and for how long. Although no hard research data are available on this topic, personal experience over a number of years suggests that the student who does not follow up an intensive program with immediate further study and/or use of the language, will relatively quickly lose the skills acquired in the intensive program. This rapid loss of facility seems to be related to the lack of "sink time," an amount of time sufficient for complete assimilation and review of the material presented. Such a lack is inherent in the intensive course and particularly in the intensive summer course, which typically condenses a year's work into a period of about eight weeks.

While these factors of fatigue and loss of facility are unavoidable features of any conventional intensive course, there is a revolutionary new intensive learning methodology, just barely out of the experimental stages, which claims to eliminate both factors entirely. This method is called Suggestopedia, and was developed in Bulgaria by Dr. George Lozanov, a psychiatrist and psychotherapist and director of the Sofia Research Institute of Suggestology. The Suggestopedia method of language learning is carried on, often with adaptations, at a number of locations in the United States. There is, for example, a Lozanov Learning Institute in Dallas where several weekends a year language classes are taught using this method. Professor Harold Raley of the University of Houston has also taught a number of such classes. A number of other universities and public schools are involved in developing and researching the method. In addition, the <u>Journal of Suggestive-Accelerative Learning and Teaching</u> has published much research concerned with validation of the Lozanov method in a number of different fields of endeavor.

In spite of the existence of a considerable body of writing on the method, it remains little known among American foreign language teachers. For this reason, I include here a brief description of what it is and how it works.

The principles of the method, which take into consideration the age and goals of the students, are as follows:

"1) Joy, absence of tension and psycho relaxation.

2) Unity of the conscious-paraconscious and integral brain activation.

3) Suggestive relationship on the level of the reserve complex.

The principle of 'joy, absence of tension and concentrative psycho-relaxation' presupposes joy with learning, mental relaxation and non-strained concentration. The emotional release creates conditions for undisturbed intellectual mnestic and creative activity without causing the fatigue and considerable consumption of energy that accompanies strained attention" (Lozanov 1978: 31-32).

This method, perfected in the early 1960s, combines such disciplines as yoga and parapsychology. A typical class of not more than a dozen participants meets in a relaxing setting such as a room equipped with carpeting, comfortable chairs arranged in a circle, and classical music. This setting is designed to enable students to relax and focus all their attention on the task at hand. Other factors which are introduced to produce this effect of relaxed concentration include physical exercises and breathing exercises. A typical class lasts four hours and includes a review of previous material, a presentation of new material through dialogues, and a kind of seance in which new material is memorized at an unconscious level. It is during the seance that most of the assimilation of new material takes place. Features of language instruction which we consider to be quite normal, such as language laboratories or pattern drills, are avoided in this system.

The seance lasts about an hour and has both an active and a passive component. Classical music provides a constant background, and the teacher reads new material to the class as the students perform yoga breathing exercises. A translation for each target language phrase is given, and the students read the material silently as the teacher reads aloud.

This active component is then followed by a passive component. Again, against a background of classical music, the teacher acts out the dialogue while the students meditate on the text with their eyes closed. By imagining the dialogue situation the students internalize the material, which they are then able to use for communication, even though they have not done any of the typical exercises which we consider so essential. The material is absorbed unconsciously while the students' brain functions are in the so-called "alpha state" (Bancroft 1978).

This method of language instruction has become known in the United States largely through the writings of Sheila Ostrander and Lynn Schroeder, whose books Psychic Discoveries behind the Iron Curtain (1971) and Superlearning (1979) have done much to transfer this technology here. Proponents of this method argue that an entire foreign language can be learned in just one month with high levels of retention a year later and with minimal stress on students (Ostrander and Schroeder 1979: 33). Documented research as well as positive personal experiences of practitioners tend to support this claim.

Pilot studies conducted at Iowa State University by Donald Schuster and Ray Benitez-Bordon in the early 1970s tended to corroborate the claims of the superiority of the Lozanov method (Schuster and Benitez-Bordon 1976a: 3). Further studies by the same researchers in 1975 showed a 250% increase in learning efficiency in Spanish under the Lozanov method as compared to traditionally taught Spanish (1976b: 10). Although these results are considerably less than the 500%-5000% increase in language learning efficiency cited by Ostrander and Schroeder (1971: 291-296), they are nonetheless impressive.

Additional research at Iowa State, using the suggestopedia method to teach junior high school science, yielded additional evidence that this method is a potentially powerful teaching tool not only in language instruction but also in other areas of learning (Gritton and Benitez-Bordon 1976: 83).

A private conversation with Harold Raley of the University of Houston in September of 1981 brought forth the fact that, among students whom he has taught using Suggestopedia methodology, a number of class members reported being able to say things in Spanish which they had no conscious recollection of having studied. Such reports are surprising, even to Prof. Raley.

Dr. Lozanov himself makes the following claims:

"A. Results of the Suggestopedic Foreign Language Teaching and Learning for Adults

"There can be different variants of the suggestopedic foreign language system—from courses with several lessons a week to courses of whole days' 'immersion' in the suggestopedic foreign language atmosphere. The leading factor is not the number of lessons but the psychological organization of the process of instruction.

"If we take as a basic pattern the 24 days' foreign language course with four academic hours a day, either no homework or only some informative reading allowed for 15 minutes in the evening and in the morning, the following results can be expected: (1) The students assimilate on the average more than 90 percent of the vocabulary, which comprises 2,000 lexical units per course; (2) More than 60 percent of the new vocabulary is used actively and fluently in everyday conversation and the rest of the vocabulary is known at translation level; (3) The students speak within the framework of the whole essential grammar; (4) Any text can be read; (5) The students can write but make some mistakes; (6) The students make some mistakes in speaking but these mistakes do not hinder the communication; (7) Pronunciation is satisfactory; (8) The students are not afraid of talking to foreigners who speak the same language; (9) The students are eager to continue studying the same foreign language and, if possible, in the same course.

"This holds good also for beginners who have never learnt the respective foreign language before. It stands to reason that in teaching students who have some preliminary idea of the language, the results will be much better. The assimilation of the new material in the following second and third courses takes place approximately at the same speed" (Lozanov 1978: 59-60).

What, then, is the future of such intensive instruction? It seems at this point that its adoption as a major methodology in American foreign language instruction remains far in the future. There are a number of reasons for such skepticism. In spite of its apparent success, the method necessarily entails considerably more expense than do more traditional methods of language instruction. The necessarily small class size, which is desirable but hard to achieve even in a traditionally taught language course, present a major barrier. The specially equipped, somewhat plush classrooms, also present a problem. It is unlikely that financially strapped institutions would be willing to commit resources on a large scale to renovating space for such a purpose.

Another major problem has to do with staffing needs. Instructors need to be specially trained in the techniques of the method, including acting and yoga, and they must accept the method as a valid, viable means of teaching their subject. Such acceptance seems unlikely to come on a widespread scale in the near future and, perhaps, not even in the distant future. One need only consider on the one hand the success of the Dartmouth Intensive Language Model and on the other hand the slowness with which it has been implemented across the country, in order to understand the resistance which the Lozanov method will encounter.

There is, it seems, an unwillingness to accept radical change in the U.S. educational system. In particular, there is a real reluctance to accept learning which appears to take place as if by magic. Not that this is bad: such reluctance may indeed, by contributing to the stability of the system, actually strengthen it. Whether it is good or bad is probably irrelevant anyway; what matters is that it is a fact.

It is likely, then, that the more traditional intensive program will flourish in the future. In particular, the advantages of relative efficiency and effectiveness, both in the educational realm and in the economic realm, will keep such traditional intensive courses alive and well for years to come. They may have their disadvantages, but these disadvantages are familiar, somewhat conventional, and more importantly, safe.

NOTES

[1] The language teaching professional who is interested in a more complete discussion of the development of such programs should consult the monograph written by David Benseler and Renate Schulz, Intensive Foreign Language Courses. This publication traces the history of such intensive courses, describes what is involved in them, and in general provides an excellent, exhaustive view of the way in which typical intensive courses operate.

REFERENCES

W. Jane Bancroft. "The Lozanov Method and its American Adaptations." Modern Language Journal, 62, 4 (1978), 169-170.

Benseler, David P., and Renate A. Schulz. Intensive Foreign Language Courses. Arlington, Virginia: Center for Applied Linguistics, 1979.

Gritton, Charles E., and Ray Benitez-Bordon. "Americanizing Suggestopedia: A Preliminary Trial in a U.S. Classroom." Journal of Suggestive-Accelerative Learning and Teaching, 1, 2 (1976), 83.

Lozanov, George. Suggestology and Suggestopedia: Theory and Practice. Paris: Bulgarian National Commission for UNESCO and the Bulgarian Ministry of People Education, 1978.

Ostrander, Sheila, and Lynn Schroeder. Psychic Discoveries behind the Iron Curtain. New York: Bantam, 1971. (Orig. publ. New York: Prentice-Hall, 1970).

_____, with Nancy Ostrander. Superlearning. New York: Delacorte Press and Confucian Press, 1979.

Schuster, Donald, and Ray Benitez-Bordon. "Foreign Language Learning via the Lozanov Method: Pilot Studies." Journal of Suggestive-Accelerative Learning and Teaching, 1, 1 (1976), 3.

_____. "The Affects of a Suggestive Learning Climate, Synchronized Breathing and Music on the Learning and Retention of Spanish Words." Journal of Suggestive-Accelerative Learning and Teaching, 1, 1 (1976), 10.

INDEX

Albert, M. 226-229
Andersen, R. 112
Arjona, E. 172
Asher, J. 83

Bancroft, W. 109, 112, 233, 235
Barik, H. 170
Barkman, B. 177
Barthes, R. 74, 75
Batts, M. 171
Benamou, M. 173, 177
Benitez-Bordon, R. 233, 235-36
Bennett, W. 105-07, 112
Benseler, D. 11, 231, 235
Beresford, M. 64
Bernac, P. 70-75
Besse, H. 163, 165
Bloomfield, L. 224
Bourgeacq, J. 85
Bowen, D. 169-70
Bowen, M. 169-70
Bradley, D. 169-71
Brannon, R. 225, 228
Braun, H. 45
Brewster, W. 106, 112
Brislin, R. 169, 171
Britt, C. 5, 11
Broce, T. E. 92, 96
Brod, R. 3, 11, 106-07, 112
Brown, H. D. 167, 171
Burkey, R. 227, 229
Burmeister, I. 46
Burt, M. 108, 112
Byrnes, J. F. 89

Cadice, R. 171
Caprio, A. 116-17, 120
Carbajo, A. 171
Carton, D. 116-17, 120
Cates, G. T. 174, 176-77
Champe, G. G. 85-89
Chancerel, J. L. 165
Chapey, R. 228-29

Chase, C. 91-96
Chomsky, N. 224
Contreras, G. 31-40
Cooper, R. 109, 112
Courillon, J. 163, 165

Dalgalian, G. 164, 165
Daugherty, H. 64
De Felippis, D. 103, 112
de Lange, J. 145
Demetz, P. 20, 29
Denbow, S. 69-75
Derrida, J. xi
de Sauze, E. 226
Deveny, J. 149-158, 231-236
Deveny, T. 123-129, 149, 151-152
Dewey, H. 64
Diller, K. 226, 227, 229
DiSimoni, F. 225, 228
Drucker, P. F. 38, 40
Dulay, H. 108, 112
Dull, C. 225, 228
Dumett, R. 55
Duplantie, M. 165

Easterling, W. L. 115-121
Emrich, T. D. 37, 40
Eppert, F. 167, 171
Escandon, R. 168, 171

Fenwick, M. 104
Ferguson, M. 101, 113
Ford, J. F. 149, 152-154
Frautschi, R. L. 101-113
French, E. 140, 147
Frere, P. 147
Freud, S. 225
Frey, J. 45
Friesen, A. 169, 171

Gage, A. 149, 154-158
Galisson, R. 162-165

Galt, Alan 45
Gassner-Roberts, I, 112
Gaudiani, C. 126, 129
Germain, C. 159, 164-65
Gerver, D. 169, 171
Gewehr, W. 193
Gollasch, F. 177
Gonzales, H. 103
Goodman, K. 174, 177
Grittner, F. 167, 171
Gritton, C. 233, 235
Guilford, J. 111
Guiora, A. 225, 228
Guntermann, G. 154

Hammerly, H. 108, 113
Harris, J. 173
Hart, G. 103
Hayden, R. 102
Helbling, R. 185, 193
Hensey, F. 167-172
Herron, C. 103, 113
Hiebert, W. 13-17
Hijirida, K. 77-83
Honigberg, J. 92
Horwitz, E. K. 31-40
Hosenfeld, C. 174, 177
House, J. 168, 171
Hudelson, S. 177

Inman, M. 4-5, 11, 31-33, 40
Ionesco, E. 173, 177

Jacobson, L. 112-13
Jarvis, A. 168, 171
Jedan, D. 193
Jespersen, R. 185, 187, 193
Jordan, G. 11-12
Jordan, R. 177
Joseph, J. 11-13, 115

Keck, C. E. 41-43
Kelly, L. 101, 113, 167, 171
Kienbaum, B. E. 45-47

Kohl, H. 13, 17
Kolers, P. A. 174, 177
König, F. 131-136
Koppel, I. 103, 113
Kraetschmer, K. 223-229
Krashen, S. 10, 12, 108, 112, 227-28
Kroes, H. 137-147
Kühne, R. 11-12

Lacan, J. 225, 228
Langer, J. 174, 177
Lanham, L. W. 147
Le Blanc, R. 159, 164-65
Lebredo, R. 168, 171
Lenneberg, E. 226, 228
Leptin, G. 46
Lerner, B. 104, 113
Lévêque, A. 173
Lewis, M. 96
Lozanov, G. 109-10, 225, 228, 232-236
Lurie, J. 102, 113, 91-92, 96
Lyman, R. 20-22, 29

Mackay, R. 177
Maquet, J. 58
McKenna, K. 63-68
McKnight, P. 19-29
Melvin, B. 173-178
Menyesch, D. 46
Mersereau, J. 64
Mills, G. 167, 171
Morris, M. 227, 229
Murphey, E. 220-21

Naisbitt, J. 16-17
Neuner, G. 173-74, 178, 193
Newmark, P. 169, 171
Nord, J. 10, 12
Northey, A. 185-193

O'Connor, F. 105
Obler, L. 226-228
Orleb, E. 171
Ortmann, W. D. 193

Ostrander, N. 236
Ostrander, S. 223, 229, 233, 236

Pannetta, L. 102
Pell, C. 103
Pellissier, S. 53-61
Perkins, C. 103
Peters, G. 185, 187, 193
Petronio, G. 172
Phillips, J. 174, 178
Plank, D. 64
Poitou, D. 58
Prinsloo, K. P. 147

Racle, G. 109
Raillard, S. 165
Raley, H. 168, 172, 232-234
Rassias, J. 117
Reagan, R. 38, 40
Reboullet, A. 165
Reeds, J. 226
Reich, R. B. 37-40
Richterich, R. 159-160, 163-165
Rivers, W. 125, 129, 151, 158, 167, 171
Roessler, H. 11
Rogers, C. 224, 229
Rosenthal, R. 112-113
Rousseau, J.-J. 121
Ruchti, J. R. 4-5, 12
Rudolph, F. 103
Russell, A. J. 53-55

Saint-Exupéry, A. de 118
Sapir, E. 224
Savariego, B. 168, 172
Savignon, S. 160, 166
Schaub, R. 42-43
Schillinger, J., ix
Schmidt, R. 193
Schouten-Van Parreren, M. 174, 178
Schroeder, L. 223, 229, 233, 236
Schulz, R. 3-12, 174, 178, 227, 229, 231, 235
Schuring, G. K. 139, 141

Schuster, D. 233-236
Schutte, L. 11
Scovel, T. 108
Searleman, A. 227, 229
Selaskovitch, D. 169, 172
Simon, P. 13, 16-17, 102-03, 113
Sinaiko, H. 169, 171
Skinner, B. F. 224
Sparks, R. 227, 229
Starr, S. F. 10, 12
Stern, S. 225, 229
Stevick, E. 110, 113
Suter, B. 165
Swaffar, J. 174-75, 177-78
Sylvester, N. 168-172

Taba, H. 78, 83
Teed, C. 168, 172
Teltsch, K. 104, 113
Thomas, J. 167, 172
Thurow, L. 37-38, 40
Thurow, R. 13, 17
Trendota, K. 10, 12
Trescases, P. 159, 166
Tsongas, P. E. 91, 96

Uterwedde, H. 46

Van Parreren, C. F. 174, 178
Van Wyk, E. B. 138, 147
Verdehlan, M. 165
Vernon, N. D. 131-136
Vogel, U. 227-229
von Schmidt, W. 193

Walsh, T. 226-27, 229
Wanat, S. 178
Wandruszka, M. 169, 172
Webster, J. 195-221
Weinstein, A. 10, 12
Weiss, F. 165
Wells, J. 149-152
Werner, D. 172
Whiteley, W. 109, 113

Widdowson, H. 168-69, 172
Wilkins, D. A. 53, 58
Wilms, H. 193
Winitz, H. 226

Yalden, J. 165-66

Zeiner, E. 11
Zeller, N. 173-178